FISHER
RENWICK

First published in 1997 by
Roundoak Publishing
The Old Dairy, Perry Farm,
East Nynehead,
Wellington,
Somerset TA21 0DA

© **Copyright 1997**
Gordon Mustoe, Peter Davies
& Roundoak Publishing

ISBN 1 871565 28 6

Designed by Peter Davies

Origination by
Character Graphics, Taunton

Printed in Great Britain by
The Amadeus Press, Huddersfield

Jacket illustration:
This painting, by Transport Artist
Peter Davies, captures much of the
period atmosphere from the heyday
of Fisher Renwick's famous Scammell
'Showboats'. The scene depicts a
classic 'high bridge' Showboat,
FYR 389, 'PLOVER', about to set out
on its long journey through the night.

Bibliography & material sources:
P.L.A. Minutes & Photographic collection
Dunbar Papers, Modern Records Centre,
University of Warwick
Public Record Office BT 31/31998/98451
& AN 68 716/720
Lloyds Register of Shipping - various
documents
Tony Billings. Scammell-45 years of
Rigid 8's
Charles Dunbar. Rise of Road Transport
1918-1939
History of the Great War, Military
Operations - various volumes
C.I. Savage. Inland Transport, Civil History

FISHER
RENWICK

A Transport Saga
1874 - 1972

Gordon Mustoe

Roundoak Publishing

FOREWORD

In December 1985 I received a letter from Gordon Mustoe, asking if I had any connection with Fisher Renwick. As a result we met for what became a reminiscence session. We were both unable to do more than keep usefully in touch for some time, and I was prompted to dig further. We each became surprised and excited by each others knowledge and records. I persuaded Gordon to go back to the founding fathers and include the shipping side which ultimately spawned the road haulage.

He was lucky in having as a major source Ted Oates, a specialist road haulage manager, latterly Director of Hydrogen Supplies, but more importantly his father had been a Fisher's driver and between them they had preserved a comprehensive collection of photos and other detail. His second lucky source was myself and the family records. I was only twelve when Fisher Renwick was nationalised, which meant that I was about twenty years younger than other potential sources of recall, and was also around when this project really took off.

Gus Renwick bought the vast majority of shares in Fisher Renwick from the executors of his father, George, in 1932. Gus purchased Holystone Grange, where his only son Denis later lived as now I do, also an only son. As a result much of the company's archive sources from 1902 to the ultimate sale to Ryder (1972), have remained under one roof and not been destroyed. In addition contemporary reference books, as well as political cuttings and much Manchester Dry Docks material are still together at Holystone Grange. Deed boxes contain family wills, probate and death duty and tax settlement records. My own records dealt comprehensively with my period of involvement in the last stage - Contract Hire Vehicles.

Road haulage vehicles were purchased more or less individually, design and mechanical knowledge progressing each time. They were therefore recorded in photos by manufacturers and owners. An added Fisher Renwick feature for each long distance vehicle was the use of names which meant that they all had to have a photo. Contract vehicles were photo recorded by the body builder and shown to customers as well as being a considerable sales aid in view of the quality of the contracts.

All the buildings from Dry Dock, White City, Kingsway, all in Manchester, to 'K' Garage and Park Royal were obviously of considerable family pride, and so have photographic records. This collection of visual history makes for greater interest.

My thanks are due to Gordon Mustoe, his own helpers and our publisher. Also to those members and descendants of old staff for their personal contributions as acknowledged.

Guy Renwick
Holystone Grange
July, 1997

CONTENTS

Foreword 4

Preface & Acknowledgements 6

Chapter One 1874-1891 - Origins 7

Chapter Two 1892-1914 - Age of the Steamers 12

Chapter Three 1914-1918 - The Great War 22

Chapter Four 1919-1933 - New Steamers and the first Scammells 26

Chapter Five 1934-1939 - The Steamers decline, The Scammells take over 48

Chapter Six 1939-1945 - War, Tribulations & Development 69

Chapter Seven 1946-1949 - Peace, Nationalisation & Contract Services 95

Chapter Eight 1949-1972 - Fisher Renwick Group, The Final Chapter 108

Chapter Nine 1891-1971 - Manchester Dry Docks Co. Ltd 125

Appendices 129

Index 151

Preface

This is the saga of a company, created by the vision of its founder, George Renwick, which was to be engaged in the carriage of general freight. Firstly as a Coastal Liner service, between Manchester and London, later changing to using road transport.

Fisher Renwick introduced the concept of a 'continuous service', and is remembered for its legendary fleet of Scammells, notably its Rigid Eight 'Showboat' vans and flats. This enabled Fisher Renwick's survival, albeit in a different form, until nationalised, and then having a further successful existence as a contract hire operator.

Four generations of Renwicks were involved in the direction of this private company to its final acquisition as a flourishing enterprise by Ryder.

To have been allowed to produce the saga of Fisher Renwick is a pleasure I never envisaged when I first became interested in the company those many years ago as I watched their Scammells, and other makes in the fleet, travel by.

My earliest of memories are of the sight and sound of chain drives, but it is the Rigid Eight 'Showboats' and flats, and their distinctive names which remain uppermost in my mind and I daresay, those of many fellow enthusiasts.

The young observers who experienced the Coventry blitz of November 1940 and April 1941 were able to note the continuing passage of the Fisher Renwick vehicles going about their business - although briefly diverted - amid the devastation that was much of central Coventry, thereby somehow making it certain that all would be well in the end.

I am sure that to regard his Scammells as an equivalent to modern day counselling would have seemed quite reasonable to Major Renwick, with his own experience of the horrors of the battles of the Great War.

Usually their drivers patiently answered questions if we saw them at Meriden, and from this we learnt that they too had suffered in the blitz, severely so at Shadwell.

We also found out about the steamer service, and why and how Scottish lorries arrived on the scene. We were to note the London drivers wore yellow socks (cockney sparrows), and Scottish vehicles did not change over drivers.

Fisher Renwick have become a legend of transport; it cannot have just been their vehicles with the scheduled, continuous service, but also their general impression of efficiency.

Certainly to work for Fisher Renwick was to be regarded as belonging to the Elite of road transport.

Gordon Mustoe
Solihull,
West Midlands
July, 1997

Acknowledgements

This illustrated history of Fisher Renwick could not have been written without the help from those many people, friends and acquaintances I have had the good fortune to meet over the years.

Guy Renwick made it all possible in the first instance, by making his family records available, with full freedom to use them. He has given readily of time and encouragement, answering and checking queries which have arisen, notably with aspects of the steamer operations, and the later contract hire businesses and the garages and their dealerships. His photographs and documents, many of which are reproduced, are invaluable in providing an original account of the company, its vehicles, and its operation. However, sadly little seems to have survived of their records taken over at nationalisation.

When no acknowledgement is given for photographs, they are from Guy Renwick's records. He also generously made it possible to obtain copies from Arthur Ingram.

Henry Atkin and the late Ted Oates were involved at the start of the project, Margaret Oates continuing with encouragement and help. Murray Bulgin shared his knowledge of Scammells; Arthur Ingram, who has shared my interest, has given access to his photographs and records over a friendship of very many years.

Margaret and Roy Diamond have given valued encouragement and help with style, proof reading and the vital task of conversion to computer compatible format.

Roy Thorpe, besides giving encouragement, provided background for White City and the later Contracts operations, and introduced me to John Holding. Herbert Hinchliffe shared his memories of working with Fisher's. Tom Thomson gave generously of time and information, and introduced me to Willie Bruce, both making a major contribution with details of the Scottish operations.

Mrs R.M. Thistlewood, Archivist, BCVM Trust Archives gave ready assistance, as did Robert Aspinall, Librarian, PLA & Museum in Docklands Project, and Gabriel Drew, Greater Manchester Records Office. Richard Storey, Modern Records Centre, University of Warwick guided me to sources, and made invaluable suggestions.

Mrs B. Jones, Information Officer & Archivist, Lloyds Register of Shipping; and Mrs R. Hunt, Mobile Librarian, Mrs J. Toulson and Miss C. Burton Bibliographical Services Department, Solihull Libraries, helped beyond the call of duty, making it possible to trace source material.

The following N.F.C. pensioners were happy to give their recollections and helpful confirmation of facts about the Company, even from the late 1920's:- Alf Bingham, George Beddows, Mrs. D. Clements (on behalf of the late Bob Clements), Mrs. D. Clifton (nee Barbara Bill), Jack Crayshaw, Mrs. M. Eden, Ted Hallam, Mr. M. James, Albert Lovell, George Miller, George Murfitt, Eric Parkin, Mr. & Mrs. J.L. Parry, George (Nobbie) Robotham, Syd Shaw, Mr. and Mrs. A.C. Worth.

Peter Davies must be congratulated on his magnificent painting of 'PLOVER' and for his 'behind the scenes' work.

Finally, my thanks go to June Lawrence for her photographic skills with old and fragile photographs and documents, also for her advice.

Chapter One

Origins

Fisher Renwick began as the Newcastle-upon-Tyne based partnership of Fisher, Harbron & Renwick, formed 7th September 1874.

The 1876 Wards Directory for Newcastle-upon-Tyne has an entry "Fisher, Harbron & Renwick", Steam & Sailing Ship Brokers, Coal Exporters & Insurance Brokers. Their first office was at Rewcastle Chare, Quayside but by 1877 they had moved to 16 Sandhill. Soon after Harbron left the partnership, nothing being known about him, not even his first name.

George Renwick, Joseph Fisher and Harbron had worked together in the same type of business at Messrs Pyman & Co., West Hartlepool. The Pyman family had various interests in shipping and George Renwick retained a friendly relationship with George Pyman & Co., on occasion placing Manchester-London steamers on short charters with them, through their Newcastle Branch Office.

George Renwick was undoubtedly the driving force behind the decision that they should start their own company, and benefit from the opportunities provided by the expanding Tyne shipping industry. Even so, George Renwick could not have known then that the Newcastle based Fisher Renwick would be operating their steamers for some 65 years (1874-1939), with its offshoot operating the Manchester-London Coastal Liner service for 47 years (1892-1939). All of this in the end being superseded by the road transport service he saw introduced by his son Gustav.

The road transport service itself operated for 28 years (1921-1949), then continued as a new company under the direction of his grandson Denis, with his great-grandson Guy, providing a contract vehicle hire service for a further 23 years (1949-1972).

As a man of enterprise, it would have been interesting to have known George Renwick's opinion of Nationalisation.

The new partnership found they would do best in concentrating upon the continuing expanding London 'Sea Coal' trade, starting with chartering, then owning and managing vessels for their own charters, rather than acting as brokers arranging cargoes.

Two years later they felt able to take the decision to build their own new coastal steamers. The first to be built was the i.s.TRIO, commissioned May 1876, built by Coulson & Co., Newcastle-upon-Tyne, and engined by R & W Hawthorn. She was 158ft.2in. long by 25ft.7in. breadth by 12ft.9in. depth. The compound 2 cylinder engine 40 & 21 in. bore x 27in. stroke developed 65 h.p. at 70lb. pressure. As was normal practice at this period TRIO was schooner-rigged to assist with coal consumption.

Happily the final payment, to be made on completion of the commissioning of the TRIO would be met by the payment of half of the charter cost made to the partnership upon loading of the coal cargo. (It was the practice for this type of cargo that half the amount due for the charter was paid on loading, the remainder being paid after safe arrival and discharge of the cargo).

There was a small problem in that the actual receipt of the first cheque for this charter would not coincide with the exact time on Saturday for hand over to be made after the steam trials. The vital cheque was actually given to Coulsons the following Monday morning, the TRIO having been moved by the Partners to be loaded at the Staithes. Coulsons chose to accept the somewhat unorthodox procedure, they had received payment, and Fisher Renwick's first new Steamer was successfully proceeding to London on its first charter.

The TRIO was painted in what became the company colours - black hull, with the single funnel amidship, also black, having three white rings - supposedly one for each partner. The firm had now become Fisher Renwick Ltd.

George Renwick achieved some repute through instigating and operating the first coastal steamer to be equipped with the then new single-ended Scotch Boiler supplying high pressure steam to a Triple Expansion Engine, the saving from the reduced coal consumption released valuable space and enabled an end to use of sails to assist propulsion. He was assisted in this by Alexander Taylor, who developed the design of the concept. The engine was a product of the North Eastern Marine Engineering Co. Ltd., first located at Sunderland, and then later at Wallsend. They were also famous for being the first large engineering works in Britain to purchase electricity in bulk, for some years being the largest buyer of electricity in the country.

George Renwick had also become interested in the provision of dry dock facilities, required for repairs and surveys for their steamers. This led to his involvement with Pontoons. He became further associated with Alexander Taylor, who was designer and patentee of 'Pontoon' Dry Docks, and of later improvements to them. Together they formed a company to build and to operate the first ever Pontoon Dock at Wallsend. This operation was later extended to include two dry docks at a site between Wigham Richardson and Swan's Shipbuilders, (which was eventually sold to Swan, Hunter & Wigham Richardson Ltd).

Fisher Renwick also developed a general trade with the Scandinavian ports, in addition to its London sailings.

By 1882 the fleet had increased to eleven vessels:

i.s.BAINES HAWKINS	i.s.KATE FORSTER
i.s.BLENCOWE	i.s.CLAREMONT
i.s.LODORE	i.s.TRIO
i.s.MARIE FLEURE	i.s.TYNE
i.s.GUSTAV BITTERN	i.s.WETHERALL
i.s.WILTSHIRE	

(The 'Kate Forster' was named after George Renwick's mother and the 'Gustav Bittern' after Gustav's Swedish godfather).

By 1888 an additional nine steamers were sailing under the Fisher Renwick House Flag:

i.s.ALBERTINA	i.s.FANNY BERTHA
i.s.PANDORA	i.s.DENIA
i.s.ELLA SAYER	i.s.LOUGHBROW
i.s.SPRINGDALE (Steel)	s.s.NEWARK
i.s.TROUTBECK	

There was a turnover of Steamers as older or obsolete vessels, including TRIO and WILTSHIRE were replaced or placed on charter.

George Renwick had by now become an important member of the North Eastern shipping community and in 1882 he became a Member of the Committee of Management of the North of England Ship Owners Association. In the 1880's he was elected Chairman, a signal honour for he was not yet 45.

Sir George Renwick (1850-1930) pictured in the late 1920s at Springhill, Morpeth. First Baronet, created 1921, for political and public services. Director and Partner, Fisher Renwick & Co., Newcastle-upon-Tyne. Managing Director, Fisher Renwick Manchester-London Steamers Ltd. Managing Director, Manchester Dry Docks Ltd. Partner, Renwick Dalgliesh Ltd. Member of Parliament Newcastle. October 1900 to January 1906. September 1908 to January 1910. December 1918 to October 1922.

The Family Tree

The Renwick family arrived in Newcastle via Bewcastle, Cumberland and Tweedsmuir, Peebleshire

Robert Renwick (Cabinet Maker)
Third Son
1794 - 1864

John Nixon Renwick - Mary Smith Forster
1823 - 1875
Second Son
Cabinet Maker
Upholsterer, Furnisher
Pilgrim St. Newcastle

Sir George Renwick - Mary Jane Thompson
1850 - 1931   1877 - 1932
Second Son
Born Newcastle

Gustav Adolph Renwick - Mabel Deuchar
1883 - 1965   1885 - 1965
Fourth Son
Born Tynemouth

Dennis Adolph Renwick - Phylis Atkinson
1907 - 1983   1908 - 1983
Only Son
Born Morpeth

Guy Philip Renwick - Janet Melanie Franklin
1936 -   1944 -
Only Son
Born Hampstead

Joseph Fisher became George Renwick's brother-in-law when he married George Renwick's sister, Frances Mary Renwick

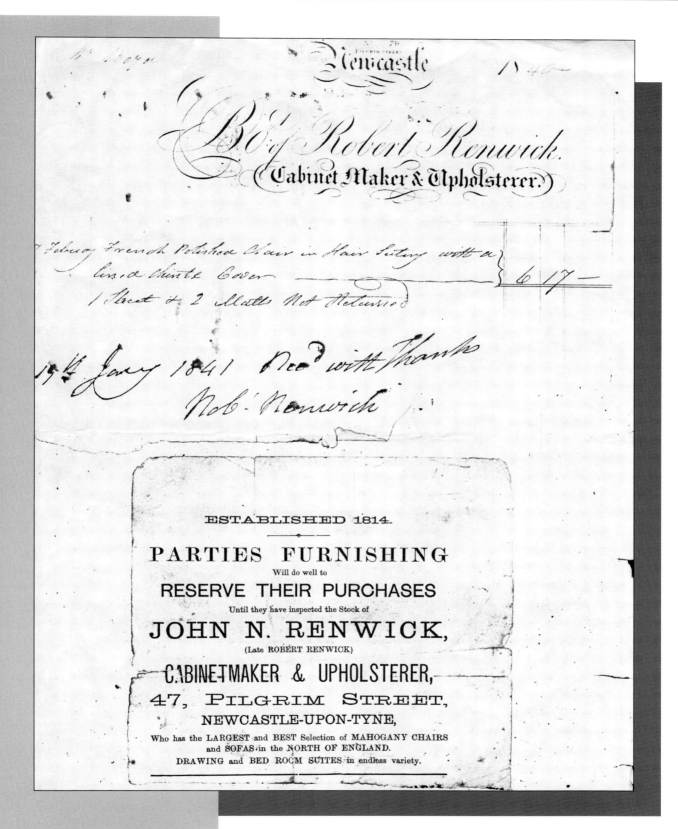

A billhead of 14th January 1841 issued by Robert Renwick, together with an impression of an advert of 1875 for John N. Renwick, dating the business to 1814.

Right: Major Gustav Adolphus Renwick (the fourth son). Chairman, Governing Director, Fisher Renwick Ltd. Chairman, Manchester Dry Docks Ltd. Sometime Chairman, Manchester Chamber of Commerce. Director and Vice-Chairman Scammell Lorries Ltd (until their acquisition by Leyland in 1955). Chairman, Berresford Atkinson Ltd. Member of Parliament for Manchester, Stretford October 1931 to October 1936. This view dates from 1953, when he was recovering from surgery for a cataract, a major operation at that time. Major Renwick is seen with his winning Greyhound 'Holystone Lightning' - Fisher Renwick employees did quite well following the 'Holystone Dogs'.

Below left: Denis Adolph Renwick (Major Renwick's only son). Director, Fisher Renwick Ltd. Chairman, Fisher Renwick Contracts Ltd., and Fisher Renwick Services Ltd., K Garage Ltd., Hendon, French Renwick Ltd., Hendon, Fisher Renwick Services Ltd., Manchester, Kingsway Garage Ltd., Didsbury, Manchester, Fisher Renwick Services (Wimbledon) Ltd., and Simpsons Motors Ltd., Upper Chorlton Road, Manchester. Denis Renwick was always responsible for the London based operations, firstly at Shadwell Basin and then at Coppetts Road, Muswell Hill. This portrait was taken some 60 years ago.

Below right: Guy Philip Renwick. A recent photograph. Guy Renwick was closely involved with the direction and management of various aspects of Fisher Renwick Contract Hire. Director, Fisher Renwick Contracts Ltd., and Fisher Renwick Services Ltd, K Garage Ltd., and French Renwick Ltd., Hendon, Fisher Renwick Services (Manchester) Ltd., Kingsway Garage Ltd., Didsbury, Manchester, Fisher Renwick Services (Wimbledon) Ltd., and Simpsons Motors Ltd., Upper Chorlton Road, Manchester.

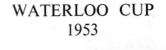

WATERLOO CUP
1953

Newcastle-on-Tyne, 7th Sept. 1874.

Gentlemen,

We beg to inform you that we have this day established ourselves here as General Merchants, Coal Exporters, Steam-ship Brokers, &c.

Mr. Harbron and Mr. Renwick having been connected with Messrs. Pyman & Co. of West Hartlepool and Newcastle, for a period of eleven and nine years respectively, have gained great experience in all branches of trade connected with this district.

We hope to receive a share of your favors, and assure you that any business entrusted to our care shall have our best attention.

Referring to our signatures at foot,

We remain, Gentlemen,

Yours faithfully,

Fisher, Harbron & Renwick.

Mr. Fisher will sign

Mr. Harbron will sign

Mr. Renwick will sign

Bankers:- The North Eastern Banking Co. Limited.

Left: The 'Partnership Notice' announcing the newly formed partnership of Fisher, Harbron and Renwick and their readiness to commence business. The Partnership would have ensured it was sent to all potential customers.

Right: The i.s.TRIO, commissioned May 1876, built by Coulson & Co., Newcastle-upon-Tyne. Her compound engine was built by R. & W. Hawthorn. Although the picture has artist's licence, it does show the use of 'Schooner rigging'. This was necessary at that period to keep coal consumption down and to reduce the space needed for the coal bunkers.

Chapter Two
1892-1914 – Age of the Steamers

Fisher Renwick's Manchester-London Cargo Liner service arose because of the building of the Manchester Ship Canal. George Renwick together with Joseph Fisher travelled from Newcastle for a specially organised tour of that portion of the Ship Canal open as far as Runcorn, and to inspect the facilities, albeit temporary, provided at Saltport. The tour was also intended to show the dock facilities planned for Manchester, George Renwick being attracted to those to be located at Pomona, for coastal traffic, he also noted the lack of any provision for a dry dock.

Saltport, (so named with the hope of obtaining the Salt Union traffic), was built at the junction of the Weaver Navigation with the Ship Canal, by Frodsham Ferry, to provide a temporary dock and quay until the remaining 26 miles 5 furlongs of the Canal to Manchester was constructed. There were some 700 linear feet of quay space which would have been a scene of chaos, with a mixture of steam and sailing ships queuing for space to berth.

The first cargoes were mostly pine timber, grain, pottery, salt and iron. There was access to the G.W.R. and L.N.W.R. Joint Main Line, although Manchester-London Steamers were to transfer most of their cargoes to lighters using the Bridgewater Canal (now owned by the Ship Canal Company). Lighter traffic at Manchester and London benefited from the Free Water clause. The quay jetty was finally demolished in 1905.

Although none of the other ship owners who went on the tour showed any interest, George Renwick saw the potential for a Manchester-London and return Coastal Liner Cargo service. He also perceived he could provide the dry docking facilities for ships using the Canal.

George Renwick was well known to be successfully involved with coastal shipping, and with the operation of Pontoons and Dry Docks, and the Directors of the Canal Company were sufficiently impressed, (indeed delighted) to give Fisher Renwick the right to operate the service between Manchester and London, and for George Renwick to provide the dry dock and marine engineering facilities.

The agreement for the dry dock was finalised 19th. October 1891, with the purchase of 17 acres of land having a 463 yards frontage onto the Canal, at Mode Wheel Locks, 2 miles from Pomona, and also a site at Ellesmere Port, 3 miles 5 furlongs from the Eastham Docks entrance, adjacent to Ellesmere Port Dock.

Virtually all the £120,000 initial capital, (£42,000 coming from the Promoters) was provided through Newcastle investors, who unlike those in Manchester were aware of the importance of dry dock provision to the successful operation of a port. The land was made available at a very low value, with the condition that two Ship Canal Directors, at this time J. Bethell and Alderman J.W. Southern were appointees, and that 10% of the net profits would be paid to the Canal Company.

There was a further instance of George Renwick's commercial acumen - the first agreement to purchase the site had to be renegotiated because the Pontoons and Dry Dock Company had arranged to purchase a much greater area than in the event could be justified for their needs, and the Canal Company was then able to sell the retained area to among others Glovers Cables, the C.W.S. Flour Mill, the Shell refinery, and B.O.C.M. (British Oil and Cake Mills), raising further now desperately needed funds to complete the final stage.

The Manchester Pontoons and Dry Dock Co. Ltd. was formed, with its first facility an improved steel Pontoon, 300 feet by 70 feet by 16 feet, and capable of handling vessels up to 5,000 tons. It was designed by Alexander Taylor, with patented improvements to weigh less than his previous Pontoons in use. Following its launch by Mrs. George Renwick in August 1893, at Edwards & Co., Howden-on-Tyne, it was towed 1,000 miles to the Ellesmere Port site, where the supporting workshop had been built and equipped with the latest machinery. Their first ship to be handled was the three masted sailing ship BEESWING. Taylor became a Director and Engineer to the Company.

The pontoon was also capable of being used for building lighters etc., and small steamers. It was to remain in use up to the 1950's. Following the opening of the Canal, the No.1 Dry Dock at Mode Wheel, 535 feet long and 65 feet wide was officially opened on 14th February 1894 with the s.s.MARTIN (Pacific Steam Navigation Ltd.). The second Pontoon, able to take vessels up to 260 feet long, and having 12 ton steam cranes available, opened on the 12th September with the s.s.BITTERN. The workshops and engineering facilities included a foundry. No fewer than 17 appropriate trades were available, and much non-marine sub-contract work was also to be undertaken. The Dry Docks were to be recognised as vital in keeping ships available to sail during both Wars. The name was changed to Manchester Dry Docks in 1906.

To achieve his second objective, George Renwick formed The Manchester and London Shipping Co. Ltd., absorbing the existing Fisher Renwick Manchester business, Fisher Renwick continuing to operate from Newcastle. A meeting appointing its first Secretary, R. Teasdale, (also to be acting

Secretary of the Dry Dock Company), was held on 15th July 1891. A meeting on 2nd October allocated shares in the Company to George Renwick, Joseph Fisher, George Forster Fisher, William Henry Renwick and Mary Jane Renwick (George Renwick's wife).

The Steamer service was able to commence with little delay using steamers transferred from the established fleet, the only exception was the VOLUNTEER(i), chartered to Fisher Renwick and also transferred for a period. The first sailing to London was by the s.s.LODORE on the 3rd December 1892. At first the sailing was every Saturday from Saltport Dock, loading on Fridays. (A handbill advertising details of this first service survives).

Use of transferred steamers enabled George Renwick to determine the most suitable type for the new service. The preference was for the 'raised quarter deck', which had the boiler and engine amidships. This type had one disadvantage making it unsuitable for collier coal cargoes - the tunnel requirement for the propeller shaft reduced the space available in the aft hold (it also made it difficult to use grabs for discharging coal or other bulk cargoes). The need to allow for the reduced cubic capacity when allocating weights in the holds to ensure stability was much easier with the varied cargoes carried by Manchester-London Steamers.

The new service was successful and the sailings increased to twice weekly, with a Wednesday sailing each way, loading Tuesdays. The London wharf was located at Victoria Wharf, Shadwell Basin, a seven year lease having been agreed with the London and India Dock Co., from December 1892 for what was to be known thereafter as Manchester Wharf, Shadwell Basin, together with Transit Sheds 54, 55 and 59. The Transit Sheds were vital for a coastal liner service as some categories of consignments from the cargo after discharge onto the wharf needed to be taken into a covered area to be sorted and then loaded for final delivery; the reverse occurred if loading was taking place. To be competitive with the rival railway service it was also necessary to be able to provide a warehousing facilities.

The approach to the Basin from the Thames was through a lock, intended to handle steamers up to 2,500 gross tons, and then past the adjacent Glamis Road swing-bridge. Office accommodation was provided at the Glamis Road end of the wharf. The lessor became part of the Port of London Authority (P.L.A.) in 1908. Fisher Renwick were to be associated with Shadwell until the purpose-built depot became available at Coppetts Road, Muswell Hill (able to benefit from the experience of the successful layout of the recent White City depot, Manchester). The lease was renewed as it expired, with some changes to the number of sheds occupied, as trade fluctuated.

Shadwell was a recognised dock for coastal services. At the time it was convenient for horse drawn deliveries for the City of London and Town (West End) traffic. Although Shadwell was not rail connected, there was convenient

Above: A copy of the Trade Bill announcing the start of the Manchester & London Shipping Co's Cargo Liner service from Saltport on 3rd December 1892. Fisher Renwick are shown as being the owners of the Steamer Company. The conditions seem less onerous than those imposed by present carriers.

access for transfer traffic to or from the Port's internal railway system, or to the appropriate railway depot or receiving agency.

The start up of the steamer service also benefited from being able to use Fisher Renwick's Newcastle office, which had moved to Maritime Buildings, and finally in 1904 to Collingwood Buildings, with its experienced staff to prepare the returns for the weights and categories of traffic making up each cargo, required for calculating the Port and Dock dues, Trinity House Light dues, and Board of Trade and Customs returns. These, insurances and other details and facts required for effective and profitable operation were all prepared by Newcastle, who had the capability to prepare accurately and speedily export shipping documents, tally sheets, and the cargo manifests and loading plans certified by the steamers Captain or First Mate/Officer. The Captain was ultimately responsible for the cargo as detailed in the Manifest, the officers had to be most alert in overseeing stowage and disposal of the cargo to ensure there were no problems over the quantities, nor any damage to consignments whilst in their charge.

Newcastle was also able to provide the earlier Marine Superintendent support to attend to the care and needs of the steamers. There was some benefit from the Directors' relationship with the dry dock for its services, and for some items of steamers' deck and engine room stores and equipment.

Although Saltport was always very congested and somewhat inconvenient, it did allow potential customers to be convinced of the practical benefits of using the new service. Among the varied traffic consigned to Saltport on one voyage in February 1893 was tea for D.Melia & Co., tobacco for B.J. Robinson, and wine for Mr. Leroy, (special arrangements were made for this to be transferred to a bonded warehouse). It is also worthy to record that the first consignment of cotton to arrive at Manchester using the Canal, was some 269 bales of Chinese cotton consigned to Malcolm Ross & Co., and transhipped at Saltport from Fisher Renwick's BLENCOWE.

The Salt Union, for whom the facility at Saltport was provided, were not persuaded to transfer their business from Liverpool, which had offered very attractive rates to keep the traffic. Fortunately the Salt Union did agree that their charge for all consignments of sacked salt would be the same F.O.B. Manchester as F.O.B. Liverpool. Fisher Renwick carried a share of this traffic, with consignments being transhipped from Salt Union's own lighters using the steamer's own derricks, almost to the end of their liner service.

The Ship Canal was finally completed, and following the official opening ceremony on 1st January 1894, with the procession along the Canal led by the Royal Yacht preceding 23 ships including a Fisher Renwick steamer with Directors, family members and customers on board.

The Manchester wharf moved to Pomona Dock, where a lease was taken of 4 Dock East and (Transit) Shed 4, which became known as London Wharf. The Offices were conveniently near at Cornbrook Road. The steamers' 'Port of Registry' became Pomona Dock, Manchester. Again Fisher Renwick were to remain there until the move to their new White City depot in 1940.

Fisher Renwick Steamers used solely on the Manchester-London service by 1905 comprised:

s.s.FISHREN   s.s.FUSILIER   s.s.HUSSAR
s.s.TROOPER   s.s.VOLUNTEER.(ii)   s.s.YEOMAN

The patriotic fervour following the Boer War led to the military sources for the names chosen for new steamers.

Both Pomona and Shadwell were responsible for the reconciliation of accounts due, and for the payment of wages and all the incidental expenditures necessary for the operation of the business.

The twice weekly service, sailing Saturdays and Wednesdays, was carrying an increasingly wide variety of traffic, mostly transferred from competing railway services. The canvassers, (and Directors) built up an extensive customer base, notably textiles, especially drapery and piece goods, and from London, groceries and provisions. Areas of the steamer holds provided a stable environment for transport of temperature critical traffic.

Drum cables became an important traffic, to be retained by the road service up to (and indeed beyond), nationalisation. Heavy crane provision was also needed - large boilers and pressure vessels were carried almost to the final days of the steamer service. At Pomona this was supplied by the Canal Company with steam cranes. At Shadwell Basin the Port Authority provided hydraulically operated heavy cranage. In practice each steamer's own derricks were usually used, especially when transhipping to and from lighters, and later the Scammell lorries.

Manchester had no tradition of dock labour, so the Canal Company took the bold decision that it would be the sole employer and provider of labour, albeit using the casual system. To this end, experienced dockers were recruited on a temporary basis from Barrow, Glasgow and even Liverpool. This was to cause resentment from the hundreds of unemployed men, who considered jobs were being taken from them, nor did they appreciate the need for training. Their agitation only ended with Manchester Corporation hiring many of them for temporary engagements with the Parks and Cleansing departments and also working on roadworks, much of these being for the approaches to the Docks and the Trafford Park Industrial Estate.

From the start of the service Fisher Renwick employed their own stevedore, usually with an assistant, up to three checkers/tally clerks, and a dock labour foreman at both their wharves. However the majority of the dock labour was at first carried out with casual employment, with only a few on permanent or regular engagement. There was an increasing use of permanently attached dock labour as circumstances permitted.

Both George Renwick and his son, Gustav Renwick, disliked any use of the 'casual' system, but had little option but to accept the practice. Although placing more of the dock labour on their own permanent employment lists, they always expressed their concern and dislike of the casual system at 'Steam Owners Association' meetings, and at the Chamber of Shipping Annual General Meetings, taking every opportunity to explain the disadvantages as they found them. One of their greatest continuing concerns was the question of piece-work rates when working their steamers.

On many occasions unfavourable comparisons were made between the cost per ton handled at London Wharf, Pomona, where a policy of day rate was able to be used from the start, and at Manchester Wharf, Shadwell, with its long existing tradition of piece-work, (at the peak it was estimated some

FISHER RENWICK MANCHESTER – LONDON SERVICE
S.S. LODORE.

The first steamer to load on the berth between the above Ports, left Saltport Dec. 3rd. 1892.

Left: The s.s.LODORE, commissioned in 1875, built and engined by Wigham Richardson. Weight 656 tons, length 200 feet. Her boiler pressure was 75 psi. The compound engine was rated at 99 h.p. The LODORE is shown moored at the Ellesmere Port facility of The Manchester Pontoons and Dry Dock Company before moving to Saltport to load for the first sailing to London from the Canal.

40,000 piece-work rates existed for London Dock work).

At London, through the long established use of the casual system, hiring was possible for a day, half day, or until 1911, even less if the work finished. Because of the Liner service with the need to keep the wharves cleared, Fisher Renwick were able to provide more stable employment than was usual, particularly at Shadwell, with employment there being highly regarded. There the labour problem was further complicated when severe weather conditions caused a steamer to arrive late, missing the tide for the entrance to Shadwell Lock - there could be up to a twelve hour wait between tides. The converse could arise and exceptionally favourable conditions could give an earlier arrival than planned.

Manchester Docks, being new, did at least provide some facilities for its labour and those visiting the Dock as part of their working day. London Docks, it is fair to state, required its dock labour to work in unpleasant, difficult and often dangerous conditions, especially in bad weather. The discipline was harsh, there were no canteens or even shelter for meal breaks, and the sanitary conditions were primitive beyond description.

Manchester Wharf, Shadwell, at least is known to have allowed its dock labour to use an area of one of the sheds for breaks, and they were allowed to use available lavatory and washing facilities.

There were advantages gained by Fisher Renwick from their consideration for their workforce with less pilferage and damage to cargoes, (important for reducing insurance premiums and customer comparisons with their record to that of the Railway companies). It is also worth mentioning that the good relations the Steamer Company enjoyed with their dock labourers meant that conditions at Shadwell were never to be the direct cause of a labour dispute or walk-out. There were to be many dock or tug strikes within the dock system over the years. Even during the worst of these Shadwell seemed to be able to remain open although with some difficulty on occasion.

Gustav Renwick began his long association with Manchester-London Steamers when he attended a Directors' meeting in 1906. He had previously been at Newcastle. (In 1905 he married Mabel Deuchar, daughter of James Deuchar, Brewer of Montrose, who operated their own coaster, LOCHSIDE, for many years carrying their beers to Newcastle). The meeting was held at Cornbrook Road. It was now the practice for the Steamer Company to vary where these meetings were held, Newcastle, Manchester and London premises all taking their turn, with other locations on occasion. Loadings had so increased that Mr. Devries, the Stevedore at Pomona, and his three assistants were granted an increase in their wages of 2s.6d.

At both London and Manchester some customers preferred to deliver or collect their own consignments, other traffic came or went by rail, some would be transhipped from lighters, taking advantage of the Free Water Clause. The greatest proportion of collections or deliveries was carried out by Fisher Renwick, using contractors for this facility. At Manchester, Cowan & Co. was used, their depot and stables being conveniently near in Cornbrook Road. In London R. Evans & Son were used, with an increasing use of Hays Wharf Cartage Co. and their associated company Henry Smithers, particularly from 1918. Indeed Hays Wharf were to be used, especially for the City and Town deliveries, until the move to Muswell Hill in 1942.

The Canal Company's Bridgewater Department provided the lighter service for transhipments, though it was known for steamers to go alongside other vessels berthed in other of the Ship Canal docks to transfer cargoes directly. The Maritime Lighterage Company were used at London for any transhipments.

The growth in traffic meant the Company felt able to enter into an agreement on 25th October 1906, between it and The Tyne Iron & Shipbuilding Co. Ltd. to build a new steamer named CARBINEER, for a contract price of £17,500. Agreement to sell the s.s.VOLUNTEER(ii) was reached early 1907, the proceeds being put into a special account towards payment for the new steamer. The Company also purchased 100 Manchester Dry Dock Co. Ltd. Fully Paid £10 Preference Shares. A superannuation scheme was introduced in 1907, a pioneering instance of the Company's interest in its employees' welfare.

There were only to be two sailings in Christmas week 1907, these being Thursday p.m. 24th December in each direction, the next sailing to be 28th December.

When the lease for Shadwell was renewed for a further

three years from 1908, with the newly formed Port of London Authority, it was extended to include the use of Sheds 56, 57 and 58. A new brick and slated office not exceeding £600 was to be provided for the Company to be usable before 31st December 1908. The lease included a clause that this would be painted every three years. Someone must have remembered the earlier differences of opinion about the need for this, the Dock Company having written to Shadwell on 2nd March 1906 suggesting the Steamer

Company's offices, facing Glamis Road should be painted. G.F. Fisher, the Director responsible for the London operations at this period, reported to George Renwick that he had declined to do this.

The Wharf was to be used solely 'for manipulation of goods discharged from or intended to be shipped into their

Steamers'. At the time this was not seen to have any future implications for the Company. The replacement of the older steamers by new, larger ones and the success of the new service led to the decision to wind up the Company and register a new Company - Fisher Renwick Manchester-London Steamers (1908) Ltd., registered 22nd June 1908,

Left: The YEOMAN, built 1901 for Fisher Renwick, Newcastle, by Wood Skinner and fitted with a 135 n.h.p. triple expansion engine by the North East Marine & Engineering Co. Ltd. Weight 1009 tons, length 220 feet. Her boiler pressure was 180 psi. Seen at Pomona with her side being scraped and painted in between sailings. Two platforms can be seen rigged over the side for the crew doing this work and a ladder, for the occupants of the boat at the stern. The YEOMAN would have had empty bunkers, and have been lightened as much as possible for her to be so high out of the water.

Below opposite: The CARBINEER, built 1907 by Tyne Iron Shipbuilders Co. Ltd. with a North East Marine & Engineering Co. 144 n.h.p. triple expansion engine. Weight 1266 tons, length 230 feet. She is seen at Pomona waiting to load. Although three crew members are visible, there seems no sign of activity. The CARBINEER had the distinction of being the first new steamer bought for the Manchester-London liner service.

Below: The LANCER, built 1909 by Tyne Shipbuilding Co. Ltd with a North East Marine & Engineering Co. Ltd. 163 n.h.p. triple expansion engine. Weight 1363 tons, length 230 feet. She appears to have just finished transferring cargo from a lighter.

were as follows:

s.s.CARBINEER	s.s.FUSILIER	s.s.HUSSAR
s.s.MUSKETEER	s.s.TROOPER	s.s.YEOMAN

Fisher Renwick, Newcastle, were shown to own:

s.s.ELLA SAYER and s.s.WHITBY, with a number of other vessels under charter to them.

The "object of the Company was to take over a going business of a Steamship Line, Warehousemen and Wharfingers now carried on by 'Fisher Renwick & Co.'s Manchester - London Steamers Ltd.' at and between Manchester, London and Southampton". The Southampton call, already rarely made, was soon discontinued, there was sufficient traffic offered for London, and the extra time required and delays incurred were a disadvantage.

An early customer was Westinghouse (of U.S.A.), who had built a new factory at Trafford Park in the

with a capital of 165,000 shares, divided into 82,500 Ordinary Shares of £1 and 82,500 7% Preference Shares of £1. The Registered Office was Cornbrook Road, Manchester, the Head Office remaining at Fisher Renwick Ltd., Collingwood Buildings, Newcastle-upon-Tyne.

Steamers owned and operated by the Company in 1908

expectation there would be a demand for equipment and plant for railway electrification and for electric power generation. The steamers carried much of the equipment supplied for the 'Underground's Lots Road Power Station.

Because of changes in the customers and developments in the products they required, there were increases in the weights and bulk of their loads, allowing the railways a virtual monopoly, even to locating their own inspector in the works, (which in 1917 became Metropolitan-Vickers), to deal with any problems. (The railways were increasingly to lose the traffic to road transport after the 1926 General Strike, when Norman E. Box was able to take advantage of the situation and prove he could provide a long distance road transport service competitive with that provided by the railways).

There was not much concern about the loss of this particular traffic, not least because Westinghouse's problems made them slow in paying their accounts, also the success of the steamers in carrying this type of traffic meant they were securing other customers in similar types of business. Considerable quantities of drum cables were now being taken to Shadwell, and almost as many carried from there. The empty drums were to be one of the few instances of Fisher Renwick, in either the steamer days or with their road transport, handling 'returned empties'.

Textile piece goods and drapery traffic increased, as did groceries and provisions. The need to deal with 'smalls' consignments or the more fragile or delicate traffic was met by the use of wooden box containers, 6 feet by 6 feet by 6

Above: A later view of the LANCER shown passing the opened Trafford Road Swing-bridge (at the entrance to Pomona). The LANCER has by now received some modifications to her 'bridge'. The covers and security of the deck cargo carried on this sailing is also to be seen. Unfortunately, nothing is known about the small steam launch moored in the left foreground.

feet, these proving to be very successful, being taken to customers' premises, or filled or emptied on the wharf. They continued to be used until the road continuous service became established. There was always to be an imbalance of available traffic between Manchester to London and from London to Manchester. This meant that the canvassers were always allowed to be less fussy about the type of traffic, including parcels and 'smalls' carried onwards from London, a situation remaining to 1949.

Fisher Renwick Manchester-London Steamers Ltd., (the '1908' was omitted with effect from 12th June 1909, following an E.G.M.), were operated efficiently. Another new steamer, the s.s.LANCER was placed in service. Crews worked hard, as was the custom of the day, but with the advantages of serving on well equipped and well maintained vessels. Their five year surveys were always to Lloyds 100 A1 standard, including the re-approval of the loading lines. They were also fortunate in being spared the excessive economies of many coastal ship owners or managers. Thus they were not given notice of 'lay off' 24 hours before docking, nor having to sign on at 12.01 a.m. of the sailing day, thereby avoiding payment of a day's pay, and also they had the opportunity to see their families fairly regularly, even if briefly.

They had extra, paid, duties when alongside the wharf. These included handling their steamers winches and derricks, covering hatches or rigging temporary tarpaulin shelters so that work on cargo could carry on during bad weather conditions. After carrying some traffic, notably cement, it would have been necessary for them to clean out the holds before stowing began on the new cargo. Painting of the steamer's hull, particularly the lowest areas was carried out in the brief period the steamer was moored and empty, (and therefore high out of the water).

The crew for a steamer would comprise at least Captain, First Mate/Officer, Second Mate/Officer, Chief Engineer, Second Engineer, Three Firemen, one at least would also act as Donkeyman, a Bosun with at least 4 Seamen, and a Steward/Cook. Watches were 4 hours on and 4 hours off, except for the Firemen who worked 4 hours on and 8 hours off, but were then expected to assist in trimming the bunkers, and in clearing and disposing of ash etc. at the end of a watch. This could be unpleasant, with acrid fumes produced when sea water was used to quench the hot ash and clinker raked out of a furnace, made more difficult by the necessity to ensure working steam pressure was kept up with only one furnace to maintain steam. It was also physically demanding, particularly when removing the ash from the boiler area before tipping it into the sea.

Crews on coasters were expected to provide their own provisions and to cook their own meals. This could apply equally to officers. The crews on Manchester-London Steamers could at least look forward to their cooking being done for them by the steward, so whatever the sailing conditions during the passage they could usually expect a hot meal. On some of the steamers it became the practice for the steward to arrange to feed the crew for an all-in charge.

The Captains were expected to possess 'Pilots' Licences for navigating the Thames and the Mersey, and for passing

Left: The HUSSAR, built 1903 for Fisher Renwick by Tyne Iron Shipbuilding with the N.E. Marine & Engineering Co. 149 n.h.p. triple expansion engine. Weight 1255 tons, length 220 feet. Two lighters are moored alongside transferring cargo, probably salt. The stove is lit in each lighter, ready for the lightermen to cook their meals when finished.

Below left: TROOPER in a sad situation beached at Runnel Stone Bay, Cornwall, following a collision, reported to be because of low visibility in fog, with the BRITISH HERO partly visible to the right. The TROOPER's crew, probably with advice if not assistance, is fixing the wooden shuttering for a concrete patch to enable her to be refloated to proceed to her destination to be unloaded before repairs are made.

Below: The damage to the FUSILIER after colliding with the DRAKE in the river when attempting to turn to enter Shadwell Basin 2nd May 1909. It was caused by a very swift running high tide, with a gale force wind. Again a midships collision, the damage that may be caused at the point of impact when this happens is clearly seen.

the Ship Canal. This saved time, and the Pilots' Fees, and was reflected in their salary. (This was not always the practice with some coastal shipping companies).

The 36 miles passage along the Ship Canal would take several hours for each direction. There were five sets of locks. The lowest set at Eastham, where the Canal and the existing Mersey Channel converge, would be left open for several hours each side of high water for the largest ships, which relied on the Estuary tide, to enter or leave the Canal. The Canal became tidal as far as Latchford Locks, rising 56ft. 6in. above sea level.

Passage along the Canal required the steamer to pass Trafford Road Swing-bridge, the (original) Railway Swing-bridge, Mode Wheel Locks, Barton Swing-aquaduct and Bridge, Barton Locks, Irlam Locks, Latchford Locks, Knutsford Road Swing-bridge, Twenty Steps Swing-bridge, Northwich Road Swing-bridge, Stag Inn Swing-bridge, Chester Road Swing-bridge, Moore Lane Swing-bridge, Old Quay Swing-bridge and finally Eastham Locks, to enter the Estuary. It was sometimes necessary to tie up at a lay-by so that a larger ship may pass. Passage along the Canal, particularly passing swing-bridges, could be hazardous in windy conditions.

Navigating the Thames and its Estuary could be even more hazardous. The entry into the Shadwell Basin Lock was difficult to say the least, needing a ninety degree turn,

which would be even worse in a high wind and a strong tidal current. Yet there were only two records of an accident to a steamer entering the lock, one of which was admitted to be the responsibility of the Port Authority, rather than the steamer's Captain.

The other occurred on 2nd May 1909 when the FUSILIER

Above: SENTRY, commissioned in 1924 and built by Tyne Iron Shipbuilding, with a North East Marine & Engineering Co. 193 n.h.p. triple expansion engine, was the last steamer built for Fisher Renwick. Seen at Pomona with YEOMAN tied up opposite alongside the wharf, the photograph shows the difference between the 'shelter deck with freeboard' silhouette of SENTRY with the 'well deck' of the YEOMAN.

Left: A side view of SENTRY taken to show the versatility of her derricks for handling cargo.

was in collision with the s.s. DRAKE in the river, turning into Shadwell entrance. The P.L.A. 'Rendered considerable service', claiming £515 for the costs. After much negotiation George Renwick was able to record they had agreed to £150. The Authority also distributed £25 to their staff involved. Happily there were no casualties from the accident, but there were claims to be met for damage to cargo being carried.

Before the Great War, and even up to the late 1920's, the upper reaches of the Thames from the Pool and Shadwell to Erith and Purfleet were busy not only with ships, but also with many hundreds of barges and lighters. The barge traffic was complicated by the P.L.A. rule that 'Unpowered Barges' had to be taken through dock locks by tugs. This meant a steamer passing a lock could suddenly find itself obstructed by a barge having cast off from its tug.

The passage down river started by leaving Shadwell Basin Lock, then passing the Lower Pool, past Limehouse Cut, Limekiln Dock, Millwall and the Surrey Commercial Docks, round by Limehouse Reach and the Isle of Dogs, passing the West India and Millwall Docks, by Greenwich Reach, then Blackwall's East India Dock (and the Trinity House Wharf),

past Bugsby's Reach then Royal Victoria & Albert and King George V Docks, past Woolwich Arsenal, (avoiding the Free Ferries), by Gallows Reach then Beckton Gas-works, Samuel Williams Dagenham Dock (the Ford Works was not started until 1930), and past Halfway Reach. These Docks no longer exist, the area now being known as Docklands, with Canary Wharf a distinguishing landmark.

Although there was still some considerable way to go past Tilbury Docks, and Gravesend Reporting Station to the Nore Estuary and the Sea, the course of the river was now relatively easier and less busy.

Relations between the Canal Company and Manchester-London Steamers were sometimes strained, as in May 1909 when there were problems with the Canal Company not passing on Cartage Rebates for Consignees who did their own cartage. George Renwick gave instructions to deduct any credits due from Canal Company Accounts, and to insist on their being allowed in future. The Lancashire & Yorkshire Railway was dealt with in the same way.

The end of 1909 was celebrated by the appointment of an additional 'type-writing clerk' at Cornbrook Road, and a

Board decision to approve buying a 'typewriting machine' for use for Manchester-London Steamers business at Fisher Renwick's Newcastle Office. Gustav Renwick was appointed a Director, Manchester-London Steamers on 10th October 1911.

During that year on the night of 6th May 1911, a fire was discovered in the coal bunkers of the YEOMAN whilst berthed at Shadwell. A stand-pipe on the wharf, and the Tug HERALD 'extinguished the outbreak'. Two further 'outbreaks' occurred during the night, without damage to property or any injuries.

A Dock Strike in July and August 1911 was noted with gratuities for £5-5-0 being paid to Ships Officers and Engineers for loading the LANCER and taking her down to Barton Bridge, and the YEOMAN down to Mode Wheel Locks, (to load cable drums at Glover's Cable Works) and then returning her to berth at London Wharf. There were later difficulties when both the MUSKETEER and CARBINEER were not able to discharge at Pomona due to their 'ship labourers, wharfmen and others being out on strike through intimidation or sympathy with the dock workers and carmen'. The crews of the steamers were not however 'paid off'. The weekly wages for the First Mates was increased to £2-15-0 from £2-12-6, and for the Second Mates £2-5-0 from £2-2-6.

Up to the Great War the business proved to be very successful. There were periods when strikes or trade disputes caused loss of trade, and there were periods of recession, but generally trading conditions were good with a mostly sustained stability in costs. Although Cowan & Co. requested an increase in their cartage rates, this was due to poor harvests causing a considerable increase in the cost of horse feed. Following negotiations with Gustav Renwick they were allowed an increase of one penny to 2s. 3d. per ton from 13th May 1913.

The rates charged by Manchester-London Steamers varied as necessary, a special rate for drapery at £2-1-8 per ton to compete with that quoted by the Railways was available around 1911/1913. While 'Trade Freight and Export Textile Goods' to London had a rate increase of 1s. 0d. to £1-7-6 quoted in 1913.

Despite the competition from railways, profitable rates were available, and the Steamer Liner service together with the personal attention given to customers' requirements enabled Manchester-London Steamers to obtain and keep customers. Even in the periods of recession when steamers were taken off line, Newcastle would find work for them by transferring to other trades with profitable charters 'out' being made. The

Home Sea Trade limits conveniently allowed the Coaster Captains to sail across the English Channel to the Elbe-Brest limits, to take advantage of the opportunities for other profitable work.

Above: Fisher Renwick 'Manchester and London' used containerisation on its steamers from its earliest days. Two distinct designs are on these horse drawn flats. They were 6ft by 6ft by 6ft, with doors at one end only. The locks for security are clearly visible. Used for consignments of valuable or fragile traffic, often drapery from Manchester, they would be loaded on the wharf or taken to a customer's premises. Some later steamers would allow two to be loaded on top of each other but, in any case, they were robust enough to have traffic stowed on top of them. The horse flats, although lettered for Fisher Renwick, belonged to Cowan & Co, the Steamer Company's Pomona Dock cartage contractor.

Below: This attractive trade card was given to customers both as a reminder of the steamer service and also as a means for collections to be made. The postal service at this period, before 1914, was such that a postcard posted before lunchtime in business or commercial districts would be delivered with its instruction before mid-afternoon. Use of the telephone or telegraph was less common. (The card is also a reminder that the customers are using the Ship Canal).

Chapter Three
1914-1918 – The Great War

The declaration of War, 4th August 1914, changed everything, and was ultimately to end this prosperity for coastal liner services. The Railways were placed under government control on 4th August, one consequence of this being that no increase in their charges for goods traffic was made until 1920. There were to be unpredictable changes in the traffics available to carry, indeed there were to be periods of severe recession and much of the munitions traffic which might have replaced the pre-war business was unsuited, or unavailable, to coastal services.

At the start of the War, Fisher Renwick Manchester-London Steamers fleet comprised:

    s.s.CUIRASSIER (new 1914) s.s.HUSSAR s.s.LANCER
    s.s.MUSKETEER s.s.YEOMAN

and Fisher Renwick, Newcastle, now operated:

    s.sELLA SAYER s.s.AMSTELDAM s.s.SPRINGHILL,

with a changing number of vessels being chartered 'in' as required. All three were among the merchant ships armed for defensive purposes and all three were to be lost through enemy action. The SPRINGHILL, on passage to London, was sunk by a mine on 24th August 1917 (4 miles N. by E, $^3/_4$ mile E. from Scarborough). Five of her crew were killed. The AMSTELDAM, on passage to London, was torpedoed 18th October 1917 (6 miles N. from Flamborough Head). Four of her crew were killed. The ELLA SAYER, on passage from Penarth to Dunkirk on charter to the Admiralty, was torpedoed 29th April 1918 (15 miles E. by N. from Royal Sovereign Light Vessel). Two crew were killed. The HUSSAR was sold in 1916, having been replaced by s.s.HALBADIER. In addition, the NEWMINSTER ABBEY, only in service for one year, was torpedoed on 2nd February 1918.

The absence on active service of many employees caused a great strain upon those remaining, who had to cope with circumstances quite beyond anything in their previous experience. As an instance of what was happening, R.Evans, Head of Henry Evans, one of the Shadwell cartage contractors, reported he was having great difficulty in delivering consignments from Shadwell. In some cases the Railways had refused to take traffic. Henry Evans were increasingly short of labour and horses, and it was considered this would get worse as more men volunteered for military service and left. Also horses were being requisitioned, and suitable replacements difficult to obtain.

The situation at Shadwell was not helped when the HALBADIER, on one of her first passages, had arrived at Shadwell a day earlier than expected, and could not discharge her cargo because the wharf was still full of cargo left from the previous steamer that had berthed there.

Also at this time, Gustav Renwick volunteered to join the Newcastle Commercial Battalion (16th) Northumberland Fusiliers) and a new Company Secretary was appointed, Henry Coulson, his salary to be £120 per annum. This was due to the ill health of his predecessor, R. Teasdale, who sadly died shortly afterwards.

A lack of cargoes during Autumn to Christmas 1915 resulted in the HUSSAR being used for sailings to Dieppe, until ordered back to Pomona on 12th January 1916 to relieve a back-log and load for London.

With a continuing lack of traffic for the Liner service, the steamers were often taken off-line and placed on charters. The YEOMAN, was for a period, used for storing grain, and from Summer 1916 the pattern of sailings was usually one from each end weekly. Some office staff, of necessity were laid off, although some volunteered for the Army. The introduction of food rationing became a further hardship for the steamer crews to endure, partly eased soon after by their being issued with 'Special Ration Cards' for 'Weekly Seamen', i.e. the steamer crews supplying their own food. However, there was limited space made available on any steamer for storing provisions and no refrigeration available.

The ROLL OF HONOUR, Fisher Renwick Manchester-London Steamers Ltd., provides evidence of the patriotic commitment by their staff to serve their country. It cannot show their injuries, or the scarring effect their war experiences may have had upon them. The ROLL is approximate to the year ended 1916. The names of the steamer crews are not included, although they had their own casualties. The ROLL is also of interest in showing how the numbers of 'Permanent Dock Labour' had increased, and the difference in numbers between London Wharf, Manchester and Manchester Wharf, London.

The death in Mesopotamia in January 1917 of T.D. Fenwick was recognised with the Company paying a lump sum of £100 to his widow, her allowance of £1-0-0 per week continuing. The Company made up the difference, when necessary, between the salary/wage and the military pay for all employees for the duration of their war service.

The continuing effects of the war influenced the Steamer Company's decisions for allocating its charitable donations. The Seamen's Hospital, East Greenwich; The Soldiers' and Sailors' Buffet, Victoria Station (the main terminal for Troops going to, or coming from the Western Front) and the East Lancashire Disabled Sailors' and Seamens' Homes were added, and that to the 'Lifeboat Institution' was increased.

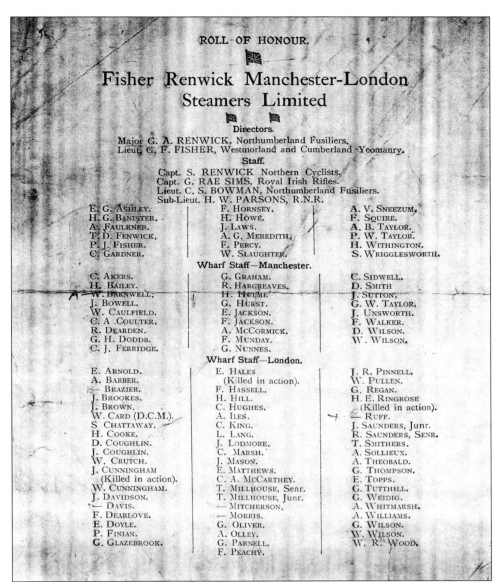

ROLL-OF HONOUR.

Fisher Renwick Manchester-London Steamers Limited

Directors.

Major G. A. RENWICK, Northumberland Fusiliers.
Lieut. G. F. FISHER, Westmorland and Cumberland Yeomanry.

Staff.

Capt. S. RENWICK Northern Cyclists.
Capt. G. RAE SIMS, Royal Irish Rifles.
Lieut. C. S. BOWMAN, Northumberland Fusiliers.
Sub-Lieut. H. W. PARSONS, R.N.R.

E. G. ASHLEY.	F. HORNSEY.	A. V. SNEEZUM.
H. G. BANISTER.	H. HOWE.	F. SQUIRE.
A. FAULKNER.	J. LAWS.	A. B. TAYLOR.
T. D. FENWICK.	A. G. MEREDITH.	P. W. TAYLOR.
P. J. FISHER.	F. PERCY.	H. WITHINGTON.
C. GARDNER.	W. SLAUGHTER.	S. WRIGGLESWORTH.

Wharf Staff—Manchester.

C. AKERS.	G. GRAHAM.	C. SIDWELL.
H. BAILEY.	R. HARGREAVES.	D. SMITH.
W. BARNWELL.	H. HOLME.	J. SUTTON.
J. BOWELL.	G. HURST.	G. W. TAYLOR.
W. CAULFIELD.	E. JACKSON.	J. UNSWORTH.
C. A. COULTER.	F. JACKSON.	F. WALKER.
R. DEARDEN.	A. McCORMICK.	D. WILSON.
G. H. DODDS.	F. MUNDAY.	W. WILSON.
C. J. FERRIDGE.	G. NUNNES.	

Wharf Staff—London.

E. ARNOLD.	E. HALES	J. R. PINNELL.
A. BARBER.	(Killed in action).	W. PULLEN.
BRAZIER.	F. HASSELL.	G. REGAN.
J. BROOKES.	H. HILL.	H. E. RINGROSE
J. BROWN.	C. HUGHES.	(Killed in action).
W. CARD (D.C.M.).	A. ILES.	E. RUFF.
S. CHATTAWAY.	C. KING.	J. SAUNDERS, Junr.
H. COOKE.	L. LANG.	R. SAUNDERS, Senr.
D. COUGHLIN.	J. LODMORE.	T. SMITHERS.
J. COUGHLIN.	C. MARSH.	A. SOLLIEUX.
W. CRUTCH.	J. MASON.	A. THEOBALD.
J. CUNNINGHAM	E. MATTHEWS.	G. THOMPSON.
(Killed in action).	C. A. McCARTHEY.	E. TOPPS.
W. CUNNINGHAM.	T. MILLHOUSE, Senr.	G. TUTTHILL.
J. DAVIDSON.	T. MILLHOUSE, Junr.	G. WEIDIG.
DAVIS.	MITCHERSON.	A. WHITMARSH.
F. DEARLOVE.	MORRIS.	A. WILLIAMS.
E. DOYLE.	G. OLIVER.	G. WILSON.
P. FINIAN.	A. OLLEY.	W. WILSON.
G. GLAZEBROOK.	G. PARNELL.	W. R. WOOD.
	F. PEACHY.	

Left: The Roll of Honour, Fisher Renwick London-Manchester Steamers Ltd. issued about December 1916. It is not complete for the whole of the War, nor does it include Steamer crew. The Roll shows the effect the War had already had upon the Company, and there were another two years to endure.

Command of his Battalion, was badly wounded by shell shrapnel during the Battle of Messines Ridge 7th June 1917, and was mentioned in Dispatches. George Renwick had played a major role in assisting to raise both the Quayside and the Commercial Battalions. He was made a Chevalier of the Legion of Honour. An appreciative gesture from the Company was the decision that the authority of Gustav Renwick, and also Percy Fisher to issue and sign cheques on behalf of the Company was not withdrawn during their absence whilst on active service. Captain Septimus Renwick, in the Scotts Guards, was to be awarded the Military Cross.

The photograph of George Renwick, (with the Parliamentary 'Portcullis' cap badge), with his sons, in their various Regiments, is reproduced on page 25.

Shipping came under the direction of the Ministry of Shipping, which among other things would have controlled any profits. A Home Trade branch was set up in June 1917, under the direction of A.H. Read (Chairman; British & Irish Steam Packet Co.Ltd., and of Powell, Bacon & Hough Lines; Member of the Mersey Docks & Harbour Board), which could and did use its powers to direct coastal shipping, although controls were not introduced until 1918. These were probably to be more beneficial to the non-liner coastal companies, rather than those who operated regular services between ports.

The problem coastal services found in obtaining available traffic in competition against the Railways through their ability to continue quoting at their 1914 rates, was alleviated when the Railways were instructed to stop accepting goods which could be carried by coaster, this being followed by a

Previously the death in action of J. Cunningham, E. Hales, and H.E. Ringrose, all members of the Shadwell permanent dock labour force had been reported. W. Card, also at Shadwell, was to be awarded the D.C.M.

More pleasant news was the opening of the Dry Dock Co.'s No.3 Dry Dock - urgently needed by then - by the s.s.WOODLEIGH (on charter to Fisher Renwick, Newcastle), Mrs. G. Renwick cutting the ribbon at the ceremony.

George Renwick M.P. was a member of the Parliamentary Commission which visited the Western Front during Autumn 1918 to investigate the conduct of the war.

All five of George Renwick's sons had volunteered for service in the Army at the start of the war, happily and incredibly all survived, despite taking part in all the worst battles of the Western Front. Major Gustav Renwick, who had joined the 'Commercial Battalion', Northumberland Fusiliers - one of the fated 'Pals' units - and now Second-in-coastal steamer subsidy being given from December 1918 to 30th June 1920, when an increase in the railway rates was introduced. This certainly benefited the coastal services by helping them regain some traffic, but was really too late. Ironically it also eased some of the problems the Railways were experiencing in coping with their traffic, and also eased the congestion, which occurred when a convoy (the grouping of merchant ships to sail together protected by warships) arrived at a port. It was as late as 1917 before the convoy system was introduced as part of the war against the U-Boats, despite the benefits to be gained being known nearly a century earlier. The heavy losses of shipping arguably nearly caused the defeat of the Allies by Germany.

In 1913 some 13,000,000 tons of non-coal traffic was carried by coastal liner services between British ports, of this Manchester-London Steamers carried some 160,000 tons (Coasters carried a further 2,000,000 tons of non-coal traffic). By 1918 the volume carried was down to some 5,000,000 tons, with Manchester-London Steamers only carrying some 75,000 tons.

At about this time A.H. Read made an offer to buy Manchester-London Steamers - this was rejected. Read's plan was to create what became Coast Lines. George Renwick preferred it remain an independent company.

The U-boat menace was made very clear with the HALBADIER, on passage to Shadwell with general freight, being torpedoed 6th January 1918 (28 miles SW. by W. and $\frac{1}{2}$ mile W. from Bardsey Isle) without warning, five crew members were lost, the Chief Engineer, Steward and a Fireman were killed

immediately. The HALBADIER was unfortunate, if not unlucky. In April 1917 when entering Shadwell Basin Lock and with her stern hard against the floating boom - kept against the lock wall to act as a fender - she caused the boom, which was greasy because it was overdue for attention by the Port Authority, to turn on its side, damaging her stern and causing £150 damage to the lock wall. No claim had been received at the time the accident was reported by the Dock Superintendent, but the P.L.A. approved a settlement be agreed on 'best terms' - no report of a claim or settlement has been located.

Her destruction did not, however, prevent Fisher Renwick writing to the Canal Company for the payment of repairs to damaged sustained by HALBADIER on 3rd November 1917, when a swing-bridge on the Canal was closed before she had passed through, fortunately without injuries being caused.

The loss of the HALBADIER led to the Ministry of Shipping eventually permitting the s.s.BLAIRMORE, now owned by Fisher Renwick, to be transferred to Manchester-London Steamers. Although useful at the time it was not seen as a long term answer, the BLAIRMORE was longer than their other steamers, causing difficulty in entering and berthing at Shadwell. Her operating costs too were greater, thereby reducing profitability and leaving less margin for sailing with less than a full cargo.

At the Armistice, George Renwick made the decision to purchase the shareholdings of the Fisher family, (there were five Fisher sisters among them), although this was not to prevent Fishers working for Fisher Renwick. To serve as a

Above: The right-hand section of the Bronze statue being prepared for the journey to Newcastle-upon-Tyne. The driver, Fred Walpole, is standing at the front of his Peerless. This was an epic trip for the time (1923). The journey took 32 hours. The petrol required for the 300-mile journey was also carried, requiring a considerable number of 2-gallon petrol cans. The very special job was remembered for being completed within the time planned and without delays through breakdown. He did however have to rewind the Peerless' magneto on arrival at Newcastle, no small tribute to Driver Walpole's abilities.

Left: George Renwick with his five sons. From the left: John (seated), William, Gustav, (Sir)George, Septimus and George(ii). Note (Sir)George Renwick's M.P. cap badge - the 'Parliamentary Portcullis' indicated he was a member of the Commission enquiring into progress of the War on the Western Front in 1918.

Below: Front and rear views of the Renwick Memorial, and Sir Gatcombe John R.A.'s finished bronze statue, at the original Barras Bridge location. The dedication reads "NON SIBI, SEDPATRIA" ("Not for themselves, for their Country"). It was unveiled by the Prince of Wales, July 5th 1923.

thanksgiving offering for the safe return of his sons, and to commemorate the sacrifice of those killed, Sir George and Lady Renwick had erected the RENWICK WAR MEMORIAL. The bronze figures were by Sir Gatcombe John R.A. Originally at Barras Bridge, it now stands in front of Newcastle-upon-Tyne Civic Centre. Sir Gatcombe John was a famous sculptor with many Royal and official commissions to his credit. Sir George chose him because he was moved by the newly completed memorial to the ENGINE ROOM CREW in Liverpool (originally intended for those who went down with the TITANIC, but now dedicated to those who died in action). The cost of their gift was never disclosed.

Chapter Four
1919-1933 – New Steamers and the First Scammells

Following recovery from his severe wounds received in June 1917 and his consequent demobilisation, Major Renwick, as he now became universally known to all employees, returned to be a director of Manchester-London Steamers on 21st March 1918. He was given responsibility for the Manchester operation. (He was also appointed a director of the Dry Dock company).

His experience during his war service, particularly while acting as Adjutant, was to be of great help in developing the relationship with employees, which was to contribute to the company's ability to survive. More importantly his army experience was to lead to his use of road transport as a means of partly overcoming the difficulties facing the company.

He found the Steamer Company coping with different and difficult conditions from those prevailing at his departure in August 1914. The Armistice did not bring a lasting improvement in trading, railway competition - through their low rates - worsened, and shortages of cargo, particularly from London, remained a problem.

Major Renwick had the unhappy task of dismissing employees, some of whom had already been laid off, whilst others accepted cuts in their pay. The Assistant Stevedore at Shadwell, who wished to return to Manchester had his furniture 'taken round in the steamer'. The Directors forewent their fees.

Nevertheless the lease for Manchester Wharf, Shadwell was extended for a year, with a rebate of £500 for not using No.58 Shed. This was because of the falling off in drapery traffic, and the reduced need for storage.

A national railway strike in the autumn of 1919 showed the potential for using road motor transport and, for the first time, that the railways were no longer going to be indispensable for movement of goods.

It is not possible to establish exactly when or how Major Renwick established his friendship with Lt. Colonel A.G. Scammell, or later with E.W. Rudd, but there is circumstantial evidence that in the preparation for General Plumer's 1917 campaign, prior to the Battle of Messines, they both would have had the opportunity to have met with each other, when observing French Army use of their Knox Tractors in moving their light tanks and also the Schneider caterpillar artillery tractors. (This was in direct contrast to the British practice of using rail transport to reach as near to the Front as possible, and then relying on

self movement of the, admittedly heavier, British tanks).

E.W. Rudd, Chairman and major shareholder of a well known London based road transport contractor, held the British agency for Knox Tractors, moving to Aberfeldy Street, Poplar, which he had taken over from Charles Fryer & Co., London, (with whom he had been connected). His firm E.W. Rudd were operating some 30 Knox articulated units, particularly on distance meat carrying and also on groceries contracts. The use by Rudd of drawbar trailers behind their Knox articulated units when used on local work between the London Docks and Smithfield Market had inspired Scammell to provide for this option as an additional benefit of using Scammells.

It is reasonable to assume that Colonel Scammell, who was Managing Director of G. Scammell & Nephew; Percy Hugh, G. Scammell's Technical Director, and E.W. (Edward Whitten) Rudd used Rudd's experience of operating his Knox units in the design of the new Scammell motive unit and carrier (Scammell preferred to use the description 'carrier' as being more descriptive of the function of this component of their flexible six-wheeler) thus forming the basis of the Scammell Lorry. This had been designed to carry the gross weight evenly over the three axles, so that no axle weight would exceed the then maximum legal weight of 6 tons, with a 7 ton payload at 12 m.p.h.

The obvious similarity was the method used to mount the 'carrier' (trailer) turntable by using separate half-elliptical springs supporting the steel frame of the turntable or fifth-wheel, and bearing directly upon the rear axle, rather than the chassis of the unit. This became a patented feature of the Scammell unit, allowing 'fore and aft' hinging of the carrier. Whereas the Knox unit had a shortened chassis, with half cantilever springs taking the weight of the rear of the unit on the rear axle, which prevented any hinging.

The Scammell four cylinder 47 h.p. petrol engine had the same 5in x 5in bore and stroke, as the Knox, but at first used cast iron pistons. It also had o.h. valves with twin detachable cylinder heads. These had copper rings acting as joints. The water passed through an external transfer pipe bolted on the near side of the engine. The drive was by a cone clutch, three-speed gearbox via a jackshaft (countershaft), which included the enclosed differential to a Renold chain-drive.

The Scammell unit had two brakes, one, the foot-brake, worked as a transmission brake on the bevel shaft. The second - operated by the outer of the side handbrake levers - functioned via internal expanding shoes in the hub of the driving wheels, another difference from the Knox, which used the countershaft (jackshaft) to carry the unit's brakes.

The Knox, however, had electric starting, a benefit not shared by the Scammell for many years. The trailer (carrier) brakes for the Knox were hydraulic, and operated by pumping the hand operated brake lever. Although effective, it was not always conveniently operated by the driver, and really needed a second man. This method of operating the trailer brakes was used because the Knox was intended to pull trailers made by other makers, and particularly in America, converted horse drawn waggons.

The Scammell carrier brakes were operated mechanically. The carrier was connected to the turntable by a hollow fulcrum pin and the carrier axle brakes used identical internal expanding brakes as on the unit, these being operated by a bell and crank lever which pivoted on a bracket bolted to the turntable below the hollow fulcrum pin. The bell crank acted on the push rod inside the pin, which by sliding up and down inside the hollow pin would cause a second bell-crank on the carrier to operate a rod connecting to a compensating bar, which in turn caused the cabling to each brake to function.

Meanwhile, the Fisher Renwick Manchester-London Steamers fleet at 1920 comprised:

s.s.BLAIRMORE   s.s.CUIRASSIER
s.s.LANCER   s.s.YEOMAN

Fisher Renwick, Newcastle were now operating the s.s.EVERELDA, the rest of their business being carried by chartering in, or broking. Fisher Renwick did not change the name of ships they purchased on re-registration, continuing to use the original name. The coal strikes in 1920 affected the steamers hopes for improving traffic, particularly as the wire traffic from R. Johnson & Nephew ceased. After the strike the rate had to be adjusted to prevent its loss to the railway, who were anxious to obtain it.

The question of taking the YEOMAN 'off line' was considered in April 1920, but Major Renwick decided to keep three steamers 'on line' temporarily despite their not having full cargoes as he believed regular sailings were the only way of ensuring the company kept its share of available traffic.

The Directors' meeting on 25th June 1920 was notable for the review by Major Renwick of the likely effect of withdrawal of the Coastal Service Subsidy scheme, a possible increase in railway rates, and the opportunities for any increase in cargo for the LANCER, the only steamer now 'on line' at that date. He also told the meeting that there were now firms running Motor 'Lurries' between Manchester and London, and he was of the opinion that the steamer company should also provide motor transport between Manchester and London. He also proposed introducing smaller vehicles for the collection and delivery services, with Scammell Lorries also being used to collect heavier traffic.

The Chairman, George Renwick, agreed that Major Renwick should see what would be needed - he would try to inspect the Scammell 'Lurry' being shown at the Darlington Royal Show that following week, part of a national tour demonstrating the 'new Scammell Articulated Lorry'.

Sir George Renwick, as he became in the January 1921 Honours List - his baronetcy being conferred on him for public services - was happy with the idea of using motor vehicles for a local service. This was becoming the norm for local firms, and the purchase of Ford T flat lorries - assembled at Trafford Park, Peerless chassis and two Daimler flat lorries, went ahead. They were intended for use at both Manchester and London. (Major Renwick almost certainly had become familiar with the Peerless marque's lorries as they were used for his Battalion's transport needs and had a good reputation when operating in the difficult conditions of the Western Front - although these examples were ex-American Expeditionary Force vehicles, the bus bodies removed being used by Lancashire poultry farmers). However, Sir George Renwick was less happy about purchasing and operating the larger Scammells.

He finally agreed that the Major obtain the first four Scammell Lorries himself, and be allowed to operate them as a separate company, Fisher Renwick Transport Ltd., operating from both Pomona and Shadwell. A decision which would eventually secure the future, indeed the survival of the Company.

Major Renwick had already arranged that the first prototype for demonstration should be tried by Fisher Renwick Transport Ltd., and this duly arrived, although in grey primer it was so lettered. It was operated with the six ton drawbar trailer, which it apparently had no problem in pulling. The trailer had the newly patented Scammell arrangement of twin turntables for the two axles to assist handling and manoeuvring.

The Scammell lorry was designed with a very low reverse gear ratio so that the engine could tick over, allowing its driver adequate time for the manoeuvre. Oliver North, Scammell's Chief Designer, strongly advocated 'the Scammell six-wheeler with the rigid rear carrier axle could be reversed as readily as one with steerable rear wheels, and in many cases more readily'.

Whilst the trial fulfilled his (and Scammell's) expectations, the Manchester Police were less than happy. With other forces they were instrumental in securing the change - which became part of the Heavy Motor Car (Amendment) Order, 29th May 1922 Regulations - for that type of vehicle operation to become illegal. The Order, however, did legally recognise the concept of the Scammell Flexible Six Wheeler provided that the six-wheeler complied with the limiting requirements:

Total vehicle laden weight must not exceed 18 tons. Maximum speed with rubber tyres, 12 m.p.h. Maximum axle weights - Front, 4 tons; Middle, 8 tons; Rear, 6 tons.

The weight on the middle axle must exceed the weight on the rear axle. E.W. Rudd was reported to be less pleased about losing the ability to pull drawbar trailers.

Fisher Renwick Transport's first four Scammells were registered NC 3744, NC 3718, NC 5037 and NC 5895. These were delivered in August and September 1920. The four motive units, which had windscreens and cape hoods, were supplied with flat carriers, 17ft long by 7ft 6in wide. At least one of these was supplied through N.M.U. (Northern Motor Utilities) of York.

Each Scammell had a driver and second man, who was also a competent driver. They were recruited from the many experienced ex-army drivers available. They all received instruction from a Scammell Lorries demonstration driver

Left: A unique photograph of the demonstration Scammell, with its drawbar trailer. It is just possible to distinguish that the trailer's rear axle was also to be used as a turntable (a patented feature) to assist in reversing or manoeuvring. The trailer carried 6 tons. Although in primer finish, it is lettered for Fisher Renwick Transport. This very early and successful version of a double bottom met with the disapproval of the authorities, notably the Police, and was discontinued. The combined payload was 13 tons.

servicing, and maintenance of their lorries. Hence their ability to perform the first virtually non-stop long distance services between Manchester and London, which usually took about 28 hours. During these first years they would 'telegraph' their progress from major towns. It is known little time was lost through breakdowns during this early 'experimental' period.

Fisher Renwick did not use the description 'Trunk', always preferring to use 'Long Distance' and then 'Continuous' or later 'Direct' service. They also made the Steamer Liner service collections and deliveries of regular consignments of wire, export drapery, and groceries at both Pomona and Shadwell, as well as proving most effective in handling awkward items such as cable drums, boilers and fabrications such as Keirs, which were then carried round on the steamers.

One of the first of these long distance road trips which gained the attention of customers was the delivery of a full load of Liptons packeted tea from London to Manchester. The first ever overnight non-stop journey.

This success attracted competition, with Horniman & Sons pointing out they had received a quotation "to convey their traffic in lock-up box vans, delivery in Manchester to be effected the day after collection in London, at 60 shillings per ton C & D". Major Renwick responded by reducing their rate to 55 shillings per ton, retaining the traffic, and being able to use a new tilt bodied carrier. By contrast the LANCER had sailed from Shadwell with about 40 tons of tea consigned from various firms for delivery in Manchester.

The Callender Cable drum traffic was now going to Manchester by rail, despite the cable company being "highly satisfied with the Steamer service". Most of it was soon regained, Fisher Renwick's service and limitation of damage outweighed any cost saving from using the railway. The Scammells, together with the new special purpose carriers known as Cable Floats, proved to be an effective aid in achieving this.

Particular attention was given to maintenance by Major Renwick and there are many references made by him concerning the provision of garaging and workshop facilities for Pomona at Cornbrook Road and at newly leased premises in Medland Street, Shadwell.

He rigidly enforced that there must be no overloading, or 'kerbing' of the solid tyres then used on the heavy lorries at this date, these being the major causes for tyre and wheel problems. This also applied to the use of the lighter Ford T

as was practice at that date. For a long period their pay was £5-0-0 per week, with an element of Job and Finish, (the right to go home if the allocated work duty was completed earlier then allowed, and other usual tasks were also completed). This rate was double the average wage paid at this period.

They were also expected to carry out the routine weekly

and Peerless lorries. Failure to adhere to this instruction continued to be a disciplinary offence to the final period of Fisher Renwick Services contracts.

Although Scammell Lorries had appointed various agents, including Pollen & Crisp for Manchester, the only Scammell sales, service and spares depots up to the 1930s - apart from the factory - were at Birmingham, (Wharfdale Road) and Manchester, (Stretford). Their Depot at Glasgow was not relevant to Fisher Renwick's needs at that time.

Following the successful trials of the prototype Scammell articulated unit, in which Fisher Renwick, or rather Major Renwick was associated, Colonel A.G. Scammell established Scammell Lorries specifically to manufacture his new Articulated Lorry. Its success meant removal from Spitalfields and a new works was built at Watford. His connection with the family business Geo. Scammell & Nephew ceased from 1922, although the Design and Sales Office remained at High Holborn. The new Company, Scammell Lorries Ltd., became a quoted public company in April 1922. Colonel A.G. Scammell was Managing Director, Percy C. Hugh, the Chief Engineer, and another of the six Directors appointed was Edward Whitten Rudd. Albert Isaac Belisha, the Company Broker, was known to have been a friend of these and also of Major Renwick. Although not yet a Director, Major Renwick was an original shareholder in the new company.

E.W. Rudd had previously roused the ire of the Rudd board through his involvement in selling horses to E.W. Rudd Ltd, so he was no doubt happy to report to his Board that he was no longer the agent for Knox, (This was no great sacrifice, the Budget of 1915 saw the 'McKenna' Budget introduce a 25% duty on all imported motor vehicles). He would, however, continue to act as the Agent for Knox spares. This would have been a profitable venture as many Knox Tractors, including Rudd's and Pickford's were in use up to the 1930's. The Knox Agency reverted to their original Agent, Bramco, who were located at 1 Ellys Road, Coventry. This company also had a connection with E.W. Rudd.

Major Renwick's Scammells were soon seen to be operationally and commercially successful, with an additional fifth unit, NC ?? (full registration unknown) being bought, together with his all purpose tilt carrier, and the special cable floats. His success may have been eased by his being able to use the Steamers' Cornbrook Road Office services, and their customer base at the start of Fisher Renwick Transport. His attention to detail, and accurate costings, with the presence of an experienced workforce for any work with the loads would also have been a factor. He soon also added a Ford T flat lorry at Shadwell to make collections for the Scammell's long distance operations.

The evidence of the success of Fisher Renwick Transport was being provided by the detailed accounts Major Renwick gave at meetings of the Directors. This led to Sir George proposing the business be bought by, and become an integral part of, Fisher Renwick Manchester-London Steamers Ltd. as from 1st May 1922. Five Scammell Articulated Lorries, and the Ford T, three carriers, and the garages with their leases were taken over for £11,151-7-9d.

On the shipping front, the BLAIRMORE whilst 'off line' had run aground near Ijmuiden, Holland, and was in dry dock being repaired at Amsterdam, these were to take over two

Below: Scammell NC 3744, with the cable carrier, showing its versatility by carrying a Keir. The photograph was taken on a fine day, hence the open house windows. The cobbled road surface leaves much to be desired, the tram track projecting above the road. Not an ideal surface for solid tyres.

Left: Major Renwick's first Scammell unit NC 3744 with the new cable carrier, the identity of the elegant gentleman with the gold hunter is not known, although he also appears in a later photograph. The address on the ramp is that of the garage in Cornbrook Road. A nice touch was the Steamer Company's house flag being painted both sides of the winch.

Above: Having arrived safely at Pomona the Keir is being loaded onto the s.s.YEOMAN. The photo is full of detail showing how this was carried out. Note the rigging of the derrick, and the three point slinging, with the crew and dock labour working as a team. There is debris from some of the consignment of cotton unloaded, but not yet cleared. The low deck of the carrier was 15 feet long.

months, to mid March 1922 and were to cost some £13,000.

Trading conditions were generally poor during 1923, and there was new, increasing competition for traffic from other motor road transport firms whom Major Renwick considered had greatly improved their organisation. The Steamers were not only losing traffic, but were having to reduce rates, or offer discounts to fight the railways, which, following the 1921 amalgamations, were aggressively seeking traffic. Dock strikes too created problems.

An attempt was made to increase the Steamer Liner traffic by again introducing a Southampton call from December 1922, but this was soon suspended. Apart from insufficient traffic, (despite promising canvassing prospects), it also "suffered from the rapacity of the dock labour particularly in regard to overtime". Southampton Docks were built by the London & South Western Railway, being greatly developed as part of the Southern Railway.

The news emanating from the road transport service was more uplifting, Major Renwick gave figures for a trip to London and return made by a Scammell which showed a fair profit with a full load. Further details were given of one trip from London to Manchester with a load of Bovril and Margarine, leading Sir George to consider "it may be prudent

to keep one or two Scammells in London to deal with urgent consignments".

Two new Scammell articulated 12 ton lorries were ordered - one for London, 'ENGINEER', XM 8895, the other for Manchester, 'GUARDSMAN', XM 9590. These had four speed gearboxes, using different sized sprockets for the chain drive, and were equipped with the newly developed, more efficient and more powerful 70 h.p. engine with aluminium pistons. They were also fitted with heavier section cast steel wheels with 12in. wide solid rubber tyres for the unit's rear axle and the carrier axle. All motive units from this date used the improved design turntable, this was now a steel pressing, and claimed to be stronger and to wear better with less parts, yet weighed less. They still had hoods but were soon converted to cabs. Acetylene headlights were also fitted. Both vehicles were ordered with 22ft. carriers. Major Renwick drew up the details for the all-purpose body, with steel stanchions, loose hoops and tarpaulin sheets. One was lettered for Shadwell, the other for Pomona. An additional 12 ton cable float was also ordered. This to have 1 inch diameter wire cable, with spliced hook, and separate cable shackles. Also, following a visit to Slough, four more Peerless lorries were purchased, two for Manchester and two for London. The latter were to help in lowering costs for local cartage.

Negotiations continued during Autumn 1923 with Cowan & Co., Henry Evans & Son, and the Maritime Lighterage Co. for reductions in their rates. Major Renwick obtained reductions of 6d per ton at Manchester and 4d at London. He was unable to get any agreement from the Lighterage Company so had obtained a quoted rate of 1s. 0d. per ton from Griffiths & Co. In the event the Maritime Lighterage Company agreed to the reduction sought. Other costs were less predictable however, the price for steamer bunker coal increased by fluctuating amounts, sometimes as much as an increase of one tenth in the price per ton.

An order was placed with W. Dobson & Co., to build a new steamer similar to CUIRASSIER for £35,000, to be named 'SAPPER', for delivery mid-January 1924 and despite the continuing poor trading conditions, Sir George had felt able to order a further new steamer in October 1923 from the Tyne Iron Shipbuilding Co. Ltd., to be named SENTRY at a cost of £34,000, half to be paid on completion, the balance in installments over two years. 'SENTRY' was to be the last steamer built for the Company. Both vessels were to be equipped with full electric lighting.

Sir George Renwick, convinced that there would be a continuing demand for new ships, also entered into a partnership with Stanley Dalgliesh to open a new, purpose built Yard at Hebburn, Renwick Dalgliesh Ltd. The depression following its start meant that no ship was built, indeed no order was ever received. The yard was taken over by National Ship Builders Ltd., set up to rationalise the industry, and closed. Both partners lost their considerable investment in this enterprise. His related purpose to develop

Below: Scammell NC 3744 being used for its main purpose, to deliver the cable drums which, in this instance, have been brought from Shadwell on the CUIRASSIER. She would have moored that side of 4 Dock, using her own derricks to unload. It was hard work hand winding the carrier's winch but, at that date, the best way to do the job. (Compare this with a later photograph showing the use of a Pickfords 'Rapier' mobile crane handling cable drums at Shadwell).

what became the Team Valley Industrial Estate was eventually fulfilled after his death, and sadly not by him.

At the March 1924 Directors' meeting, Lady Renwick who always showed considerable detailed knowledge of the operations, queried comparative labour costs at the Wharves. Major Renwick also considered these costs a problem, particularly at Shadwell. He reported that he was going to stop piece-work on cargoes, and use permanent labour on day rates, however, these did have an element of incentive included in them.

Because of heavy investment in various capital items, the Directors' meeting on 24th August 1924 approved the creation of £60,000 of 6% Redeemable Debentures to be authorised, these to be issued as required. The meeting was followed by Directors and family members taking a short cruise along the Ship Canal following the delivery and acceptance of the SENTRY.

On the motor transport front, another cable carrier for use with the Scammell units was purchased in December 1925.

As the 1920's progressed it became apparent to some, including Major Renwick, that there was continuing decline in the cotton textile business, and therefore in the traffic available. This was not to be a series of temporary slumps, perhaps disguised by the effect of strikes, particularly the 1926 General Strike, but would be a permanent decline. A major factor was to be the boycott of Lancashire cotton goods by India as part of its campaign to gain independence. (India was able to do this by substituting purchases from Japan, and by starting to create its own manufacturing industry, purchasing old, superseded machinery from Lancashire together with new machinery from Japan).

There was a noticeable, if gradual change in cargoes available, sometimes not acceptable for the steamers, which were facing increasing competition from the railways. They were not only quoting attractive rates but also actively targeting the steamers' customers, particularly for groceries

and provisions. All this made it difficult to make a profit. Sir George gave instructions that canvassers 'should arrange that large urgent consignments could be dealt with by putting part on the lorries, with the balance going by Steamer'.

It is interesting to see the extent to which Sir George had now become an enthusiastic convert to the operation of the Scammells.

As Major Renwick's earlier forecast that road transport, using larger vehicles, could replace the steamers became all too accurate, his concern for the future for the company made him concentrate upon developing the road service. In March 1926, the first four Scammell lorries were included in a part-exchange arrangement for one new 12 ton, motive unit, NE 6097, and one 10 ton unit, NE 6871, and its carrier. All the units now had the box cabs, and double split windscreen. Another 10 Ton unit, NE ??, was ordered a month later, this had a 17ft. Liverpool type flat carrier. Although Colonel Scammell was now advocating the use of

'giant' pneumatic tyres for large commercial vehicles, and Scammell exports were being fitted with 40x8 Dunlop tyres, the new orders for Fisher Renwick were to continue to use solid tyres for some time.

Major Renwick may not have been a practical engineer, but he had the ability to identify problems from hearing of his drivers' and fitters' experiences and knowledge of faults. Their suggestions for improvements, or the need for any modification to be made to the specification were considered and in turn passed to Colonel A.G. Scammell. Notable was

Below: Fisher Renwick Transport's 'pride' of Scammells, NC 3744, NC 3718, NC 5037, NC 5895, and NC ?? lined up at 4 Dock, Pomona, all coupled to flat carriers, shortly after delivery of the fifth. They may all be described as immaculate, although the first ones would already have covered thousands of miles on the earliest long distance journeys. The background detail shows a number of Cowan's horse drawn flats with sheeted loads. The railway trucks in the distance contained Guinness barrels.

the need for extra and stronger exhaust brackets to secure the exhaust system to the Unit chassis. A rack to carry 9 two-gallon petrol cans was fitted at an early stage, (at this date petrol was not always conveniently available, especially at night, it would also have been more expensive). As late as 1925 the A.A. was operating a 'Roadside Petrol Filling Station', provided with a 500 gallon storage capacity, on the A45 on the Coventry side of Dunchurch.

Increases in taxation caused concern especially for a future petrol tax. It was suggested that the increases would put costs up by 5d per ton. However, the Heavy Motor Car (Amendment) 1927 introduced changes in braking, and in the maximum length.

Scammell Lorries themselves were also suffering difficult trading conditions, and made a loss in the financial year to May 1926. A consequence of this was a reduction in the value of their Ordinary Shares by two-thirds from £1 to 6s. 8d. Shortly after Major Renwick was appointed a Director of Scammell Lorries Limited.

Steamer trade during 1927/1928 was such that LANCER spent much of her time laid up at Pomona. No suitable charters being found and her insurance cover was limited to 'harbour risks'. Paradoxically rising costs, including that of bunker coal, made it necessary to increase rates by 6%, and these were able to be held.

The Ship Canal had to close Pomona whilst heavy repairs were made to the Trafford Swing-bridge, the steamers using a temporary berth in the main Docks. The Canal Company also used this closure to extend London Wharf, doubling the available berth space. This was to become very useful for the increasing use of the Fisher Renwick lorries.

The increase in competition from other road transport operators caused less concern to Sir George and Major Renwick than did that from the Railways. Their continued rate cutting was particularly damaging to the Steamer service, which was their intention. They were assisted by their ability to introduce charges for all destinations, including collection and delivery, to gain or keep traffic. This was a concern which also affected competing 'smalls' carriers; Bouts, Suttons and Suttons (Manchester) and Carter Paterson all suffered. McNamara seemed to have established some form of agreement with the railways,

Below: Was it a jack-knife, or did the fulcrum pin fracture? We are unlikely ever to know. The accident happened sometime earlier during daylight, obviously during wintry conditions. The motive unit, NC 5037, remains upright. It is now lettered as part of the Steamer Company, and has also been named FUSILIER. It is of particular interest because it shows detail of the carrier braking system and the impressive size of the brake drums, which were interchangeable with those of the unit.

Above: Scammell S12 ENGINEER, XM8895. One of two 12 ton units with the new 70 h.p. engine and 4-speed gearbox. The hood was soon to be replaced by a cab. Both units had carriers with all-purpose bodies, designed by Major Renwick. The loose hoops and sheets, if not being used, were stored in the bow front of the body. The success of the covered body led to coachbuilt box bodies being introduced.

particularly the London & North Eastern Railway (this seemingly originated with the Great Central Railway), and were apparently less affected.

Denis A. Renwick joined Fisher Renwick Manchester-London Steamers in 1928. Major Renwick persuaded him to move from his job with Coast Lines (part of Sir James Sutherland's grand design for the future of the Liner Coastal trade), where he was manager of The Free Trade Wharf. He was to remain at London, marrying and setting up his home there. He was given ever increasing and total responsibilities for the London operation. (He was appointed a Director at the Meeting of 15th July 1929, aged only 21 years).

A decision was made in January 1926 to have the BLAIRMORE 'survey passed' for her Lloyds rating and then offered for sale. This sale was finally completed early 1928, resulting in a surplus in account of £5,987 for reinvestment, and for the first time the asset value of the Motor Vehicle fleet, less depreciation, was given as £13,555-3-3d.

At the Directors' Meeting of 16th May 1928, Major Renwick mentioned that he had the opportunity to invest in Marston Road Services as a means of acquiring an interest in 'outside transport work', however after careful assessment he had decided to withdraw from the negotiations. (He considered the business to be under-capitalised). This was to be a wise decision in view of the subsequent history of

Marston Road Services, which underwent various re-organisations and changes of name until acquired by Ralph Donaldson-Hudson and his son, John in 1933.

Expansion and replacement of the fleet took place, including thirteen of the latest large capacity Scammell S15 'eight wheel' articulated lorries. These had the 70 h.p. 'high efficiency' engine, four speed gear-box, and roller bearings. They were so named because their carriers were the first British examples made with the 'four in line' wheel layout. The two oscillating axles had their semi-elliptical springs attached to their mountings on longitudinal pivots. The company's carriers now included box and flat types, two semi low-loader cable floats, and a specially bodied carrier - the front half having a box body, the rear half 4ft detachable sides and a tilt. This replaced the original, successful tilt carrier introduced in 1922.

The thirteen Scammell S15 were almost all supplied during 1928, they were as follows:

'HALBADIER'	UL 185	S15 Flat 25'6" long.
'VOLUNTEER'	XV 5213	S15 Flat 25'6" long.
'MUSKETEER'	?? ??	S15 Flat 25'6" long.
'FUSILIER'	XV 5547	S15 Flat 25'6" long.
'CAVALIER'	XV 9921	S15 Flat 25'6" long.
'PIONEER'	YV 5155	S15 Box 26'10" long, 7'9" high.
'BRIGADIER'	YV 5156	S15 Box 26'10" long, 7'9" high.
'MERLIN'	YW 5024	S15 Box 26'10" long, 7'9" high.
'LANCER'	YW 5207	S15 Box 26'10" long, 7'9" high.
'PARTRIDGE'	YW 5208	S15 Contractors Sided.
'DRUMMER'	YX 5267	S15 Contractors Sided.
'PHEASANT'	GK 642	S15 Cable Float
'DRAGOON'	GU 9561	S15 G.P. Half Tilt.

These new vehicles made it possible for the company to

Above: A flat drawbar trailer for cable traffic, lettered for Shadwell, the picture believed to have been taken in 1926. The original was a Dyson Trailers publicity photograph. The trailer is shown outside the works at Liverpool. The works no longer exists, and Dyson are now part of King Trailers. It is a safe assumption that it is being delivered to Pomona, to be taken by Steamer to Shadwell.

introduce the pioneering concept of their Continuous Road Service between Manchester and London, which although also competing with the steamers, effectively answered competition from Bouts, etc.

Major Renwick specified a fifty gallon tank, equipped with a hand rotary pump to be fitted under each carrier chassis, again to ensure they had no problems over petrol supplies. A little later when the first Rigid chain-drive chassis were purchased they were specified with an additional petrol tank.

These S15s proved to be ideal for the new traffics which were being obtained. These included 'Dominion' Cash Registers, Carborundum Grinding Wheels, Brooke Bond Tea (they opened a tea blending and packing warehouse at Trafford Park), paper converted products including Shand Kydd Wall Paper, and increasing consignments of Kelloggs Corn Flakes and other of their products, imported from Canada, until their new factory was opened in 1937/1938.

The naming of the early Scammells was Major Renwick's idea, these first long-distance lorries were named after

Right: One of the Steamer Company's first Ford T flat lorries, outside Shadwell. The left-hand drive chassis would have been assembled at Ford's Trafford Park factory, and was supplied by Quick's, who also built the cab and body. The ridge pole to support the sheet can be seen. The electric lights would only work when the engine was running, making the oil lights necessary.

Steamers, (not all these names belonged to steamers owned or operated by the Company however). With the introduction of rigid vehicles the change was made to using the names of waders and game birds, then almost at the end, gods, stars and rivers. Believing many more names would be required with the increasing number of vehicles, the inspiration for the bird names came from his use of a list of the General Steam Navigation Company's steamers, most of which were named after these birds.

Amongst changes introduced to provide faster communication now necessary between Pomona and Shadwell, a private telephone line connection was installed, the rental charges of which were estimated to be £1,200 per year.

The expansion and updating of vehicles also included both Pomona and Shadwell collection and delivery fleets. The first Ford Ts were replaced by the new Ford AA and B models, although the Peerless lorries, in a few instances modernised and fitted with front pneumatic tyres, were to remain in use a little longer. These new

vehicles were all intended to meet and take advantage of the changes brought about by the Construction and Use Regulations, part of the Road Traffic Act 1930. These also brought in limits for drivers' hours, although the Act did not require records of hours worked to be kept.

A greater proportion of Shadwell's local work would continue to be carried out by Hays Wharf Cartage Co. under contract. They had by now totally replaced Henry Evans & Co., partly due to their ability to provide a mix of horse vans (their Clydesdale horses were long renowned), and also specialised motor vehicles. Following the acquisition by Hays of Pickfords, the latter's Rapier Mobile Cranes were frequently hired, especially for cable drum traffic.

The wharf and yard layout and entrances to Pomona and especially Shadwell, created problems due to the expansion of the fleet and the increased size of the long-distance vehicles. The layout of the internal rail track at Pomona was to be a particular problem, these restricting the manoeuvring of vehicles. The transit sheds at both Pomona and Shadwell whilst not ideal, were easily adapted to have loading banks, although movement could be increasingly difficult.

Extensions to both garages were also completed and a welcomed reduction to £150 in the rateable value was

obtained for the Medland Street Garage, because of the de-rating benefit for freight transport allowed by the Local Government Act 1929.

The experienced wharf labour, used to stowing cargo in the holds, had no difficulty with also loading the new vehicles, vans or flats, to the maximum capacity, always with the proviso of no overloading. The handling of any of the larger consignments, boilers and cable drums, posed no problems either.

The administration and clerical routines for the road service were carried out by existing staff at Manchester and London. Accounts were prepared from consignment notes, Proof of Delivery (POD's), and the long distance vehicles waybills by the depots.

As the traffic taken by road steadily increased, evening overtime began to be necessary to load and then prepare the waybills. The traffic returns and the financial reports based on these routines were developments of the well established systems used for the steamers.

The Newcastle office was never involved with the road service, and in fact was to be closed. This was partly due to the recurring trade recessions which affected Britain and her exports - Sir George Renwick's death on 17th December 1930 being also a contributory factor.

Considerable difficulties continued with railway competition, particularly the L.M.&S.R., on this occasion because of their rates for multiple-shop grocery deliveries from the Margarine Union, within a thirty mile radius of Manchester.

Major Renwick was also expected to act within the framework of the Coastwise Shipping Act, and the Railways Conference Scheme, to his considerable regret.

Some help with steamer costs was obtained by the P.L.A. arranging a Rates Compounding Agreement effective October 1930. Fisher Renwick being able to present their manifests and analysis of goods specified, with a detailed calculation of Port Dues and Rates payable. The P.L.A. allowed a 12% commission for this. The previous rate of 4d paid by the steamers was reduced to 2d per ton outbound, 1½d. inwards, based on the steamer's net registered tonnage.

A lease described as garage space, but actually to be parking space and occasional space for storage of the cable drums, allowed a roadway to be made at Fisher Renwick's expense, and included demolition and re-construction of the 'lockman and oilers cabins'. A ground rent of £154 and rates etc. for a 21 year lease was agreed.

Four of the new Scammell S10 Six-wheeled Articulated Lorries fitted with 40x8 pneumatic tyres, including two

spares, were ordered mid 1930 at a cost £6,400. The carriers had box van bodies. The extra reserve tank was again fitted. This enhancement was introduced by Scammell themselves in 1930 as part of the updating of their range. Four of the S15 lorries were taken in part exchange with an allowance of £3,221 being given.

Two more S10 models were purchased the next year. Their success meant four more examples soon joined the fleet. Some were to be fitted with 13.50x20 giant pneumatic tyres on the driving and carrier axles.

Above: A Peerless, XH 7252, with Fred Walpole, as always smartly turned out, together with a second man. They were in this case delivering Kolynos toothpaste to Butler & Crisp, once a well known chemists, in Clerkenwell. The cab provides minimal protection, and dates it to the mid-twenties, it also shows it was one of the many ex-army Peerless lorries reconditioned by the Slough Trading Co. and sold by them as Peerless dealers. The solid rear tyres have recently been replaced. The picture reflects the effect of the ravages of age on the glass plate negative.

Above: This impressive line-up depicts the Fisher Renwick Shadwell collection and delivery fleet. The second of the two Peerless lorries on the left has Fred Walpole standing beside it. The five Ford Model T flats, like most early examples of the marque, feature left-hand drive. The second and third appear to be well loaded, presumably with textile goods. The third man from the left, next to Fred Walpole, is believed to be Fisher Renwick's mechanic. It is not possible to identify any of the other drivers. Hays Wharf were also being used as cartage contractors at this time.

Right: A mixed line up of Fisher Renwick vehicles at Pomona. The Scammell is thought to be the S10 'YEOMAN', NE 6871, supplied in 1926. From this point in time all new Scammells to enter the fleet were named. Note that the two Peerless flats and the Daimler have had full cabs and screens fitted. The solitary Daimler in the foreground would have had the well-known Knight sleeve-valve engine, and appears to be fitted with electric lighting. In this instance the identity of the drivers is not known.

Above: A happy group of the Directors and families with the Captain and some crew, on board the SENTRY after her acceptance, on a trip along the Ship Canal following a Directors' Meeting on 25th August 1924. In the front row are the Marine Superintendent, I.Lowden, the Captain and Sir George Renwick with Lady Renwick. Major Renwick is in the second row, third from right, wearing a bowler hat.

The Scammell S10 Articulated Lorries bought 1930/31:

'GROUSE'   GJ 8257   S10 Box.
'BLACKCOCK' GJ 8258   S10 Box.
'SNIPE'   GJ 8259   S10 Box.
'WOODCOCK' GJ 8260   S10 Box.
'MALLARD'   GK 643   S10 Box.
'LAPWING'   GK ??   S10 Sided. (on 13x20 tyres).
'WIDGEON'   GN 892   S10 Box.
'GREYHEN'   GN 893   S10 Box.
'PTARMIGAN' GN 894   S10 Sided. (on 13.50x20 tyres).
'MOORHEN'   ?? ??   S10 Sided.
'CURLEW'   GT 202   S10 GP/S. Tilt.
'PLOVER'   GT ??   S10 GP/S. Tilt.

The carriers' box bodies had semi-low loading floors, with suitable wheel arches for the tyre size. The height was not to exceed 12ft 5in. The side panels used 'Plymax' sheets and a double planked floor was fitted. Louvred ventilators, two in the front and one in each rear door were specified - a necessity with the increasing quantity of fruit traffic being carried. There was some change-over of carriers between motive units, mostly as traffic fluctuated.

The introduction of the Scammell Rigid Six, retaining the

chain-drive, and equipped with 13.50x20 pneumatic tyres on the 'K' type wheels, (these had the bolt-on detachable rims), marked a change of policy in choice of vehicles for the long distance service.

The first three ordered were placed in service October 1930, one was delivered in 1933, and a further fifteen between March 1934 and October 1935. A second-hand example, GY 2093, was delivered in January 1936, this had a sided body. After the experimental use by Fisher Renwick of

Left: Scammell S15, 'LANCER', YV 5156, at Pomona. This too is coupled to a van-bodied carrier. The forlorn Peerless in the background could be waiting to be refurbished and fitted with a cab. It is not known why the building behind is shored up. The mystery gentleman at the front of the carrier was also seen with the Major's first Scammell.

Below: Scammell S15, 'PIONEER', YV 5155, at Shadwell. The Scammell built van body was of 1,400 cubic feet capacity. The spring mountings of the 'Four-in-line' suspension of the carrier axle can be seen, as can the 50-gallon auxiliary petrol tank mounted under, and at the front of the Carrier chassis. Electric lighting is now standard. Starting though, is still by hand. The speed limit is now 16 miles per hour.

Left: A busy scene at Pomona. Scammell S12, 'HUSSAR', NE 6097, with a later cable carrier unloading Glover cable drums ready for the waiting steamer, (either SAPPER or SENTRY judging by the number and position of the derricks). Loading of this consignment is already proceeding. The Peerless is one of the later purchases, now supplied fitted with a cab. Its load of textiles is being off loaded into the warehouse to be stored until required by the steamer. The photo shows both vehicles have split windscreens. The cobbled surface and railway track was a disadvantage.

a Gardner L2 diesel engine, the majority were supplied with Gardner 6LW diesel engines. The only known identities of these vehicles are:

'REEVE', AXT 671,

'SHELDRAKE', and registration numbers AXT 676, AXT 853 and ALW 665.

Their box bodies were built by Scammell and had boxed interior wheel arches to reduce deck height from the floor. The transverse bearers had steel channel pressing with a steel angle and the bottom body aluminium 'Plymax' panels were bolted to this. The interior was lined with tongued and grooved pine boards. Ventilators were fitted, two in the top at the front, two in the tops of the rear doors.

Not all of the eighteen examples purchased new were fitted with box bodies as four were supplied as flats.

The Directors' meeting of December 1932 noted that this was the first Board meeting at which, following their deaths, neither Sir George nor Lady Renwick had been present.

Major Renwick, now Chairman, had purchased all their shares in the Company from their executors using a loan from Lloyds Bank, Newcastle-upon-Tyne. It was also the occasion for his comments on the possible consequences of the Road and Rail Traffic Bill, then going through Parliament. A short renewal of the lease for Manchester Wharf, Shadwell, less the North Quay and Transit Sheds 58 and 59, was agreed for the year to 31st August 1933.

A new seven year lease for the Wharf was agreed from September 1933. This now included re-occupation of Shed 58, with continuing use of all Shed 57 (paying Imperial Lighterage £60 for their costs in transferring from part of Shed 57 to Shed 53), use of a 25 ton electric crane, and removal of the hydraulic Crane (P.L.A. 132) at Fisher Renwick's expense.

Right middle lower: By way of contrast with MALLARD above, Scammell S10 'CURLEW', GT 202, has the single axle semi low-loading box van carrier fitted with single 13.50x20 low-pressure tyres. It is a matter of personal preference as to which looks better. This example is also fitted with ventilators.

Right: Rear views of Fisher Renwick vehicles are rare. This view of S10, 'GREYHEN', GN 893, supplied 1931 shows both the style of lettering used and the arrangement of the van carrier's twin 'barn' doors and tailgate. There were petrol tanks both sides of the unit. In this instance, no ventilators were fitted. This view also shows the speed limit as 16 m.p.h.

Opposite top: One of the last S15 units, 'DRUMMER', YX 5267, with a sided carrier photographed at Tolpits Lane, Watford. The auxiliary petrol tank under the carrier chassis is again clearly visible. Differences to note are: the hub covers are now plated, making the outfit look even smarter and the bonnet sides now have wire mesh for cooling, replacing the louvres previously provided.

Opposite middle upper: The Scammell S10, 'MALLARD', GK 643, supplied 1930, fitted with 40x8 high-pressure tyres. The van carrier now has a semi low-loading drop frame to provide 1,250cu ft capacity within the height limit of 12ft 5in. A single large ventilator is fitted at the front in this case. The radiator casing is now the split casting type. Two spare wheels are provided.

Left upper: 'PTARMIGAN', GN 894, supplied 1931, had single 13.50x20 low-pressure tyres on the driving axle and carrier. Front tyres were 36x8, a single spare of each size was provided. The sided body was 25ft 6in long, the 2ft 6in high sides being in three sections each side.

Left middle: The first of four Scammells to be named 'LAPWING'. It has a dropside carrier, in this instance with the Scammell twin-axle rubber suspension bogie. This is the only known example to be purchased, all the other carriers in this batch being single axle.

Above: This photograph is included not because it shows 'GREYHEN', GN 893, in trouble, but because it now has a drop side carrier, and also shows detail of the braking system which has changed little in the ten years or so, when compared with the earlier view of the accident to 'FUSILIER'. The location or cause is not known. The damage to the front axle resulted from the impact. What can be seen of the load also confirms the mix of types of traffic carried.

Chapter Five

1934-1939 – The Steamers decline, The Scammells takeover

Above: Scammell S15, 'PARTRIDGE', YW 5208, after being refurbished and fitted with pneumatic tyres. The cable float too has been refurbished and fitted with a double axle bogie. The considerable number of drums awaiting transport appear to be all Callender, waiting for passage to Pomona. What was in the boxes? The holder for the float's 'A' licence is on the bow front. This was Fisher Renwick's practice. Major Renwick considered it avoided problems with the declared weight of the particular carrier if this licence was displayed on the motive unit.

Two significant events occurred in 1934, the first, the Road and Rail Traffic Act 1933, effective from 1st January 1934, introduced changes affecting the future of the carriage of freight by road and applied to every operator. Principally these were the introduction of Carriers' Licences, and the requirement to keep records of drivers' hours worked. The Act made it illegal to operate goods vehicles, of any unladen weight, unless they had one of three types of licence to be granted by the Area Licensing Authority.

For Fisher Renwick this meant the 'A' Licence. This was

only granted to operators carrying for 'hire or reward', it was to be valid for five years, and allowed operation without restriction within the terms of the licence. Trailers, (carriers), also had licences with details of their unladen weight.

The other two classes of licence, which did not apply to Fisher Renwick, were the 'B' licence for 'limited carriers', allowing the holder to carry his own goods, or other peoples goods for reward, subject to the conditions as to type, and for whom or where to or from. The 'C' licence was only for any holder to carry his own goods. No charge could be made. An exception was made for farmers to carry neighbouring farmers' 'goods' for reward. The Act also required drivers to keep records of their hours worked, and operators were required to check them.

The railways were now authorised to negotiate an Agreed Flat Rate with customers, if they were able to carry all their traffic, regardless of destination and distance. Announcements of businesses seeking agreement became a feature in the trade periodicals.

It is known that the application GC 5311A from Fisher Renwick, Manchester, to the North West Licensing Authority claimed "36 Vehicles (103 tons) and 10 Trl. (39 tons): these in use Year beginning 1st April 1932, with a discretionary allowance of 3 Vehicles (20 tons) and 1 Trl. (3 tons), with 8 V. to be acquired. To be used for General Merchandise, Manchester and District, London and Home Counties, Manchester and London."

In the event they were granted (AD 3-13) 42 Vehicles and 11 Trailers, comprising "13V. at 2 tons, 3V. at 2T., 8V. at 4T., 3V. at 4T., 1V. at 4T., 3V. at 8T., and 1 Trl. at 3T., 6 Trl. at 3T., 1 Trl. at 4T., 2 Trl. at 4T., and 1 Trl. at 5T., and vehicles to be acquired 4V. at 2T., 2V. at 4T., and 2V. at 7T."

In quoting AD 3-13, this indicated the details of Fisher Renwick's original application was the 13th dealt with listed in the third issue of the new lists known as Applications and Decisions required to be published weekly by each Traffic Area to inform those interested of applications for the various licences, the decision, or give notification of the date and time of related public sittings.

Commendably the applications for both the North Western and The Metropolitan Traffic Areas were amongst the first to be made, and to be granted. Unfortunately the Ministry of Transport disposed of the files of Applications & Decisions (A.D.) it held, and despite every effort by the present South Eastern & Metropolitan Area Staff, it has not been possible to trace details of the application made to the Metropolitan Area. However, it is known that the terms of condition of use were as for the North Western Area.

The second event was the reduction in the share capital through a Re-construction by Members Voluntary Winding-up on the 1st August 1934, (now possible by a resolution of

Above: The change-over point at Meriden on the A45. The Cafe is today a very attractive private residence, "The Olde Pound Cottage", although still recognisable. The photo was taken after an extension was built. Three Fisher Renwick Scammells are visible. Not all the cheerful group were Fisher Renwick drivers, one being an R.A.C. Patrolman.

the Directors, following the Companies Act). The new company took on the assets and business of the 1908 Company, the main consequence being that the value of the ordinary shares were reduced to a nominal value of 10 shillings.

The Rigid Six Scammells now proved particularly successful following the increase in the speed limit to 20 m.p.h. Their fuel economy, when fitted with Gardner LW diesel engines, was the beginning of the end to any cost advantage the steamers may have had for the heavier bulk traffic, e.g. cable drums, and boilers. As to the salt traffic,

this was to be given up without much regret.

The 13.50x20 low pressure pneumatics on the 'K' type detachable steel rims were less popular, a puncture, particularly on a front wheel could be dangerous, the wheel would immediately drop by some 11 inches. They were also awkward and heavy to handle when being fitted or repaired. The Major (as he had become more frequently termed), was later to specify 36x8 or 40x8 tyres on three piece wheels as standard, rather than the optional large low pressure tyres.

The Rigids proved more suited to the long-distance work with the traffic now being carried than the equivalent Scammell Articulated Lorries, and no more were to be purchased with the exceptions in 1943, until the Seddons in 1947.

As part of the continuing replacement and updating of the fleet, the local collection and delivery vehicles were also being replaced. The new Bedford WTL 3 ton chassis was used for vans. Some Fordson 7V 3 ton vans were also placed in

Left: The new Extension at Shadwell, being used for handling the cable drum traffic. Hays Wharf are now able to provide the Pickfords 'Rapier' mobile crane to handle the drums, in this instance a consignment of Glover's Cables from Manchester. There are various vans apparently parked-up in the background.

The directors of the Slough-based Peerless Trading Company, the ultimate source of the Peerless lorries still used, had separated, some acquiring the agency for Studebaker Lorries. These American built chassis had six-cylinder petrol engines, five speed gearboxes, and effective hydraulic brakes. They were a little heavy but have been described as 'fast and nippy'.

Major Renwick having had the 3-4 ton model on trial was sufficiently impressed to order these as replacements for the now obsolete Peerless lorries. The Studebaker chassis were fitted with flat, van and Luton van bodies by Cornbrook Coachworks, a few survived to be nationalised.

Some AEC Mammoth Major six wheel chassis were purchased, but found wanting and soon exchanged following the introduction of the Scammell lightweight Rigid Six Wheel Chassis. This was in direct contrast to Fisher Renwick's competitors, notably Bouts-Tillotson who chose to standardise on AEC.

The purchase of some 12 Leyland Hippo and Octopus vehicles which were found to be suitable for Fisher Renwick's duties, was in great part due to the fact Scammell was not offering a comparable chassis at that time.

Trade for the steamers had become increasingly difficult, and Major Renwick was now expressing his serious anxiety that it was becoming "less fashionable" to use the Coastal service, even to the point of the company no longer providing this sea service. At July 1936 Fisher Renwick Manchester-London Steamers Fleet comprised;

s.s. CUIRASSIER   s.s. LANCER
s.s. SAPPER   s.s. SENTRY.

The steamer journey took 700-800 miles by water, compared with 184 by rail, and 186 by road. Allowing for collection and delivery days it could take some 5 to 7 days for delivery which was no longer acceptable. As a result the LANCER was withdrawn and sold, the resulting surplus in the Capital reserve of £4,336 was re-invested.

At this period 33 vehicles were bought costing £19,164, and 21 old vehicles sold to realise £2,567. This illustrates how the rapid improvements in vehicles affected the depreciation charge allowed for by prudent operators.

Problems when applying for variations of existing vehicle 'A' licences were eased by the declared weights of the old, heavier, Scammells and their carriers, and the ex-army vehicles. The 5% unladen weight allowance for new, replacement vehicles was equally beneficial.

The Scammell Units 'MERLIN' and 'PARTRIDGE' were updated by Scammell, and their two semi low-loading cable floats were altered from the 'four-in-line' solid tyred configuration to have twin axle bogies on 36x8 pneumatic

service, these were used mostly in London. The new factories being developed along the A4, A5, and A40 trunk routes meant longer trips from Shadwell, and to a lesser extent the same thing was happening at Manchester.

Both these types were used on long-distance work when necessary, as allowed under the terms of the 'A' Licence. Their 30 m.p.h. capability allowed dual use. This intensive use, particularly of the Bedfords, meant some were soon part-exchanged for new vehicles.

Left: A puzzle picture. Clearly taken at Pomona, at some later date, 'PARTRIDGE' is now looking quite work worn, although the tyre treads have little wear. The near side sidelight does not match. The photograph was probably taken for a reason but we are unlikely to find out after this distance in time.

Right: This Leyland Bull dropside, GK 3157, number 139, was the first heavy non-articulated vehicle, entering the fleet in November 1930. It gave good service. Scammell were able to take it in part exchange for a Rigid Six RC13 box van in 1933 - because of its unladen weight and the pending applications for a new 'A' licence ?

tyres. 'MERLIN' remained at Pomona, 'PARTRIDGE' at Shadwell, then to Coppetts Road. They too were included among the vehicles to be nationalised.

Scammell Lorries Ltd. were making little or no profit at this period, despite Share Rights Issues in 1928 and 1929 to finance new designs, and production facilities. Major Renwick used his knowledge of operating Scammells to influence features and types of chassis available.

This included his supporting the introduction of the 'Mechanical Horse', and the subsequent introduction of the 6 ton version, and then later in 1938 the Bedford-Scammell version, though Fisher Renwick was never to operate these in service. He was particularly concerned with the introduction of first, the new Lightweight Rigid Six, and then the Rigid Eight after Fisher Renwick had been forced to place rival makes of chassis in service.

The new Scammell range of 'Lightweight' Articulated and Rigid lorries was introduced at the 1933 Commercial Motor Show. These were the first Scammell lorries to have the drive-line comprising the Gardner 6LW diesel engine coupled to O.D. North's new six-speed gearbox and its separate gate, and double reduction spiral bevel and epicyclic driving axle. A feature was full air-assisted braking on all wheels on the three or four axles. Single low pressure tyres were at first standard.

The bonneted Rigid Six had the driving axle mounted on front end balance beams, and used Panhard-rods to control sideways movement. The back end of the beams held the independent stub axles, the suspension used rubber discs under compression. Single 13.5x16 tyres were standard, as was Dewandre air braking. A 'Saloon' cab (standard for articulated and rigid versions) was fitted. Windscreen wipers were also standard. Flats had pressed steel cross beams and raves for the transverse planked floor.

Fisher Renwick were to buy a number of the Lightweight Rigid Six lorries between November 1934 and 1936. At least four of those ordered had box bodies, with double floors and ventilators front and rear. These were named:

'HAWK'   'EAGLE'   'PETREL'
'REDSHANK'   'REDSTART'

The vans had an unladen weight of 6tons-7cwts-1qtr. One of the Rigid Six flats was 'KITE', BLL 248. The flats were 5 tons-13 cwts. Always without a spare wheel. Other registration numbers allocated to these were:

BLL 835	BLN 693	BLO 690	BLT 949
BLY 525	BUC 793	BUC 794	BXV 520
BYU 933	CGD 341	CGD 342	

A distinctive feature was they all had chromium plated hub caps. However, following the introduction of the Rigid Eight, Fisher Renwick were to base all their future Scammell purchases on the Rigid Eight model. (Scammell Lorries were the first manufacturer to use the description as the Model name 'Rigid Eight').

The Lightweight Rigid Eight equalled anything available from the other lorry builders, and met Major Renwick's preferences. It is understood that the Armstrong Saurer 'Samson' rigid, being built at Scotswood, Newcastle had impressed him on trial, especially the air-braking operating on all four axles. It was thought, however, to be rather heavy. He was also aware that Vickers were considering the future of their involvement in Armstrong Saurer, because of the arms contracts to be placed.

Despite his long and successful operation of Scammell articulated lorries, he now preferred the rigid type for their long-distance operations. It is 'lore' that the Major made it clear that aspects of the initial design of the five chassis to be built for the first production batch of Rigid Eights did not impress him. This applied particularly to the cab, and especially the rear hung doors, and the awkward access. The limited visibility provided by the narrow windscreen and the position of the controls, also received his unfavourable comment.

Indeed Fisher Renwick's first order, which would been for this original version, was cancelled following the trial of a prototype. This meant that the first Rigid Eights were to be placed in service by Fisher Renwick in 1937 and only after Scammell had made the detailed modifications those first operators were to find desirable, if not necessary.

The revised chassis version which was to become virtually the Fisher Renwick standard was 17ft 6in in length between bogie centres. It retained the load equalising front bogie with two tubular section axles. The early ones used the compressed rubber suspension, this was changed about 1940 to coil springs. It was fitted with the now optional rear steel sprung suspension with a balance beam, still with the spiral bevel double reduction epicyclic driving axle and a trailing tubular axle, all fitted with 36x8 tyres. There was full air-assisted braking on each axle, the front wheels had Girling brakes, the rear axle drums had 17 inch toggle operated fabricated brake shoes. The rear bogie, using rubber suspension and the single low pressure tyres, remained an option favoured by many customers.

The chassis provided 25ft of body space. It had the new coachbuilt saloon type cab with the doors mounted on the front pillar with adjustable windows, twin two piece windscreens with a windscreen wiper, bucket seats, horn and interior electric lighting. The CAV 12 volt system provided two head lights, two side lights, and a single tail light. Spot lights came later. Instruments included oil gauge, air pressure gauge, and gearbox oil pressure gauge. The cab also had an interior light with a blue lens to the right of the driver's head. (This was switched on if he was late for the change-over, enabling the other driver to recognise him, and

stop. This was of course before the Police and Emergency services obtained the sole use of blue lights, putting a stop to this practice). A tool kit and 5 ton hydraulic jack were supplied as standard.

The Flats had the wooden floor mounted on pressed steel crossbearers with pressed steel chock rails. The cost to Fisher Renwick of the first batch of chassis, after their discount, was £1490-0-0. The flat body cost £150, including painting.

Scammell also built the first of the Fisher Renwick Rigid Eight van bodies. These also used the pressed steel cross bearers and chock rails and the interior length of the body was 24ft 6in and 14ft height. The body was panelled with 'Masonite' panels. All the bolt heads had to be flush and ventilators were a standard fitting.

Shortly after, chassis only were sometimes ordered, these were fitted with the Cornbrook Wheelwrights 'Showboat' Luton bodies, or as flats with their distinctive Cornbrook styled cabs. These had the front wings supplied by Scammell. Their delivery ended the practice that all the Fisher Renwick Scammells had their bodies built by Scammell at Watford.

Following the experience of these first Rigid Eights on the continuous service, 'Duflex' clutch plates, and bronze bushes for the rear suspension balance beams were specified. A little later Tecalemit automatic lubrication systems were usually specified.

The first Scammell Rigid Eights were delivered to Fisher Renwick between September and November 1937 and comprised the following:

Left: The effect of the 1932 legislation on vehicle design is shown by this 1934 Bedford WTL tilt van, specially bodied by J.E. Lombell to meet the 50 cwt unladen weight 30 m.p.h. limit at that time.

Below: This photo was taken by the P.L.A. and is believed to have been taken to show the use being made of Shadwell by the Steamer Company for their long distance motor transport service. The various vehicles identifiable date it at 1934-1935. At least three Scammell S10 articulated lorries on pneumatics and a Leyland Octopus are visible. The lighter in the foreground is laden with Guinness barrels. *(Courtesy of Museums in Dockland. PLA collection).*

'GADWALL', DJH 768 (Van) 'GARGANEY', DJH 769 (Van) 'SCAUP', DNK 162 (Sided) 'SCOTER', DNK 165 (Sided) 'TEAL', FGO 169 (Flat) 'MALLARD', FGO 171 (Flat) and one further flat, 'LAPWING', the registration number of which is unrecorded.

Thereafter Fisher Renwick were to have the largest single fleet of Rigid Eights in service up to nationalisation. Their use of the Rigid Eight chassis with the alternative steel leaf-spring rear bogie suspension with 36x8 and later 40x8 tyres proved to be ideal for use with the high capacity van bodies, particularly with the 14ft 3in high 'Showboats'.

As prosperity increased, with industry benefiting from re-armament orders, the traffic continued to change. In London, Beechams became customers for their pharmacy and toiletry products. Personal hygiene products too became a regular 'bulk' load, as did fruit and produce for Manchester Market, at that time the largest wholesale market other than Covent Garden. Special journeys for soft fruit in the season for Marks & Spencer shops in the North West Region became a regular valuable contract. This traffic used those Leyland, Scammell, and Studebaker box vans which were fitted with ventilators, and were usually taken by senior drivers.

Left: A Ford B, with an unidentified (Baico?) forward control conversion. Since it was supplied by Quicks, it would be reasonable to assume they also built the Luton van body. The front conversion cab blends in well with the normal control wings, in contrast to the awkward appearance of the rear wings.

A popular duty occurred each Christmas, when a box van would be allocated to collect a cargo of 'brace of pheasant' from the Major's estate for distribution to most Manchester and London customers. The labelling and delivery was carried out by the two depots.

A special fruit service from Faversham (Kent) to Dundee was introduced using specially bodied Studebaker forward control vans, weighing under 2ton 10cwt, and therefore able to travel within the 30 m.p.h. limit. They were expected to complete the journey within 24 hours. There were, of course, three driver changes to achieve this. The pressed steel forward control cab was described as a 'Camel-back', and the 6.3 litre petrol engine, five speed gearbox and excellent hydraulic brakes made it ideal for urgent deliveries. They had pressed steel one piece wheels, which were weight saving compared with the cast steel spoked hubs with the detachable rims fitted to the earlier chassis. Known names for these include 'CIRIUS', 'LYRE', 'MARS', 'MERCURY' and 'NEPTUNE'. Some known names for the new Commer Superpoise normal control box vans placed in service about the same time included 'CERES', 'CANOPUS', 'VENUS', 'HERCULES', 'HERMES' and 'CETUS'.

New light industries were replacing the textile traffic. Hoover had expanded their product range, manufacturing the

many new domestic electrical products being introduced to ease housewives' chores. They and E.K. Cole and HMV with their radios and gramophones, together with the heavy, fragile gramophone records became good premium rate customers. They expected fast reliable service, and they received this.

At Manchester, the new factories opening at Trafford Park included Kelloggs providing light bulky consignments, ideal for 'Showboats'. Manchester Oil Refineries produced industrial oils packed in steel drums, many of 45 gallon capacity. These made ideal loads, or part loads for the flats, many of which had double planked floors for these, and also for the cable drum traffic. Paint, chemicals, lard and machinery were also carried. Carpets and felts partly replaced cotton goods, with clothing to and from London being another increasing high value traffic. Tyres, particularly Firestone, also became a regular consignment in both directions. Tyres being taken to Manchester for local

distribution, and cotton tyre fabric back-loaded to their new factory on the Great West Road. At this time it was usual for garages to be supplied with virtually daily deliveries of small quantities of tyres. This work was to be retained until 1972 with specially bodied contract hire vans. Thomas Hedley, later becoming Procter & Gamble, also provided a considerable amount of work, providing loads for the flats, requiring careful sheeting and roping.

Other new traffic, including Heinz products from Harlesden, was gained through Fisher Renwick doing the local distribution for Manchester. Increasingly, consignments were received for local distribution as sub-contractors to other operators. Conversely, Manchester Carriers were using the service to take their consignments for London. Some traffic for Scotland including Heinz was given to J. & H. Hinchliffe and to Youngs Express Deliveries Manchester depot before Fisher Renwick were able to carry the traffic themselves.

In 1938 Fisher Renwick had 120 vehicles on their 'A' licences, operated from Pomona (N.W. Area) and Shadwell (Metropolitan Area). The problems of using Shadwell were a reason for continuing use of Hays Wharf Cartage as contractor for 'local' collections and deliveries, and for the remaining dock work. It also enabled considerable use of the 'A' licenced smaller vehicles for long-distance work.

Hays Wharf vehicles and horse vans were kept at their depots and stables convenient for Shadwell, but away from the Wharf. Their horse vans were by now a mix of the traditional tilt vans with wooden, steel rimmed wheels, and modern aluminium-panelled vans, with pressed steel 'artillery' pneumatic tyred wheels. The leaf sprung axle hubs had roller bearings and the rear axle had foot pedal operated hub brakes. These vans were also used by Pickfords and Carter Paterson. Later, virtually identical vans were placed in service by the Railways parcels depots.

The horses were sometimes nervous when the larger vehicles, particularly the 'Showboats', manoeuvring to gain access to a shed, or to leave the basin, would come near them. Sadly one or two incidents of injury to a horse occurred through their becoming uncontrollable in such situations.

Hays Wharf also used some different,

Above: A line up of six new Fordson 7V vans taken in 1936. These were to be based at Shadwell. They had a long life, some being nationalised. They were reputedly popular with their drivers, who did not seem to experience problems with starting the V8 petrol engines, unlike some users of these vehicles.

Right: The Ford T's were replaced by Ford B flats. This photo was taken at Pomona. VR 5212 was registered at Manchester in 1931 and GN 9497 by London County Council in 1930. The drivers seem delighted with their lot. The Fords are gleaming and the photo was taken on a fine day since both windscreens are open.

Left: This photo of 'REEVE', AXT 671, was taken when parked in The Highway, Shadwell, late 1934. Believed to be one of the first Fisher Renwick Scammells to be retro-fitted with a Gardner 6LW. Fred Walpole, now a Senior Driver, is seen with his second man. Although the continuous service was now operating, the change-over was not yet in full operation. The box van body, with a lowered floor and boxed wheel arches, has twin ventilators back and front. The fruit traffic from London is now becoming increasingly important.

interesting vehicles on their Fisher Renwick contracts. Amongst them were a Shelvoke & Drewry flat, with 'tiller' steering. A Garner low loading type flat, with a narrow cab, was especially used for collecting wool bales. Most of this particular traffic was said to have been lost to a competitor. The Fisher Renwick drivers blamed this on those drivers working a 25 hour day!

The decision to end the Steamer Liner service became inevitable. The costs of the Continuous Road Service were lower. The steamers, having carried up to 160,000 tons per year in their heyday were now down to 40,000 tons per year. Negotiations with the ultimate purchaser were discontinued because of the 1938 Munich Peace crisis. In the event Major Renwick was able to successfully conclude the sale of the Steamer Liner service to Coast Lines by a willingness to accept extended payment.

This, of course, meant that Fisher Renwick were now motor transport operators only. With no legal right under the terms of the leases to occupy their Wharves etc. at either Pomona or Shadwell. They did, however, continue to act as cargo brokers in London, and to load and discharge the steamers at Shadwell. In both Manchester and London they were to continue to organise and carry out the collection and delivery of cargoes carried by the steamers.

Major Renwick made it clearly understood that once the steamers were sold, expansion could only come by acquiring existing road transport businesses, for their licences. New and good freehold sites at White City, Chester Road, Old Trafford and at Coppetts Road, Muswell Hill - conveniently near the North Circular Road - were obtained.

The greatest competitive benefit gained was the reduction in the transit time. This was particularly so with increasing use of Rigid Eights, and refinement of the change-over, usually at Meriden, avoiding for most purposes 'Nights Out'. The concept of change-over for drivers also allowed 'double-shifting' of vehicles. The system was that vehicles worked in pairs, and swapped drivers approximately half way between Manchester and London, usually at Meriden, although some changes were made at Bacon's End, with a few at the start of the Coventry by-pass. There were two drivers allocated to each vehicle at each Depot, the long distance man was able to return home within the legal driving day. The other, the day man, was responsible for loading and unloading, ready for the next journey. The two drivers would work 'week about'.

The change-over also avoided the need for Manchester drivers to deal with the problems of the approaches and access to Shadwell Basin. The London drivers were also familiar with the practices of the P.L.A., and of the P.L.A. Police interest in passes for vehicles entering or particularly leaving the Dock entrance. The local Council also tended to react badly to Fisher Renwick (and others) practices, e.g. carrying out light repairs, and transferring loads whilst parked on Glamis Road or The Highway. They were especially irritable in complaining when inspection lamps were made to operate by the 'tapping' of their electricity supply from the street lights!

Unfortunately no record of Fisher Renwick's accounts have been found. It is known that Major Renwick's control of

Left: The preferred replacement for the Peerless lorries. The contrast was striking. These Studebaker normal control lorries were to give good service, mainly used at Manchester, and some survived to be nationalised. This one, number 144, has a dropside body, and is seen outside the Cornbrook Road offices, delivered when new from Cornbrook Wheelwrights.

Above: Another new Studebaker normal control, this time with a Luton tilt body by Cornbrook Wheelwrights. The number 147 shows it was Pomona based. Understandably, they were popular with their drivers. The difference in the capabilities between these and the Peerless lorries, aided by the benefit of hydraulic brakes and pneumatic tyres was to be used to full advantage.

An impress-ive, gleaming 'SHELDRAKE' at Scammell's Tolpits Lane factory. Yet to be registered and accepted by Fisher Renwick.

costs for both local and the long distance vehicles ensured they never operated at a loss. The Major's attention to overhead costs included carrying a considerable insurance excess for the vehicle insurance, and Fisher Renwick fought claims whenever there were grounds for this; a practice dating from the earliest steamer days. Major Renwick had by this time been appointed Director of the Omnibus & General Insurance Company.

The intensive operation of the Continuous Service required adjustments to both the bank working and to the clerical routines, as the traffic was increasingly carried by road. For the bank work, late shifts and part-time working were introduced. For the clerical staff a mixture of overtime and part-time evening working was introduced to prepare the all important waybills.

The typing was done on 'Elliot Fisher' typewriters, which had a flat typing surface which came down on to the flat roller. (The flat roller allowed the waybill to be removed if it was unable to be completed, so that the next one could be prepared for the next load, after which the previous one could then easily be replaced and finished). Waybills were prepared from a copy of the sequentially

Above: Following the successful operation of the Rigid RC13 chassis, the Lightweight Rigid Six with O.D. North's six-speed gearbox and double reduction rear driving axle, using rubber disc suspension, was to become the choice of new vehicles for the long distance service. 'REDSTART' was amongst those supplied having a Scammell built box van body. All of this batch of box vans were fitted with ventilators.

Above: This Bedford WTL 3 ton van 'ORION', CGO 339, was based at Shadwell. Note the oversize petrol tank (despite the increase it made in unladen weight) for when used on the long distance service. The 30 m.p.h. limit it was allowed, by being under 2 ton 10 cwt unladen, made it ideal for urgent traffic.

Right: The majority of the Studebakers had flat bodies. This one has a full load of wheelbarrows (still awaiting fitment of wheels), presumably en route to the docks to be loaded onto a steamer. The unknown driver should be satisfied with the way they are loaded.

numbered consignment notes used for collections, originally in triplicate, perforated three to a page. One was kept by the customer, one was used on the bank and for P.O.D.'s., the third was used for the typists to prepare the waybill, and then for costing and invoicing. The notes from the returning vans or flats went to the traffic desk, and were allocated to a long-distance vehicle. The other copy was then passed to the office to be used by the typists.

The waybill was 'concertina folded', to make up a top copy with three carbons, one copy was kept as a record, one went for 'charging', and two went on to the receiving depot. After every collecting vehicle had returned and the consignments checked and reloaded, the waybills for each loaded long-distance vehicle could be finished, put in an envelope for that vehicle and driver, or placed in a wallet - together with any internal mail - for dispatch by a later vehicle. It was possible for up to six waybills to go with the last vehicle of that group to leave. This was usually at 10.00 pm. (22.00hrs). It was always a senior driver, and it was not unknown for him to take a Scammell or occasionally a Leyland being repaired, but not quite finished. This was more likely to be a vehicle which had developed a problem on the way, and did not belong to where the repair was being completed. It would, however, be safe to use, although this may have meant nursing it during the trip. (Unfortunately this would occur with any problems the Leylands had at Shadwell, and later Muswell Hill. The London workshop tried to avoid touching them if possible).

This special leather wallet remained in the 'Showboat' until handed to the Bank Foreman on arrival. The opposite applied to the drivers tool bag, which on change-over would be the first thing removed by the driver, to be placed by him in the cab of his new vehicle. Until 1946 'Fishers' (as it now tended to be known) would expect to help each other if there was a problem, or indeed any other driver in trouble whoever they worked for. This also applied to the express coach services when operated, notably Standerwick and Scout.

The P.L.A. had reluctantly allowed one petrol pump at Shadwell, a diesel pump came later. The use of the garage and workshop at Medland Street about five minutes away, just for refuelling, was not encouraged. In any case they too were cramped, being also used for body repairs.

Despite the demands made upon Major Renwick in discussions with Government departments, and increasingly the Emergency Road Transport Organisation which was drawing up plans for the obvious approach of war, the Company used 1939 to consolidate.

Major Renwick had played no known role in the formation of the various road transport operators' associations. These at this time included the ARO (Associated Road Operators'), the CMUA (Commercial Motor Users' Association), the NCEC (National Conference of Express Carriers), and the NRTEF (National Road Transport Employers' Federation). However, he was on familiar terms with the leading

personalities in the industry, and was supportive of the establishment of the Standing Joint Committee, formed January 1938, to have, amongst other roles, road transport's representation on the Road & Rail Central Conference. This was a result of the Railways Square Deal campaign to deal with increasing road competition.

The Transport Advisory Council 'Reports on Rates and Services'-1937 concluded the railways, organised as four large undertakings with their rates controlled by regulation, based on average costs, were now finding it difficult to cope with the increasing competition from road transport. The road transport industry had no large companies to compare with the railway companies, being mainly small firms,

needing only to cover their costs to remain in business.

The success of the Joint Committee was to lead to the formation after the war of the RHA (Road Haulage Association) and the TRTA (Traders' Road Transport Association) now the FTA (Freight Transport Association). Major Renwick's independence from these associations gave him freedom to express his own viewpoint on the industry, a factor appreciated by the Government and Ministers.

Good progress had been made with the construction of the new White City Depot, and it was expected to be available in Spring 1940. The more complex work for the adaptation of the former Sewage Works at Coppetts Road was reported as going well. This was Denis Renwick's special concern.

Above: Hays Wharf Cartage continued to provide local cartage services. This new horse-drawn van would have provided a contrast even to many of the motor vehicles still in use in the Docks area. The body used aluminium panels; the pressed steel artillery pneumatic tyred wheels were mounted on roller bearing hubs. The foot operated hub brake worked on the rear axle. The electric lights were battery operated. The welfare of the obviously cared for horse included ear protectors against irritation from flies.

The first acquisition in the company's policy of acquiring existing road transport businesses was completed on 1st September 1939. This was the purchase of the long established business of John and Herbert Hinchliffe, with depots at Ramsbottom and London. Their immaculate fleet comprised mostly AEC four and six-wheeled flats; their 'A' licence was for General Goods, England and Scotland. They were well known to Fisher Renwick and to Major Renwick,

having acted as sub-contractors to each other, with Hinchliffes carrying Manchester bound and Scottish traffic for Fisher Renwick. Also, about the same time, Cowan & Co. were phased out as collection and delivery agents at Pomona. (Their warehouse and other premises were to be demolished in 1995). War was declared 3rd September 1939. This time Major Renwick was expecting the worst! Indeed it was to mean much extra work for him.

Above: Another P.L.A. photograph, this time of the Shadwell extension being used for parking, in this instance four unidentified Scammell lightweight Rigid Six lorries. Although the background is blurred, it does show the amount of river traffic still using the Upper Pool and the Tower wharves. The vessel (a portion of which can just be seen) going through the entrance to the Basin is the tug NEPTUNIA. *(Courtesy of Museums in Dockland. PLA Collection).*

Right: Although not a Fisher Renwick vehicle, this is one of the first five Scammell Rigid Eights built. It is included to show the limited vision and awkward access before the revised version, with newly designed saloon cab, became Fisher Renwick's preferred long distance vehicle. Despite accurate claims for the roll stable rear bogie with rubber suspension and 13.50x20 tyres, Major Renwick preferred steel rear suspension and twin 36x8 tyres. The vehicle is carrying Thomas Hedley soap products. Hedleys also used Fisher Renwick to distribute from their Trafford Park plant.

Below: Leyland Hippo 'TERN', when new. The success of the diesel engined Leyland Hippo and Octopus in Fisher Renwick's service, together with the Scammell Rigid chain drive 'Sixes' meant that no more articulated Scammells were to be purchased by Fisher Renwick for operating the Continuous Service.

Below: Two Leyland Octopus flats at Shadwell, carrying 'wide' loads, brought to Shadwell by steamer. Both are of the earliest 1934 version Octopus chassis, with the single drive rear bogie. 'KITTIWAKE', CVR 802, was to be nationalised as a White City based vehicle, after fourteen years service. The other Octopus cannot be identified. Although clean, both the Leylands show signs of being worked hard. A Scammell chain drive RC13 Rigid Six box van is seen parked behind.

Above: The first Rigid Eight, 'GADWALL', DJH 768, supplied September 1937. Although a familiar photo with its Scammell built box van body, it is included because it shows Major Renwick's ideal chassis with which to ensure the success of the Continuous Service in overcoming opposition from the rail and other road services between London and the North West. Sadly, the success also meant the end of the company's Steamer Liner service. The improvements to the model required by Fisher Renwick aided its commercial success.

Right: Schedule of collection and delivery Groups/Districts served by Pomona, December 1937, for Manchester-London Steamers.

Right: The sided Rigid Eight, 'SCAUP', DNK 162, supplied November 1937. Scaup had a hectic life during the Second World War, being used on a contract to take bituminous felt to the many new airfields being constructed in Eastern England. The 2ft 6in drop sides were in three sections.

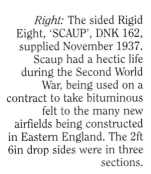

MANCHESTER—LONDON STEAMERS LIMITED.

Manchester Wharf,
Shadwell,
London, E.1.

Phone: Royal 7003 (6 lines).

Cornbrook Road,
Manchester,
15.

Phone: Trafford Park 1864.

GROUP No. 1.

Ardwick	Collyhurst	Irlam o' th' Height	Pendleton
Barton on Irwell	Crumpsall	Levenshulme	Rusholme
Blackley	Eccles	Longsight	Salford
Broughton	Fallowfield	MANCHESTER	Stretford
Burnage	Gorton	Miles Platting	Trafford Park
Cheetham Hill	Harpurhey	Moston	Whalley Range
Chorlton-cum-Hardy	Heaton Park	Old Trafford	Withington

GROUP No. 2.

Altrincham	Denton	Hyde	Prestwich
Ashton on Mersey	Didsbury	Kearsley	Radcliffe
Ashton-under-Lyne	Droylsden	Irlam	Reddish
Audenshaw	Dukinfield	Lees	Royton
Bolton	Elton	Little Hulton	Sale
Broadheath	Failsworth	Middleton	Stalybridge
Bury	Farnworth	Monton	Stockport
Chadderton	Flixton	Moses Gate	Swinton
Cheadle	Godley	Newton (Hyde)	Timperley
Cheadle Heath	Hale	Northenden	Urmston
Cheadle Hulme	Heaton Chapel	Oldham	Walkden
Clifton	Heaton Mersey	Partington	Whitefield
Davyhulme	Heaton Norris	Patricroft	Worsley
	Hollinwood	Pendlebury	

GROUP No. 3.

Accrington	Castleton	Horwich	Rawtenstall
Adlington (Lancs)	Chorley	Leigh & Bedford	Rochdale
Astley	Church	Leyland	Shaw
Atherton	Clayton-le-Moors	Littleborough	Tyldesley
Bacup	Cloughfold	Lostock Junction	Wardle
Bamber Bridge	Darwen	Milnrow	Wardleworth
Baxenden	Glossop	Mossley	Warrington
Blackburn	Haslingden	New Hey	Waterfoot
Blackrod	Hazel Grove	Oswaldthwistle	Wigan
Burnley	Helmshore	Preston	Woodley
	Heywood	Ramsbottom	

GROUP No. 4.

BLACKPOOL AND SURROUNDING DISTRICT.

Blackpool	Kirkham	Cleveleys	Fairhaven
St. Annes on Sea	Lytham	Poulton Le Fylde	Freckleton
	Fleetwood	Thornton Le Fylde	

BY ROAD FROM MANCHESTER.

219104. 500. W. & S. Ltd. 12/37.

Left: 'LAPWING', one of the first Rigid Eights. It had a short working life with Fisher Renwick, the name later being given to an Alexander Brown ERF flat. Rigid Eight flats were used for every type of traffic, including cable drum traffic. This was the second vehicle to bear the name.

Below: This photo was taken at Shadwell after delivery of 'GADWALL' and 'GARGANEY' to show Fisher Renwick's capability to provide suitable vehicles to meet tight time limits for the seasonal fruit contracts to be operated. The vehicles are a Scammell Lightweight Rigid Six, a Leyland Octopus, the Scammell Rigid Eight and a Studebaker - all ventilated box vans. The forward control Studebaker has only one spotlight for night driving. This needed a smaller battery, helping to keep the unladen weight below 50 cwt, in order to stay within the 30 mph limit. The passenger seat was also removed. The Octopus and Rigid Eight both have a spotlight fitted. A consignment of drums for Glovers Cable awaits delivery.

Chapter Six

1939-1945 – War, Tribulations and Development

The War immediately resulted in many vehicles whether on A, B, or C licences being requisitioned, mostly for Military service. The Civil Defence services also took many vehicles. It is believed that the only Fisher Renwick vehicles to be commandeered were two or three Bedford vans. This would have been possible because Hinchliffe's fleet is believed to have been taken for Military service. They were not operated by Fisher Renwick, nor were they recorded being in service with other operators.

There was a commitment, however, to make their vehicles available for Civil Defence duties. Their long distance vehicles would also be ready for movement of essential goods if needed, should the other forms of transport become inoperative through any enemy action.

Very quickly there were unpredictable changes in traffic. Another effect of war was the legal requirements to paint the edge of the mudguards white, and also the front bumper if fitted. Otherwise a broad white stripe outlining the bottom line of the cab was acceptable. A single approved headlight mask, and the reduction of the side lights to the size of a one shilling piece was all the lighting now allowed. Spot lights were also restricted unless there was heavy fog. Three weeks later, on the 24th September, fuel rationing was introduced. Road freight transport was allowed a ration of 75% of the estimated pre-war use. Long distance traffic was now expected to be transferred to rail. In practice there was a basic ration of 50% of the pre-war purchase, three units of fuel per week for every half ton unladen weight of the vehicle.

This should have allowed operating use of some 180 miles per week, and an operating supplementary allowance of a third could be allocated on evidence of need. The Fisher Renwick Scammells would run more miles than this in a day. This was, of course, totally inadequate for operating any long distance and trunk service. There were considerable arguments on the need for extra supplies.

The very severe snowfalls in January and mid-February 1940 also created difficulties exacerbated by the blackout regulations and following the fall of Dunkirk in May/June 1940, and the start of the Blitzes the operating difficulties increased.

Despite the Government's attempts to plan for the needs of war, it soon become obvious that little had been done to check the physical capacity of the main or cross country rail routes. To some extent the same thing applied to long distance road transport, although there were details available for the number and type of vehicles in use.

Although the pre-war planned Emergency Road Transport Organisation had been created to save fuel by limiting long distance/trunk services and light running, by the use of rationing to encourage diverting vehicles to essential traffics, it also served to obtain details of available vehicles in each Traffic Region.

The development of the schemes which led to the formation of the Road Haulage Organisation is complex. The first was the Meat Transport Pool. Its success led to a Committee being set up in May 1940 under the Chairmanship of Sydney Garke which suggested a voluntary comprehensive scheme for the operation and control of road transport. The Garke Report did not meet the approval of the Ministry of Transport. However, events following Dunkirk caused a Consultative Committee to be appointed in August 1940 which arranged for the pooling of road transport at the ports. Major Renwick was involved with this.

Before long it was obvious that it was necessary to ensure the organisation of road transport. The Government's answer was another sub-committee, again involving Major Renwick, to see if it was possible to agree to a scheme based on the Garke Report, this time without the proposals unacceptable to the Ministry. The general basis for a scheme was issued in January 1941.

This time, the Ministry of Transport intended to operate a scheme by which the Government would hire vehicles with the intention of carrying traffic on Government direction. The operation of the vehicles remained with the owners, but a Ministry organisation was to be set up including experts from the industry to control the scheme. As a result Claude Barrington, Managing Director, Transport Services Ltd. and P.J.R. Tapp, Managing Director of Market Transport Ltd. were appointed Chief Road Haulage Officers. Five Divisional Road Haulage Officers were appointed to cover the country. There was no Divisional Road Haulage Officer for the South East/Metropolitan Area. The two officers responsible in the two divisions affecting Fisher Renwick's operations were: North-Western - Mr.R.B. Stockdale (Motor Carriers Ltd), Liverpool; Scotland Division - Mr. James B. Hastie (Glasgow Hiring Co. Ltd.), Glasgow.

The first result was the Ministry took over the Meat

‘PTARMIGAN’, FXJ 689, new late 1939, seen early in the War. It is said to be parked at Meriden. The effect of the lighting restrictions at the date can only be described as horrendous - no spotlight, and only one masked headlight. The offside headlight has been removed, which seems somewhat excessive, since the regulation only stipulated the bulb be removed. The sheeting and roping must be excused by the War. The 'Showboat' is not identified.

'EIDER', GNB 925, a 1940 'Showboat' with the Cornbrook Wheelwrights Luton body. Scammell supplied the bare chassis with front mudguards and pressed steel radiator shell. These achieved legendary fame far beyond the actual number operated. The comparison with the driver's height (5ft 6in) to that of the van readily conveys the impressive nature of these vehicles. The major difference between these and later versions was the fitment of the horizontally split windscreen.

Transport Pool, which became the Meat Transport Organisation.

In May 1941 the Ministries of Transport and of Shipping were merged to become the Ministry of War Transport. This had long been advocated by Major Renwick, who rather to his surprise would usually be the only public member of the various committees etc. with knowledge of coastal shipping.

In July 1941, the new Minister, Lord Leathers, set up the Road Haulage (Operations) Advisory Committee. The Chairman was Major Renwick. In October 1941 it issued its Report. The recommendations were:
(1) Provision of a pool of vehicles under Government control.
(2) Arrangement of most of the long distance movement of Government traffics.
    The organisation would be in three parts :
(i) A Ministry organisation, divided into six divisions, initially sub-divided into 14 areas. (As previously, the areas were based upon the Civil Defence regions. The organisation would control the movement of traffic, and act as a clearing house for all traffic accepted. All the vehicles would be in the maximum capacity long-distance category).
(ii) An organisation set up by the industry which would actually allocate the traffic passed to it by the Ministry.
(iii) A pool of other operators, not in the scheme but who would place vehicles at short notice with the scheme.

Although the Meat Transport Pool kept its separate identity, it was to be a sub-section. The need for long distance road services became recognised as essential. Fuel supplies became available on this basis. Drivers over 35 years old were registered as being in a 'reserved' occupation. It was the best compromise Major Renwick could achieve. It became an operating organisation in February 1942.

The major objections and reasons for the subsequent withdrawal of this scheme and the introduction of the Road Haulage Organisation in 1943 were the low level of rates and the problems of matching vehicles to type and amount of traffic available at a particular time. The administration required was considered cumbersome by those involved.

The Hinchliffe Brothers, Herbert and John, had stayed to work with Fisher Renwick, at first in what may be best described as an 'independent role'. Amongst the first vehicles they were allocated to drive were the last of the rigid chain-drive Scammells and the Rigid Six 'PETREL'. Their skills in maintenance led to Harold Withrington, Chief Engineer, Manchester getting them to take any ailing Scammell to drive and also service to be trouble free. They were especially known for the ability to cope with the usual problem with the Scammell six-speed gearbox, the selector spurs. Supplies of these, and other items needed, not only for use by them, but also for the Manchester and London garages, were regularly obtained by their diverting to call at the Birmingham Scammell service depot, Tyseley. The Foreman was always willing to open up when needed if he was warned. The Scammell depots at Liverpool and Leeds do not appear to have been used by Fisher Renwick, more surprisingly the Manchester area depots had less use than Birmingham.

This meant that the Hinchliffe Brothers were never sure when they would get home with their vehicles, and sometimes several days would pass during which time they would have taken over two or three vehicles to bring up to their standards. The call up of fitters was proving a severe problem to all operators, as well as agents and makers service depots. The situation was made more difficult through the additional demand for repairs to military vehicles.

The fall of France ended the need to supply French forces with fuel, and brought an improvement in oil stocks held in this country. Each Regional Transport Commissioner, being ultimately responsible for allocations, was allowed from July 1940 to issue up to 90% of pre-war use when necessary. This was partly to assist in reaching a seven days per week production of munitions, particularly aircraft.

The German Blitz and U-Boat campaign which started in the autumn of 1940 made it necessary to bring into action the planned diversion of much shipping to the West Coast ports, (including Liverpool and Manchester). This immediately made heavy demands upon Fisher Renwick's long distance service.

Shadwell was virtually destroyed in the November 1940 blitzes, and of necessity much of the transfer of traffic had to take place in Glamis Road and The Highway. This use of these roads was not made easier by the equal need of other transport firms to adopt the same procedure. There were also the normal traffic movements. Fortunately the long relationship with Hays Wharf Cartage proved to be helpful. The Pickfords' offices and yard, Long Lane, Bermondsey, (much less used because of the move to Willow Walk) were able to be used by Fisher Renwick until it was possible to move to Coppetts Road.

Denis Renwick had already been managing the London operations with an increasingly fraught relationship with the P.L.A., because of the change from a steamer based service to the increasingly busy road transport operation. The destruction of Shadwell, despite its problems, meant he had the Herculean task of keeping the London end working. He

also had to deal with the difficulties encountered in work continuing at the now urgently needed Coppetts Road premises.

The building of these had become delayed by a requirement to modify the plans, scaling down the original proposal. These had been based on the successful experience of the White City Depot. The virtual destruction of Shadwell at least resulted in consent for a modified development to go ahead.

Although the early preparations of the site and the groundworks had proceeded as planned, it was ironic that much of the Blitz rubble from the City, the East End and Docks, was to be used by Deards to fill in and level the site.

It had now become practice during periods of bombing that drivers at both Shadwell and White City took vehicles, which were to be parked up, home for the night. This was to reduce the chance of damage or destruction through enemy action. They would also have been available if needed for priority use. The Shadwell drivers actually would load their vehicles with their 'valuables', together with those of neighbours, and drive to the nearest public open space, using their vans as a shelter. No Fisher Renwick vehicle was lost or damaged by bombing, nor was any stolen or affected for any other reason when used for this purpose. This use was officially recognised as a legitimate reason for the allocation of fuel coupons.

The drivers had an increasingly difficult time. Blitz or bomb damage caused diversions from the recognised routes. This was a problem for the 'Showboats', particularly with regard to low bridges, although flats with full, high loads could be equally disadvantaged. Worse was the 'Blackout', the light available from a single masked headlight was barely adequate in a built up area, which at least had a kerb to help visibility. Driving along a rural, if main road of the period, could be unpleasant and difficult. A right hand turn during foggy or misty periods would have been hazardous. Even adverse weather failed to stop Fisher Renwick, or indeed the other night drivers. A lesser, but still important inconvenience, was the reduction by closing, of transport cafes. Although not affecting the Manchester-London service too much, it became more of a problem for the new Scottish services.

The new White City depot was opened for operation on 6th May 1940, and immediately demonstrated its worth. When opened it was recognised as the biggest and arguably the best carriers' depot in Europe. The double-sided loading bank or deck, about 640ft long, was arranged so that local work was generally handled from one end, and the long-distance vehicles were all handled from the other end. Again a pioneering example of an idea for 'cross-deck' transfer of consignments. The space beneath the deck floor had been excavated to provide storage space, which was used at times as a Buffer Store by the Ministry of Food. Cranage was available for heavier traffic, particularly the drum cable traffic and a vehicle weighbridge was available at the front of the building.

Notably everything was inside under cover. Servicing the vehicles became much easier, a gantry for washing the Showboats, tyre air lines, and diesel and petrol pumps were available at the end of the depot. The offices moved later on 26th October 1940.

White City was also to be affected by the Blitzes on Manchester and its Dock on two occasions. The first caused damage to an exterior wall and the asbestos-sheeted and glass roof. The necessary repairs were soon completed. The roof was replaced by Fisher Renwick's own people. This became a further reason for absence from home for the Hinchliffe Brothers, when it was found they had 'heads for heights' among their accomplishments.

The need for blackout of any visible light was overcome by painting the glass areas of the roof with tar, and covering this with hessian. Working at times under somewhat restricted light was another difficulty overcome by the bank staff. Then during the second Blitz campaign in 1941 a nearby land mine caused evacuation whilst it was made safe.

It was no surprise to Major Renwick that road haulage rates were controlled from October 1940. Any increase allowed after this was only when necessary, i.e. in arrears and after tortuous negotiation with the Ministry. Also from 1941 the carriers' licences were suspended, replaced by Defence Permits. These were allocated as needed. B and C licence holders did not however automatically receive approval to carry for hire or reward.

Unfortunately the U-Boat campaign of 1941, and the heavy losses of tankers made it necessary in October 1941 to again reduce the basic fuel ration to 2 units for each ton of unladen weight. Supplementary rations were still available however, even after these worsening losses. These were allocated for Fisher Renwick's essential traffic.

It was not all bad or depressing news. Depots were opened in 1941 at Vauxhall Road, Liverpool, in a rather dilapidated former warehouse, formerly McGovern, Grove Parcels. It had the advantage of being high enough to accommodate a 'Showboat', although their access had to be gained around the back at the Vandries Street entrance, the Vauxhall Road front entrance not being high enough. The Manager was Alf. Bingham, who moved up from Shadwell. He was very familiar with the needs and problems of dock transport. Later when it was unit 10 Q 16 he would sometimes have to arrange for some 1,000 tons of traffic to be taken from the docks. Occasionally this was urgently needed food supplies with short notice of the movement. As a consequence of this new depot, some vehicles, local and trunk, were then lettered:

FISHER RENWICK
CONTINUOUS SERVICE
LIVERPOOL & LONDON

These included some transferred older, small Ford BB vans, (including 189), and a flat, (141), for local collections. For a period, recent Bedfords, a Commer sided lorry, and a Studebaker forward control van 'LYRE', were allocated to the Depot. Leyland Octopus vans 'DUNLIN' and 'DIVER' were re-lettered for Liverpool, until replaced by Scammell Rigid Eight 'Showboats' including 'PINTAIL' and 'POCHARD'. Their Liverpool based drivers were the Lewis Brothers, Bert and Norman, who although very small in stature were known for the skill in handling their 'Showboats' in confined areas. They were also remembered for standing up to the Dock Foremen when this was necessary. One occasion being when kept for hours to move alongside their ship to unload the cargo of Shand-Kydd wallpaper (unpopular with dockers because the rolls were packed in hessian covered bales, which had to be handled without use of their 'hooks', this type of traffic was heavy and difficult to hold). Norman, in this instance, decided this was not acceptable, and reversed in such a position to prevent movement of any other vehicles until he was unloaded. Eventually agreement was reached, and this delay did not occur again. Liverpool was also given the Rigid Eight flats 'TEAL' and 'TERN' from new. These were used for collections and deliveries, including dock work, as well as the service to London. When, as frequently happened, extra vehicles were needed, Scammells would have to be sent from Manchester. The Midlands too was now providing considerable traffic and another new depot was opened at Birmingham, using the former cattle housing at Castle Bromwich Hall, just off the A452, the first Manager being Teddy Goddard.

This was used by Fisher Renwick flats and vans for the continuing requirement to deliver Spitfire wings, some Lancaster wing-tips, and also propellers to the new Shadow Factory just past Fort Dunlop on the Chester Road. It was operated by Vickers Armstrong to build these aircraft until the end of the war. (It is now the body and paint shop for Jaguar). Following the take-over of the 10 vehicle fleet of Watkins Transport, who had been acting as Fisher Renwick's Birmingham Region Sub-contractors, it became a base for the increasing traffic to and from the region, including Coventry.

Opposite top: Fisher Renwick Ltd new offices and depot. The front of the newly opened White City Depot. The left-hand set of folding shutter doors was always the entrance to the depot. The dial for the weighbridge is visible behind the 'in' sign. The photo would have been taken early on a May 1940 morning, to ensure there was no traffic along the normally busy Chester Road. The cobbled road surface has a double tramtrack in the middle.

Right: An idea of the length of the loading deck can be gleaned from this scene. The 30-foot long Rigid Eight flat is lost against the some 640ft. length of the deck. The bottom left hand side was used by the long distance vehicles. The Showboat parked against the wall is waiting to be called for unloading. Various vans can be seen parked up by the entrance. A Studebaker flat can be seen on its way round to the right hand side of the deck.

Right: The bottom right hand side of the deck - always used by local vehicles. A Studebaker and an Albion flat are parked up, having been unloaded. White City was also a pioneering user of crossdeck working. This meant that there was a minimum need to move consignments. The two views of the loading bank give some idea of the wide variety of traffic now being carried. The windows seen below the deck provided some natural light to the storage area beneath.

Above: Following the destruction of Shadwell, 'PLOVER', FVR 489, is being unloaded parked in The Highway. The two Hays Wharf horse drawn vans would only be able to carry a small proportion of the contents of the 'Showboat'. It does give some idea of the terrible difficulties everyone was working under, until it was possible to move to Coppetts Road. The photograph has been the subject of retouching, due to negative damage. 'Plover' is the subject vehicle of Peter Davies' front cover painting.

Left: The rear of White City showing the attention paid to servicing the vehicles. The gantry would have been a familiar sight in bus depots, but was unusual in a haulage depot. The tyre bay was next, followed by the diesel fuel tanks and pump, with a pump for petrol where an Albion flat is being filled up (the bulk storage tank for the petrol, was of course, underground). The drivers did not fill the tanks, this was always done by a shunter.

It was usual for the drivers of long distance vehicles arriving, when the depot was closed, to park up in the Hall Drive, hiding the keys, then going to their digs. The shunter, or day man would then take over the vehicle when he arrived later. This meant the Scottish and Manchester long-distance vehicles would often be used for the deliveries, and if not already full for the return journey, would then be loaded at Castle Bromwich.

The use of Bacon's End as an alternative halt for the change-over breaks came about through the custom of giving a lift to the 'Cafe' owner's daughter, who lived in Castle Bromwich.

Direct deliveries to Coventry customers were made after the introduction of the Road Haulage Organisation. These vehicles would call at Castle Bromwich as necessary or be directed to collect their return loads. Soon after the end of the war a move was made to Pitney Street, Vauxhall, by the Co-op Dairy. Pitney Street was also the base for Holdsworth and Hanson's Birmingham Depot. The Street no longer exists. The availability of the low 'Showboats' made it easier for alternative routing of these to and from the depot and the A45 and A452.

At last, by mid 1942, Coppetts Road was fully operational. At first a van fitted with temporary seating was used to transport those who had lived near Shadwell, and they were able to transfer. Other workers at Coppetts Road managed to use public transport. Unfortunately - as had been the case at Manchester - with the move to White City, the remaining few dock employees kept for working the Coast Line traffic were no longer able to be employed by Fisher Renwick. They became part of the Dock labour force.

The cable drum traffic was a consistent traffic both ways throughout the war, with new shadow factories, airfields, etc. and the need to repair bomb damage. Both White City and Coppetts Road had crane facilities to handle these and other heavy items.

For Fisher Renwick, who remained running continuous long distance services albeit under direction, tyres remained a problem. The loss of Malaya (Malaysia) and the Dutch East

Left: The site of the former sewage works at Coppetts Road, Muswell Hill, still a rural setting even in 1941. Two R. Deard's 'B' licensed Fordson lorries, a V8 and a B, have tipped their loads of hardcore, mostly blitz clearance rubble, to level the site and fill in the settling tanks before the construction work can start.

Left: The entrance for the 'depot', the Deard's site office. The old van body would be considered luxurious for this date. One of their lorries is off for another load. The rural nature of Coppetts Road and the depot site can be seen. Some care was taken to ensure the minimum damage was done to any trees while the work was carried out.

Left: A general view of the completed Coppetts Road depot, showing a part of the loading bay. The original plan for a building similar to White City was severely limited by the restrictions for the supply of steelwork etc, because of the war. The depot was nevertheless successful when operating, and met all the demands made upon it, even after nationalisation. There was sufficient height and length for even the 'Showboats' to back up to the bank, with the folding doors shut. The rectangular building in the foreground was the office, remembered as being quite a pleasant place in which to work.

Right: A close up of part of the loading bay. The Rigid Eight box van is thought to be 'GROUSE', FXJ 951, the local collection and delivery vans are a Fordson 7V and a B. All have blackout masks fitted to their headlights. The Scammell now has two, and an unmasked spotlight, the result of more sensible attitude and recognition of the problems of night driving by the authorities - a matter in which the Major had taken an urgent concern, together with other senior figures, with some success.

Right: The loading bank in full operation. Again there is both a large amount and variety of traffic. Despite their difficulties at that time, Fisher Renwick continued to be very busy. Denis Renwick was working all hours, having to assume some of Major Renwick's responsibilities when he was occupied with Government business. The number of jackets hanging on the wall at the rear gives some idea of the number working on bank duties. Surprisingly, the white painting to the edge of rear wings of the 'Showboat' had been allowed to become almost worn away.

Right: This picture was taken on the bank at Coppetts Road at about the same time. There is a mix of 'Showboats', and local vans, including an older tilt van. Note the signs on the end wall for sorting parcel type traffic for the appropriate depot. The varied traffic is a fascinating mixture of textiles, foodstuffs, oil drums, etc., and would of course be prohibited today. The stack of cartons to the left of the No Smoking sign was from Metal Closures, West Bromwich, and would have contained bottle caps. The firm still exists, while West Bromwich, two local government re-organisations on, is now part of Warley.

Indies (Indonesia) to Japan early in 1942, caused the supply of rubber to become very restricted. At first the synthetic rubber now being used for civilian lorry tyres often failed early in their use, however it should be said that the tyre-makers, notably the American firms, were successful in overcoming these problems. By the end of the war, tyre problems were amongst the least of the worries. From mid 1942 lorry tyres were available only from authorised dealers on the basis that if a vehicle was receiving a fuel ration it was being used on essential work. Permits for replacement tyres were therefore available only on this basis. The dealer was also required to check to ensure wear had not been caused by neglect, or poor servicing of the vehicle.

In May 1942 the basic fuel ration for goods vehicles was abolished, instead the 'Issuing Office' for each District or Sub-district would issue coupons against application forms which needed accurate details of journeys, with routes, mileage and exact load to be carried. This change proved helpful to Fisher Renwick, particularly following their Scottish acquisitions.

A depot was opened at Barr Bank, Lymm, (on the A56) and between 1942 and its closure in 1944, it dealt with the transport from Scotland of wing components and propellers to the A.V. Roe works at nearby Woodford. Occasionally Rolls Royce Merlin engines for both Woodford and Castle Bromwich would be carried from Scotland. It was also able to assist White City, being convenient for the new traffic directed from the Runcorn and Widnes/Warrington chemical industry.

A depot at Balm Road Mills, Hunslet, Leeds, following the acquisition of Blackford Brothers, provided new, essential traffic including Napier aero-engines, and wool textiles and uniforms. Their small fleet comprised mostly older Leylands.

The further major acquisitions took place in Scotland, the first, largest and most important, being Alexander Brown, Townend Garage, Symington, near Biggar, Lanarkshire. He operated a fleet of some 30 modern ERF flats, changing what had been a Leyland fleet. Brown's had depots at Claypots,

Right: The interior of the spacious Liverpool depot at Vauxhall Road, in 1942, shortly after becoming operational. The restricted height of the Vauxhall Road entrance is clearly seen. The traffic office was in an ideal position to observe what was happening. The construction of the loading bank was indicative of the strict limits on the supplies of any form of building materials at that period. The deck is again arranged for cross bank working. The amount of cheeses waiting for onward delivery would have represented about a week's ration for Liverpool at that date. The elderly, unidentified Ford B Luton van would not have been sent further than Manchester, although newly lettered for both London and Scotland services.

Above: Taken in 1945, two Liverpool depot's long distance vehicles, rigid flat 'TEAL', FGO 189, and Leyland Octopus 'DUNLIN', DNC 715, at Coppetts Road before starting out on their journey to Liverpool. Sadly, the identities of the three in front of DUNLIN have not been traced. Was the schoolboy going on his first long distance ride? A Bedford WHL tilt van is also visible.

Left: The opposite side of the Liverpool depot loading bank, at a quiet period. The vehicles that can be seen include a Bedford OWL flat, and the Studebaker forward control van which is thought to be 'LYRE', both of which would be used for long distance journeys when required. The Ford Luton van has now moved over to this side. The varied mix of consignments on the bank would be segregated now.

ER RENWICK

TINUOUS SERVICE

HESTER & LONDON

A superb view of Scammell Rigid Eight 'CURLEW', FVR 591, taken in the Muswell Hill area. This classic 'high Showboat' has the integral Cornbrook cab with sliding doors and double split wind-screen and, judging by the gleaming paintwork, it would have been virtually new. It appears in full war-time guise with masked sidelights and offside headlight, together with white edged mudguards.

Left: Fisher Renwick's Symington Depot Office following the acquisition of Alexander Brown. Its size was deceptive for the amount of traffic it handled. It was for a period the first home of Alexander Brown and his wife.

also operated some dozen Bedford and Morris-Commercial vans of various types on parcels traffic. They acted as agents for Red Arrow (Birmingham), and worked their transferred traffic for United Automobile Services and also Caledonian Omnibus Co., however, this part of the Rodgers operation was not acquired, presumably because of the nature of the parcels being carried.

William Love, Bellshill, operating 6 Karriers, was acquired August 1941, followed by William Murdoch, Wellesley Road, Methill. This mixed fleet comprised Albion, Bedford, Reo 'Speedwagon' and Dennis lorries. A Dennis was fitted with a Gardner diesel engine, an enterprise which required some alteration to chassis and controls by the talented Dougie Smith.

George Wilson of Pittenweem with 8 vehicles, including an early and a more recent ERF was also acquired and the next acquisition, William Goodfellow, Methill, was transferred to Pittenweem Depot. Allison of Dundee also came within the Scottish operation, as part of Brown's business.

These Scottish acquisitions were successful businesses in their own right (apart from Allison of Dundee), and although there was merging of depots, and standardisation on Fisher Renwick procedures, the various 'new' employees experienced no problems with working for Fisher Renwick. The change to Fisher Renwick style of consignment notes, and administration of P.O.D's was easily understood.

The first Scammell Rigid Eight vehicles delivered in 1937 had beige wheels, (it has been suggested this was a primer finish?). Soon after all wheels were painted red. The Alexander Brown colours were green and red. This meant that when it came to repainting them it was only necessary to change the body colour to the Fisher Renwick navy blue (described as Vauxhall blue), and of course signwrite the names.

and Broughty Ferry, and Dundee. There was also a traffic office at 132 Broomielaw, Glasgow (this is now a virtually derelict area) and an English depot at Salford, with its traffic office at Deal Street/Chapel Street, Manchester. Brown was known to both Fisher Renwick - using each other for transferred traffic - and also to the Hinchliffe Brothers. The Brothers disclosed the fact that this flourishing business was available through the tragic circumstances of Alexander Brown's death in his sleep on 5th September 1940, followed shortly by his first born son being stillborn.

The premises of the former Brown depot at Symington remain recognisable as such today. They are now used by a fencing contractor and still in a rural setting. Browns started with two ex-RAF Leyland flats on milk collection, but were to become an ERF fleet, being the second only operator in Scotland to use an ERF (The first was Alexander Mathieson, Prestonpans).

There was further family tragedy, leading to the purchase of the Brown business. This was completed by the end of 1941, but the business had been under Fisher Renwick's management earlier. It led to an 'England Scotland Direct Service', and further smaller acquisitions.

These comprised William R Rodgers, Earlston, in the Borders, whose mixed fleet on take over comprised Albion rigid 8 wheeled flats, an ERF articulated 6 wheeled flat, and a Scammell LA 15 articulated 8 wheeled flat. Both of these also had four-in-line low-loading trailers. The firm continues in business today as civil engineering contractors. The Albions were replaced by Scammell Rigid Eights. Rodgers

The Alexander Brown, Symington, fleet at acquisition included:

Unnamed	FS 1917	Leyland Bull	4 whl.
Unnamed	FS 4811	Leyland Bull	4 whl.
Unnamed	FS 4947	Leyland Bull	4 whl.
Unnamed	WS 639	Leyland Hippo	6 whl.
Unnamed	WS 642	Leyland Hippo	6 whl.
YARROW	SY 5384	ERF CI.4	4 whl. flat.
EARN	WS 5384	ERF CI.4	4 whl. flat.
MEDWAY	BLG 800	ERF CI.68	8 whl. flat.
CAM	CMB 111	ERF CI.68	8 whl. flat.
ESK	CMB 883	ERF CI.56	6 whl. flat.
CARRON	DMA 225	ERF CI.54	4 whl. flat.
ETTERICK	DMA 275	ERF CI.54	4 whl. flat.
DEVRON	DMA 757	ERF CI.54	4 whl. flat.
Unknown	DMB 370	ERF CI.54	4 whl. flat.
LIDDLE	DMB 771	ERF CI.54	4 whl. flat.
YARROW	DMB 969	ERF CI.54	4 whl. flat.
JED	DMP 370	ERF CI.68	8 whl. flat.
TWEED	DTU 287	ERF CI.68	8 whl. flat.
TAY	DTU 288	ERF CI.68	8 whl. flat.
TEVIOT	DTU 522	ERF CI.54	4 whl. flat.
DOCHARD	DTU 523	ERF CI.54	4 whl. flat.
TUMMEL	ELG 55	ERF CI.56	6 whl. flat.
DEE	ELG 56	ERF CI.56	6 whl. flat.
ROBIN	ELG 357	ERF CI.4	4 whl. flat.
IRWELL	ELG 763	ERF CI.68	8 whl. flat.
WREN	FLG 140	ERF CI.4	4 whl. flat.
REDWING	FLG 337	ERF CI.4	4 whl. flat.
LAPWING	FLG 362	ERF CI.4	4 whl. flat.
MARTIN	FLG 363	ERF CI.68	8 whl. flat.

They were to be named following their absorption into Fisher Renwick's fleet.

The vehicles on the Scottish long distance services were lettered:

FISHER RENWICK
CONTINUOUS SERVICE
ENGLAND & SCOTLAND

The van fronts were lettered:
DIRECT SERVICE
Vehicles allocated to Scottish depots for local collections and deliveries, notably two Studebaker forward control vans,

and later some Bedford OWL vans were lettered:
FISHER RENWICK
MANCHESTER EDINBURGH
BIRMINGHAM GLASGOW
LIVERPOOL DUNDEE

This lettering also appeared on vans which worked from White City and Coppetts Road.

Because of the peculiar circumstances of the period, and 'direction' it was not unknown for Fisher Renwick vehicles to be used for journeys which had no connection with the service destinations appearing on the vehicle.

The Scottish acquisitions introduced new traffics, as well as smalls and general merchandise. These included seven vehicles on farm milk collections, and bricks. The brick traffic using lorries with drawbar trailers was soon sold off, the milk collection contract followed shortly. This was bought by Ramage, Riggside, Douglas. Only one of the four ERF lorries, 'LAPWING', went with the transfer, the other three were kept.

The unfamiliar, non-standard makes of vehicles acquired created some difficulties. Even in the difficult conditions prevailing it became possible to replace the older, particularly non-diesel engined vehicles. Scammell Rigid Eight flats and

Above: A fine photograph of Symington Depot's mechanics. Pictured from left to right are James Murray; an unidentified person but known to be living in Wishaw; Walter ('Waltie') Blackwell; foreman mechanic Joe Neill (with pipe); the redoubtable Dougie Smith and, lastly, another unidentified individual known to have worked in the office, and who transferred from White City.

high and low Showboats became a familiar sight over Shap, and then as far as Perth, Dundee, and even Aberdeen. The 'low Showboats' were also built by Cornbrook Wheelwrights and were some 13ft 6in high. They were introduced partly because of a number of bridge height restrictions on the Manchester-Scotland route and partly because weather conditions were sometimes unsuitable for the original high version. They were also useful on the Manchester-London Continuous Service. They could pass under the bridge at Church Lawton, avoiding the lengthy diversion via Scholar

Green and Red Bull Bank, Kidsgrove, to rejoin the A50.

Nevertheless high 'Showboats' were sometimes used on this service. Most of the Brown's fleet of ERF diesel flats, all with the Gardner engine, continued in use to nationalisation. They were all allocated names although some were to be replaced by Maudslay Mogul III 4w flats, including 'ANNAN', 'DOCHARD', 'ESK', 'JED', 'PERSEUS', 'TEVIOT' and 'YARROW' and Meritor 8w. flats including 'COOT', 'TEAL', 'THRUSH' and 'WAGTAIL'. They also had allocated new ERF vehicles, including boxvans' ANNAN', FTB 733 and 'NITH', FTB 732 and also 'BERVIE' and 'BLYTH', these had the AEC 7.7 litre diesel engine and gearbox, as part of the war production specification.

Sugar, sometimes with other foodstuffs from ships diverted from London (and requiring careful sheeting), jute products, metal components and paper were carried south. Tyres of all types and sizes, including aircraft tyres, were carried from the India works at Inchinnan. Willy Bruce recalls these as not being the easiest load to pack in a 'Showboat' - the various sizes were packed, the smaller inside the larger.

Horse meat, (originating at Dundee) and whale meat was also a regular cargo. This was placed on top of a tarpaulin placed on the bed of a flat, (preventing effluent drips on to the road) and then covered by another tarpaulin. At first Scammell Rigid Eight flats were used, later Seddon flats for speed were introduced, a Manchester driver taking over to go through to London.

The distinctive very dark blue tarpaulins with their white lettering were other victims of war conditions. New tarpaulins were now all unbleached grey, with limited black or white lettering.

Delivering transformers, using the Scammell Rigid Eight and ERF 8 wheeled flats, could also cause problems. Some

made a load with a very high centre of gravity. The consignor at Dundee did not appreciate the need to chain, rather than rope this load securely, nor to ensure the weight was correctly declared. It was soon learnt that they could also be careless about leaving them filled with the special oil, not ensuring they had been drained. This traffic was carried out in association with transformers and related equipment for English Electric at Stafford and Newcastle-under-Lyme.

The expansion and continuing growth of traffic being carried by the Scottish depots made it a priority that a site near Glasgow, with facilities to equal those of White City, should be provided after the war. Sites were investigated in the Rutherglen area, but later events prevented this becoming a reality.

The greater distance of the journey between London and Scotland, not least over Shap, required additional arrangements for dealing with any mechanical problems. Hudson of Milnthorpe were the preferred 'call-out' service, and were adept at getting the Fisher Renwick vehicles moving again if their services had been called upon.

The major serious fault with the Rigid Eights was a tendency for their tubular front axles to fail. These had their swivel axle stubs welded to the axle tube. The welding could and did fail without warning. This took some time to appear as a problem. Some of the accidents arising, although not involving other vehicles, on occasion caused fatal or severe injury. Scammell always carried out a thorough investigation into the reason for the failure leading to the incident. By the late war period improvements in manufacturing the axles were successful in virtually ending these incidents. Although, as late as 1948, Driver Raeburn of the Earlston Depot was killed when driving his Scammell Rigid Eight flat 'LYNE', MMH 11, this apparently hit a depression left by badly made up roadworks and 'LYNE',

Right: Driver John Dempster with an Alexander Brown ERF CI5 flat, pictured before the war carrying a full load of grain. Taken on a dry day, the tarpaulin sheets can be seen laid on top for speedy covering if the rain came. After acquisition by Fisher Renwick DMA 757 was to be named 'DEVRON', and Tom Thomson's father became the regular driver. 'DEVRON' was sold in 1948, working thereafter for a short period as a three deck sheep float (the under slung allowed too much sway when loaded) and it was passed on to Sam Anderson, Newhouse (Red Line Transport). It was used with a draw bar trailer for brick transport, the remains of the vehicle existing today at the rear of their garage.

Above: An early Cornbrook 'low Showboat', (built 1942?) 'CLYDE', FTB 844, seen at Symington depot, lettered for the England & Scotland Continuous Service. It would have been quite a contrast to the residents on seeing them pass through compared with the more familiar green and red ERF flats.

Left: A preserved Alexander Brown ERF CI.54, DNB 771, (Fisher Renwick's 'LIDDLE'). This superb machine looks as it did when first new in Brown's service. It has been completely restored and is owned by Henderson, Alston, Cumbria.

Right: A 'high Showboat' in trouble. However, this view has been included because of the detail it provides of the construction of the Cornbrook body. The variety and amount of traffic being carried on this occasion, and the skill of the loaders is all too visible.

leaving the road, fell some 80 feet to land on the foundation works for a new bridge.

Scammell fabricated quite a number of their components including the brake shoes, gearbox mounting brackets, and were sometimes at the edge of the then available welding technology.

Normally if a problem arose, the driver would ring Coppetts Road or White City, (whichever was nearest), for a fitter to come out by car, or if necessary use an available spare vehicle. Change-over of loads between vehicles was avoided if possible. A distinct difference from the English practice was that almost all Scottish-London long distance vehicles did not operate change-over for drivers, (meat and fruit being obvious exceptions, those drivers would change-over at Symington and Manchester), but stopped overnight at Manchester, then drove on to London, expecting to take four days for the round trip. The Manchester-Scotland, Earlston and Bellshill Continuous Service developed. Drivers changed over at the Jungle Cafe, Shap.

This was because the journeys over Shap, and the more difficult roads travelled especially in harsher weather, were better handled by the Scottish drivers experienced in dealing with these circumstances. The Scottish routes had some severe gradients and many sharp bends.

Although the former Brown drivers such as Willie Bruce were matter of fact about it, it required knowing the road and extra care when driving high or low 'Showboats'. Looking out for overhanging boughs, which meant pulling out into the middle of the road, whilst having a regard for any other obstacle, and not forgetting the possibly adverse camber.

Again a strange driver relying on the restricted lighting allowed, even with the later easing, would have been in an unenviable situation. One Manchester-based driver of a

'Showboat' skidded off the icy road into a burn (stream) near Abington. The van was carrying a load of broken chocolate, when Dougie Smith and the rescuers arrived early morning, not only was it now empty, but the rear doors were also absent.

A surprise benefit of the Scottish acquisitions was the quality of the drivers, and particularly the fitters and their commitment to keep the vehicles running. Another hidden benefit was the fact that drivers going to or from Scotland were able to obtain supplies of items such as rabbits, and pigeons or even irregular poultry. Other drivers kept hens and were able to supply eggs, (for administrative reasons there was no formal food rationing for the northern area of Scotland). This could mean some need for caution when a vehicle was stopped by Police, making checks (usually because of a report of a deserter, or perhaps a spy scare). The

Left: This Leyland Hippo flat WS 693, seen in Blythe & Berwick ownership was originally one of the vehicles acquired with Alexander Brown, being sold by Fisher Renwick when replaced by a Scammell Rigid Eight.

Lower left: 'FORTH', FTB 383, halted for a 'photo-opportunity' soon after being placed in service. The exact location on the A7 is not known, but it would be difficult to repeat this today, with the increase in traffic. Note the number of telephone lines on the pole, this was also the main route for the Post Office Telephones link between Central Scotland and England. The cables are now longer visible having been placed underground. Another photograph taken at the same time showed 'ROOK', FXJ 119, with 'REIVER' FXJ 336, on the opposite side of the road.

at Meriden, at what was Keelavite, on the way up. The Scottish depots also moved quantities of produce in season.

The difficulties in keeping the vehicle fleet, particularly the long distance vehicles, running became a 'nightmare'. Not only were parts difficult to obtain but there was an increasing shortage of fitters, experienced or otherwise. Interestingly some drivers were to become adept in keeping their vehicles in running order. The cost of temporary repairs was stated by Major Renwick "to be extraordinarily high", which would result in a reduction in gross profit. A special reserve fund was provided towards the costs which would arise from these deferred repairs when it would be possible to catch up with them. Spare parts became a little easier following the introduction of the Road Haulage Organisation.

reason given, if asked, for the 'Parcels' in the other side of the cab, would be "you would think with vehicles as big as these, they could get it all in the back, these are last minute 'urgents", fortunately for amongst others, including the Hinchliffes, this was always accepted, and no close examination ever made by the Police.

During the Summer and Autumn of 1942, grouping schemes were introduced for many categories of groceries and provisions. These included movement restrictions for journeys with seasonal soft fruits and plums, and for green vegetables and carrots. The Fisher Renwick pre-war involvement with fruit particularly, meant that the long journeys from Kent, and the Scottish fruit areas were to continue. Cherry and strawberry consignments for Marks and Spencer continued as approved annual special journeys. If the petrol engined Bedfords had to be used they refuelled

The Road Haulage Organisation was formed mid-1943 to overcome the difficulties of the 1942 scheme. It involved taking over by the Ministry 'well organised' businesses which became 'controlled undertakings', operating chartered vehicles. This was completed by late October 1943, with 388 Units. Including hired vehicles attached to the Units, over 14,000 long-distance vehicles were involved. These Units were to conduct their whole business on Government account. To ensure operators were prepared to offer vehicles for government service, the Ministry decreed all long distance traffic be carried by the Road Haulage Organisation.

Most Fisher Renwick depots became M.o.W.T. Offices,

with their Managers becoming Unit Controllers, having responsibility for the successful operation of their Unit. This not only meant ensuring the traffic was moved with minimum empty running, but that 'foreign' vehicles were able to get home as directly as possible. Worse was dealing with those 'foreign' vehicles that had limped into the unit with mechanical problems, and used fitter's time and spares, which in all truth could be ill afforded.

The Depots allocated as Ministry Units were:
LONDON Division 5.
5S4 Fisher Renwick Ltd. Coppetts Road, Muswell Hill N10. Manager Mr.S.H. Waters. Traffic directed to 10R Manchester and the North to 10T Preston, 10V Kendal, (not Carlisle), 11Q Glasgow, 11S Falkirk, 11T Dundee, 11V Aberdeen.
NORTH WESTERN Division 10.
10R4 Fisher Renwick Ltd. White City, Old Trafford. Managers; Mr.F. Bowden, London traffic, and Mr. H. James, Scottish and Birmingham traffic. Traffic directed for 5 London and 11 Scotland to 10V Kendal.
10Q16 Fisher Renwick Ltd. 57 Vauxhall Street, Liverpool. Manager Mr.A.E. Bingham. Traffic directed for 5 London to 11Q Glasgow, 11R Edinburgh, 11T Dundee, 11V Aberdeen, 11W Dumfries.

Top: Muswell Hill Home Guard Motor Transport Company seen 'paraded' for an official photograph. Responsible for defending the depot in case of invasion, they also had the considerable duty to provide motor transport needs for local units when required. The background view of the depot reveals it had been possible to provide a covered, secure storage area, despite the problems in getting approval and licences to build.

Left upper: Some of the Home Guard Company and their vehicles on parade, possibly being inspected before a training exercise? The availability of Bedford WTL and Fordson 7V tilt vans in the line up would have been the envy of some Army units.

SCOTTISH Division 11
11Q6 Townend Garage, Symington. Manager Mr. A. Brown. Traffic directed to 4V St. Albans, 5 London, 9T Coventry, 10Q Liverpool, 10 Manchester, 10T Preston, 12T Maidstone.
11Q7 Fisher Renwick Ltd. 81/91 Main Street, Bellshill, Manager Mr.J.L. Fox. The Traffic directions were as 11Q Symington.

One effect of the control exercised over traffic was that from 1942 Herbert and John Hinchliffe, were each driving the ERF vans 'ANNAN', FTB 733, and 'NITH', FTB 732 - these had Gardner 4LW engines, and were amongst the last

Above: 'ANNAN', FTB 733, one of two ERF CI.54 vans, always associated with Herbert and John Hinchliffe. Their exploits with these included assisting the Scammell Rigid Eights over Shap during winter. It is seen at Symington while working on United Turkey Red traffic. Later both were to be employed in carrying aircraft parts to English aircraft works.

Left upper: Ready for action? The still rural aspect of Coppetts Road was partly due to the fact that the sewage works, which the depot replaced, made its presence known to local residents, should the wind be in the right direction. It may be presumed that the interested spectators are family members of the men.

ERF war production civilian vehicles to be so equipped - changing over in Shap. At first they mostly carried products from United Turkey Red, then gun-cotton wadding, and finally aircraft components to England. Among the return traffic were Timpson shoes for Scottish shops.

They were able to help the Fisher Renwick Scammell Rigid Eights in wintery conditions. The Scammells, having only one driving axle, had difficulty in actually getting moving again after stopping for any reason when the road surface was icy and slippery. To overcome this, the Hinchliffes would join two Scammells together and then give them a tow to start them moving. Once moving,

however slowly, they no longer had a problem.

The Scammells always travelled in groups, and stopped at the Jungle Cafe for their break. The two ERFs timed their arrival to fit in, and when the weather would make it necessary, Herbert and John would go up and down Shap with two Scammells attached, preventing any problem if their progress was halted. Before changing over to the ERFs they had sometimes driven the Fisher Renwick Leylands, which would be in bottom gear most of the time going over Shap. They found judicious dosing of paraffin through the air inlet would give a useful boost in power. It did however create a thick, pungent exhaust trail.

By contrast, the Scammells of Youngs Express - the Rigid Eight being used by that company by this time - had rubber suspension and large single low pressure 13.50x20 rear tyres. Their brake drums were fitted with the chain tooth rings enabling them to be temporarily converted to double-drive.

A serious disadvantage to becoming an M.o.W.T. R.H.O. Unit was that all the Units experienced considerable delay, amounting to years, in agreeing and settlement of the annual accounts, and therefore in knowing profitability.

Some new civilian vehicles were being built for supply against Permits, Fisher Renwick were also able to purchase a few Scammell Rigid Eights, and intriguingly Permits

M.o.W.T. 12568A were allocated for two Scammell 45-ton Motive Units/Tractors and Machinery Carriers. These were ordered in April 1942, delivered in May and June 1943. It is believed they were to carry electrical equipment, but no knowledge of their use can be traced. It is thought one was named 'ELECTRICIAN' and the other 'ENGINEER'.

These Scammells were chain drive, having four-speed gearboxes, with heavy duty bevel drive countershafts using 12 and 119 teeth sprockets. They were supplied with 36x8 front tyres, and 15"x771mm single solid tyres on the driving axle. There was also a set (pair) of 13.50x 20 pneumatic tyres for when the unit was to be used as a tractor. The wide 6ft 6in version saloon cab was fitted. A ballast box was provided to be fitted over the turntable, the chassis had a heavy duty tow-bracket fitted.

Their 'DE.45 DA x 18 ft' low loading carriers were standard all welded, built by Thompsons (Dudley) Ltd. They had 12"x771mm solid tyres, and four-in-line detachable oscillating axles, the 18ft well length gave a 26ft 4in. wheel-base. An unusual extra was the well deck plate was indelibly marked with centres of gravity for various loads. One unit survives as a preserved ballast boxed tractor, fitted with the 13.50x20 pneumatic tyre conversion.

Top: The acquisition of part of the business of William R. Rodgers, Earlston, Edinburgh, led to their Scammell LA20 being included in the Fisher Renwick fleet and named 'BLACKADDER'. SH 7119 is shown with its Scammell flat carrier. The photograph was taken at Coppetts Road.

Above: 'BLACKCOCK', FGU 979, was a Scammell Rigid Eight flat with Cornbrook cab and body. Seen at Coppetts Road when new and just delivered, the M.o.W.T. Unit number is clearly visible. The Scammell is included in the schedule for 2nd March 1945 as working on long distance 'smalls' traffic.

Above: One of Rockman Brothers Bedford OL vans which were employed exclusively on sub-contractor duties for Fisher Renwick Coppetts Road depot. They may have been used for occasional long distance work. A brief glimpse of a Rockman Brothers Bedford WHL van going through Shap can be seen on the video programme published by the Shap Trust.

Opposite centre: Rodger's ERF artic 'WHITEADDER', SH 7061, seen in Edinburgh. It is understood that neither of these Rodger's articulated vehicles shown here was ever painted in Fisher Renwick livery. They did operate for thousands of miles as part of the Earlston fleet. The horse behind is not letting the photographer disturb its bait time.

Left: Rockman Brother's International K8 articulated flat, AJD 533, was operated by them as a vehicle under Muswell Hill's R.H.O. direction. It was the only International known to have an association with Fisher Renwick. It is seen parked outside a Hays Wharf warehouse which, at this time, were along the whole three-quarter-mile length between London Bridge and Tower Bridge. The conduit tram track in Tooley Street was still in use.

MUSWELL HILL, M.o.W.T. Unit 5S4
Examples of Operations and Traffic carried out on three specific periods during March 1944 to March 1945
These schedules do not include traffic given to other hauliers working under Fisher Renwick's direction e.g. Rockman Brothers

'Local' Work

W/e 3 Mar. 1944	W/e 4 Aug. 1944	W/e 2 Mar. 1945
10 V. 54 (5T.) 70 (7T.)	**6 V.** 59 (5T.)	**17 V.** 43 (14T) 66 (6T.)
55 (5T.) 72 (6T.)	60 (6T.)	46 (14T.) 73 (7T.)
62 (5T.) 73 (7T.)	62 (5T.)	47 (14T.) 77 (7T.)
63 (5T.) 77 (7T.)	66 (5T.) PLUS	50 (14T.) 172 (5T.)
64 (5T.)	73 (7T.) 5	52 (12T.) 174 (5T.)
67 (5T.)	77 (7T.) M.o.W.T.	59 (5T.)
	147-151	60 (5T.)

(inclusive) Owned and operated by FISHER RENWICK.

Note: the 5 ton vehicles are thought to be Bedford, and the 14 ton vehicles were Scammell Rigid Eights.

'Local Work' at this period was usually 'tonnage' movements. Mainly fertilizer and meal, but also contract work., e.g. 50 (Scammell Rigid Eight flat), Contract - glass containers from Greenford to Shippams, Chichester.

'Smalls' & 'General'

W/e 3 Mar. 1944		W/e 4 Aug. 1944		W/e 2 Mar. 1945	
16V. 8 Smalls	**8 General**	**5 Smalls**	**9 Gen.**	**9 Smalls**	**6 Gen.**
36	40	48	37	44	36
38	43	49	38	45	37
39	44	67	41	48	39
41	45	68	42	49	41
42	78	74	43	51	72
47	79		45	67	75
50	80		47	68	
74		81	51	69	
			53	71	

Partly Long Distance/
Partly C. & D.   also M.o.W.T.
1 V   71   147-151 incl.
                 Partly Long Distance/
71,72,75   Partly C. & D. Smalls

Long distance movements were described as 'Smalls' unless a traffic reference was used, when the description was 'General'.

Vehicles under repair or off/road for all or most of the reference weeks detailed

W/e 3 Mar. 1944	W/e 4 Aug. 1944	W/e 2 Mar. 1945
20V. 3 10 26 27	**18V.** 2 9 14 16	**16V.** 4 7 11 17
31 33 37 46	19 24 33 34	25 29 34 35
48 49 51 52	35 36 39 40	38 40 42 53
53 56 57 58	44 46 55 69	56 62 70 74
59 60 66 68		

The slight easing in supplies of spares, meant that there could be a slight reduction in the vehicles 'off road' waiting for parts. Even with a similar situation at White City, it can be seen the problems faced in providing sufficient vehicles for each day's traffic requirements were considerable.

These schedules of the Fisher Renwick Muswell Hill collection and delivery vehicles show the district/round regularly served. Some changes have taken place in the period covered as circumstances permitted. The relief vehicles were all allocated to district/rounds according to that day's traffic needs.

28 C&D V. W/e 3 Mar. 1944		28 C&D V. W/e 4 Aug. 1944		32 C&D V. W/e 2 Mar. 1945	
Van No.	**District/Round**	**Van No.**	**District/Round**	**Van No.**	**District/Round**
2	Woolwich	2	Woolwich	3	Wembley
4	Uxbridge/Slough	4	Uxbridge/Slough	5	City
5	Chiswick	5	City	6	Acton/Staines
6	Acton/Staines	6	Acton/Staines	8	Ilford
7	St.Albans/Welwyn	8	Woolwich	9	Watford/Enfield
8	Deptford/Woolwich	10	Islington	13	West End
9	West End	11	Silvertown	14	Bermondsey
11	Silvertown	13	West End	15	Leyton/East End
13	West End	15	Leyton	18	East End
14	Bermondsey/Camberwell	17	Holborn	19	North West
15	Leyton	18	West End	20	Uxbridge/Staines
16	Islington	20	Camberwell	21	Romford/Brentford
17	City	22	Kensington/Barnes	22	Silvertown
18	Bermondsey/Peckham	25	Hendon/Harrow	23	Dulwich/Beckenham
19	Park Royal	26	Islington	24	Kensington/Barnes
20	Tooting	27	Willesden	26	Islington
21	Croydon	28	City	27	West End
23	Dulwich/Beckenham	29	Watford	28	Enfield
24	Kensington/Barnes	30	Enfield	29	Holloway
25	Edgware	56	Luton/Welwyn	30	Walthamstow
28	Holloway	57	Peckham/Beckenham	31	Park Royal
30	Enfield	58	Barking	55	Woolwich
34	Western Avenue	61	Hackney	57	Hackney
35	Ilford	63	Western Avenue	58	Barking
61	Walthamstow	64	Kingston	61	Croydon
69	Park Royal	-	-	63	Western Avenue
-	-	-	-	64	Tooting
-	-	-	-	76	Luton
-	-	-	-	173	Watford/St.Albans
22/29 Relief		23,31 Relief		10,16,54 Relief	

Chapter Seven

1946-1949 – Peace, Nationalisation and Contract Services

The return to peace did not end the problems of running Fisher Renwick. A newly elected Labour government made it clear that road transport was to be nationalised, at a time and under terms then unknown. Major Renwick, through his involvement in the M.o.W.T. was able to suggest improvements thereby changing ways nationalisation could be achieved. He realised that Fisher Renwick would be included, and also that there would be opportunities for providing contract hire vehicles.

The new Minister of Transport, Alfred Barnes, who had been Chairman of the Co-operative Party, with the 35 plus Labour M.P.'s sponsored by the Co-operative movement, and later joined by the Federation of British Industries, realised that the interests they represented would be severely affected as 'C' Licence users if their vehicles were to be included, or limited as to distance, and made sure that 'C' licence users were excluded. This was achieved at the Committee stage of the Bill, when the proposed '40 mile radius' limit was dropped, and an unlimited operation for 'C' licences, to be granted on demand was introduced. An example of Government hypocrisy, it was to lead to much resentment from the rest of the road transport industry. It also resulted in increasing loss of traffic for both British Road Services, (despite setting up their own Contracts Branches), and the Railways.

Major Renwick and Denis Renwick's reactions were reminiscent of Sir George Renwick in their recognising potential for Contract hire of Vehicles on 'C' licences, hence their creation of Fisher Renwick Services to start to provide 'C' Licence and 'C' hiring margin Contract transport vehicles from Coppetts Road and White City. The new companies to be formed for this purpose, were not included in the nationalisation, allowing them to proceed with the rapid development of their new business.

The end of the M.o.W.T., and the Road Haulage Organisation came on 16th August 1946. This led Major Renwick to create a £10,000 account to settle any claims for damage or loss of 'goods in transit', the Ministry no longer existing to have any responsibility for these. Fisher Renwick had an excess of £100,000 for their vehicle insurance, and made a point of fighting any claim if there were reasonable grounds for this, saving a considerable amount on their premium. This continued to be policy with the Contracts and Services businesses, which averaged one claim per vehicle received per annum.

The change-over for most of the long distance vehicles had continued even during the most difficult periods of the war, proving the value of this system. To make the system even more efficient a teleprinter line was installed between White City and Coppetts Road, enabling printed messages for vehicle loadings etc. to be sent. There were to be changes in the pairings of vehicles, and in the depot workings, and sometimes this would cause the livery to be misleading.

The Hinchliffe Brothers left Fisher Renwick correctly assessing there was opportunity to commence their own business. (J. & H. Hinchliffe continues today, a successful

VEHICLE PAIRINGS

As earlier described, the system used four drivers for each paired set of vehicles. Recognised pairings, mostly of Rigid Eight high or low Showboats or flats included:

SHOWBOATS

GANNET - GUILLEMOT	ESK - TUMMELL
EAGLE - FORTH	TAY - DEE
PLOVER - CURLEW	TYNE - TWEED
RUFF - REEVE	DON - HAWK
SHELDRAKE - EIDER	LEVEN - COQUET
PINTAIL - POCHARD	LEADER - LYNE

BOX VANS

Later variations to pairings were:

ROOK - RAVEN	HARRIER - SEVERN
GADWALL - GARGANEY	KITTIWAKE - PETREL

FLATS

BITTERN - KESTREL	MOORHEN - WIDGEON
PTARMIGAN - GREBE	GROUSE - WOODCOCK
MALLARD - QUAIL	MALLARD - CORMORANT
CORMORANT - GROUSE	KITE - KESTREL
SNIPE - KITE	DIVER - COOT
BUZZARD - WOODCOCK	HERON - QUAIL
EGRET - BLACKCOCK	HARRIER - BITTERN
GREYHEN - TEAL	FULMAR - MERGANSER
LAPWING - HERON	PUFFIN - WHIMBREL
LANDRAIL - SCOTER	TERN - TEAL
GREBE - PETREL	LAPWING - PTARMIGAN

Note: some pairings were through runs. There were also to be some pairings of Seddon-Carrimore flats allocated to the Manchester-London Continuous Service.

family operation). A sad coincidence was one of the sons, who worked for a period for T.G.B., a once famous dealer, breaking up withdrawn B.R.S. vehicles including many former Fisher Renwick Rigid Eights for spares. Many rear bogies were purchased by Siddle C. Cook to be used as 'dolleys' or 'jankers'.

An unpleasant surprise was the tightening of fuel supplies, partly due to Government policy through the dollar shortage. The winter of 1946/1947 was one of the most severe in living memory, to be followed by flooding, creating problems, the worst affecting Shap and Scotland. Increased costs were inevitable in overcoming these, but as usual everyone put their all into the job, and the customers, who also had their own difficulties, not least with shortages of coal, suffered few serious delays.

The long-distance vehicles no longer carried spare wheels, these had proved vulnerable to theft when parked at the transport cafes. Their drivers now rang the nearest depot who made the necessary arrangements for the tyre problem to be dealt with. The increase in the number of vehicles operated, together with an increase in the turnover of drivers meant new drivers took over one of the available spare vehicles. Their lack of experience could cause further problems leading to further delays. Service vans were not used until after 1946, yet from the first use of the Scammell

Above: 'PERSEUS', JTJ 286, one of the AEC engined Maudslay Mogul lll flat lorries placed in service, November 1945. These were purchased because almost immediate delivery was available. The vehicle was supplied and bodied by Oswald Tillotson.

Right: Scammell Rigid Eight 'Showboat' 'HAWK', FTE 829, based at Bellshill (11Q7) and looking a little travel stained. The picture was taken at the end of the war, by which time the vehicle's headlight masks had been removed, and fog and spotlights added. The white painted edging too has gone. The location of the Scottish transport café is not known. It is not HAWK's driver who is seen walking across.

Below: This Austin K4 sided lorry is thought to have a Fife registration. The significance of the P6 on the cab door is not known. It has been suggested it signified it was based at Pittenween.

articulated lorries it was exceptional for them to be moved 'on the bar', except for severe accidents. Indeed considering the annual mileage the number of accidents or smashes was remarkably low, and usually caused by bad conditions, or mechanical failures.

The now urgent fleet replacement was made difficult by the long waiting lists built up for new vehicles, particularly the heavy chassis needed by Fisher Renwick. The delay for new Scammell Rigid Eights being aggravated by the waiting time for Gardner engines, although they had continued to be preferred and were obtained as available, bodied in flat and 'Showboat' versions. Although the ERFs acquired with the Alexander Brown etc, businesses had proved reliable in service, no post war purchases were made. This was mainly

Above: An early post war Bedford OLB van, carrying out local delivery work. The fleet number 50 identifies it as one of the Coppetts Road vehicles.

due to the lengthy waiting list, again due to the difficulty in obtaining Gardner engines. Maudslay chassis, powered by AEC engines were more easily obtainable and were purchased in their various models, they were found to be acceptable, although as all users of the Maudslay 'Meritor' rigid 8 found, the Lockheed braking had to be modified.

A more surprising choice was in Seddon rigid 6 ton flats and vans and articulated 10 ton tractors with Carrimore flat semi-trailers. These all received the names of rivers. This choice was partly because they were also more easily available, and the firm, originally Foster and Seddon, had also been known to Major and Denis Renwick as transport contractors. Their local agent, Halls of Finchley, also did a very good job in ensuring a back up service.

Some of these Seddon 10 ton articulated flats, 'CHELM', 'EAMONT', 'HUMBER', 'LOWTHER', 'ROM' and 'TEES' were on the White City-Manchester Continuous Service making changeovers at Meriden. The others 'EARN', 'IRWELL, 'ISIS', 'MEDWAY', 'MERSEY', 'RIBBLE' and 'THAMES' were used on day 'roaming' work, a type of operation new to Fisher Renwick.

The necessity to use available specialist repairers could also lead to problems. 'DERWENT', TMV 907, an experimental Seddon aluminium bodied Luton van, with sliding cab doors, referred to as a 'Showboat pup', proved to be a failure. The body was too lightly constructed for the task, being designed to come into the under 3 tons u.l.w. to come within the 30 m.p.h. limit. The low 'Showboat' 'DON',

FTC 636, suffered severe crinkling of some aluminium body side panels after repairs to the body. This was due to no allowance being made for the expansion caused by the temperature of a hot summer day, or night.

Cable drum traffic continued to be carried in both directions, northwards for the expansion of the National Grid, and southwards particularly for 'Underground' and railway electrification expansion or modernisation. Two of the Scammell S15 chain drive units, updated with pneumatic tyres remained in use as cable floats. That used at Coppetts Road, 'PARTRIDGE', was to be included in the B.R.S. takeover. It had a regular driver, Henry Miller - who was quite small in stature and had blocks fitted to his unit's pedals - as none of the other drivers were keen to either drive a chain drive articulated lorry, or carry out the physically hard tasks of loading or delivering the drum cable loads. The virtually identical cable float used at White City ('MERLIN') is also thought to have been taken over. Even allowing for their refurbishment, a further noteworthy length of service.

New traffic included sugar confectionery, Burton's Wagon Wheels and MacDonalds Penguin Wafers, these also using the basement storage at White City. Cigarettes, particularly from Liverpool, became an important traffic. Yeast from N.G. & S.F. Trafford Park was a perishable traffic requiring express service, as was 'Dry Ice' (solid carbon dioxide). Drivers delivering this needed to remember to wait a minute when opening the doors, to allow the carbon dioxide fumes to disperse. Delivery of periodicals, notably on behalf of Hulton Press, and the London specialist distributors, became important time sensitive distribution contracts, particularly in Scotland.

Some of this traffic was also brought in by other operators, as part of customers' policy of dividing their business. Sub-contract 'break bulk' and sub-contract local deliveries were carried out, and long distance services provided for local and 'regional' Carriers.

The Transport Bill received the Royal Assent on 6th August 1947. Fisher Renwick were amongst those agreeing to be purchased voluntarily, as coincidentally and quite independently did their competitors Bouts-Tillotson/Holdsworth & Hanson, and Youngs Express Deliveries. Other familiar carriers who were acquired voluntarily (besides Carter Paterson and Pickfords with

Right: This view, and the one overleaf, showing Scammell Rigid Eight flat MMH 167, were part of a series taken to illustrate a journalist's trip from Coppetts Road to White City. The first shows it passing through Barnet, followed by an ERF 8-wheel 'flat'. In the second (page 100) it has crossed Gas Works Hill cross roads in St. Albans, a notorious hazard with a long steep incline with the traffic lights at the top. The other vehicles are worth a second look, the ERF 8-wheeler is still to be seen at the rear of the Rigid Eight, a Co-op ERF 8-wheeler is turning onto the A5, an AEC STL is crossing, whilst waiting at the lights is a Commer Superpoise, unusually, towing a small flat drawbar trailer, apparently being used for machinery removal.

Sutton & Co Ltd), were Eastern Roadways, McNamara & Co. Ltd., and P.X. Ltd.

The compensation for Fisher Renwick was received in three stages, the first cheque issued on 24th April 1949 for £1,005,198-12-7d, the second on 18th January 1952, for £253,700-0-4d, and the last on 15th May 1953, for £18,547-7-6d - a grand total of £1,277,445-0-5d.

At their nationalisation Fisher Renwick were operating over 330 'A' licenced vehicles from freehold sites at Bellshill, Edinburgh, Kirkcaldy, Liverpool, Manchester, Symington, Dundee, Leeds and a site was owned for a new depot to be built at Rutherglen. The Birmingham depot, now at Pitney

Street, was leasehold. The value of the property accounted for much of the compensation.

Truth to tell Major Gustav and Denis Renwick would have experienced mixed feelings about nationalisation, what had been a very personal, tightly run family concern operating from two sites had by both purpose and circumstance become a considerable enterprise serving most of the country from ten depots.

This they realised required an almost impersonal style of management, totally different from their 'paternalistic' approach. Major Renwick's major concern remained Manchester, now at White City. He reputedly knew all his

Above: A splendid 1950's view of the Jungle Café, Shap, at a quiet period on a wintery day. Normally parked vehicles would obscure this view of the 'Jungle', and there was usually a wait for the phone box. Known for the quality of its 'full' breakfasts and the tea, it was quite a small building for the trade it did. To the disbelief of the owner, it did not survive the opening of the M6.

Below: One of the first of the Fisher Renwick Services Ltd. contract vans, before nationalisation. This Bedford 2/3 ton ML van was on hire to Metropolitan-Vickers wholesale division, distributors, of among other products, their Cosmos lamp bulbs.

Left: Scammell Rigid Eight 'Showboat' 'DON', FTC 634, at Biggar garage, where Fisher Renwick rented space to work on their 'Showboats' and other large vans when needed. Dougie Smith is pictured whilst carrying out replacement of the vehicle's engine. The ease with which the radiator shell can be removed can be seen. The ripples in the body side panels can be attributed to the negligence of a local coachbuilder who failed to allow for the effects of metal expansion, (due to the heat from the sun), when replacing the panels. As can be seen 'DON' continued to run with this rippled effect for some years, even after nationalisation, no doubt much to the Major's displeasure.

Above: 'TEAL', TMV 896, an AEC engined Maudslay Meritor rigid 8, new in 1948. They were regarded as not to be compared with the Scammell Rigid Eight by both drivers and fitters. The Lockheed brakes were idiosyncratic when compared against the Scammell's Dewandre air brakes.

Right: An Austin K4 flat posed outside Arlington Motors, Ponders End. It appears to have been rebodied and painted in the designated British Road Services livery for the first stage agreed acquired companies. It was not new, apart from the registration. Look at the front and rear wings, and the radiator grille. The headlights appear to have been replaced.

Right: One of the 14 vehicles supplied by A. Pannell Ltd. (better known for ash and clinker removal and Council refuse contracts), for their Fisher Renwick sub-contract work. This is Seddon Mk 5L flat AP14. Most of the others were Bedfords.

Upper middle: The last day of Fisher Renwick, Coppetts Road, Muswell Hill, before becoming Unit C33 Fisher Renwick (B.T.C.) Ltd. The photograph of the line-up of Scammell Rigid Eights waiting to set out on their northbound journeys was fortunately taken (unusually in the late afternoon - normally Sunday only journeys started during the day) by a twelve year old Guy Renwick using his Kodak Brownie camera. Nineteen are seen, others were in the workshop, or parked up to the loading bank. The only other location anywhere this number of Rigid Eights would be seen was at Fisher Renwick's White City depot. The photograph warrants close study for the differences in lights, the lettering, the loads and, for instance, the difference in height between the Cornbrook 'low' and 'high' Showboats. Also to be seen is a Rigid Eight box van with a Cornbrook cab.

Top right: Taken on the same occasion, part of another line-up showing some of the collection and delivery vehicles. Seven Austin K4 vehicles and three Bedford OL vans are seen, only one Austin is not a van.

Top left: Again taken at the same time, this photo of the Coppetts Road depot, showing the loading bays pays careful study. The rear of a (Bedford?) tipping lorry can be seen - it is not known as a Fisher Renwick vehicle, and is believed to belong to French Renwick. The Bedford van drawn forward has a Tecalemit lubrication trolley in front. Next is a Seddon, then a 'Showboat' van, and then more Bedfords. The Bedford OL van, lettered for Raymond Radio and Television, was another early Contract Services van.

Middle lower: Taken in 1950 by Arthur Ingram, the line up shows the effect of Muswell Hill now being a B.R.S. depot. At least two Fodens and an Atkinson can be seen. The Lion emblem is clearly in evidence.

employees by name, and made a point of always asking about the welfare of anyone known to have a recent personal problem. He was particularly remembered for consideration at times of illness, or if a driver had been injured in an accident. Denis Renwick had established the same relationship at Coppetts Road, probably having more problems in management with having to contend with the cockney character. Major Renwick was also faced with the fact that the business would also have required considerable investment.

The changes following the end of the War, and the increasing Union involvement in the direction of the business, not least in disciplinary matters made the decision sensible.

For whatever reason, there was a noticeable increase in losses or shortages of consumable items through pilfering, with some newer drivers less interested in the good name of Fisher Renwick for its service to its customers. This was due to the temptations created because of the continuing rationing or allocation of these products. Well intentioned attempts by employees were made to have their Fisher Renwick delivery notes signed as correct on receipt in the mistaken belief the firm would not lose. This created further problems especially if other sub-contractors such as A.H. Barlow found they were suffering any shortage.

There was an Extraordinary Meeting of the Company held on 26th April 1949. This was to fulfil the legal requirements to approve the acquisition (Nationalisation), and approve the change of name to Fisher Renwick (B.T.C.) Ltd. Mr. C.N. Christenson represented the British Transport Commission. Neither Major Renwick nor Denis A. Renwick were present.

Ironically the final Accounts for the last years of Fisher Renwick i.e. for year ended 30th June 1947 and to 31st December 1948 were to be approved by Fisher Renwick (B.T.C.) Ltd.

Senior Fisher Renwick management remained at Coppetts Road under B.R.S., and for a short time the practice of naming vehicles continued for new purchases and for vehicles allocated to the depot following acquisition of the operator. Amongst these were new Maudslay Meritor 8w. flats 'DIVER', 'LARK', 'OWL', 'THRUSH' (actually 'badged' AEC Mammoth Major III chassis, following Maudslay's acquisition by AEC), being the first new vehicles delivered to B.R.S. although ordered by Fisher Renwick.

Nationalised operators acquired vehicles included AEC (Maudslay) Mustang 6w. flats, 'FALCON', 'PIPPIT' and 'OSPREY', Foden 8w. sided 'CUCKOO' and 'SWAN', Foden 4w boxvan 'MAGPIE', ERF 6w. Artic flat 'SHANNON', and Maudslay Mogul III drawbar flat 'WAGTAIL'.

A new feature was that many of the former Fisher Renwick fleet, notably the Rigid Eight 'Showboats' and the conventionally cabbed Scammells had illuminated British Road Services signs inserted into the Luton fronts or mounted on their roofs.

A testimonial for the operational efficiency of Fisher Renwick must be the fact that almost seven years later, White City was operating as a B.R.S. Parcels Depot recognisably in the same way, apart from the B.R.S. stationery and forms, dealing with parcel and smalls traffic to the same depots, with the addition of some extra destinations. White City was by then handling some fifty long distance vehicles each weekday, these were also supported by the local collection and delivery vehicles.

Left upper: 'PARTRIDGE', YW 5208, seen for the last time, and with only the Lion emblem to show her B.R.S. ownership. The photo is known to have been taken in 1951 when the vehicle was out of service awaiting disposal. Despite her long and arduous life, 'PARTRIDGE' has clearly been cared for by her last driver.

Left middle: Photographs of any Fisher Renwick Seddon-Carrimore articulated flats are rare. This is 'TEES', TMK 586, newly painted for B.R.S. Muswell Hill.

Left: The City of London Lord Mayor's show with an immaculate 'CLYDE', albeit in B.R.S. livery, and identified as a Scammell Rigid Eight. Taken in 1949, the background provides ample evidence of the devastation of the blitz.

Above top and left upper: Two interior views of White City probably taken on the same occasion. The first starts with the front of 'Showboat' 'GUILLEMOT', GTE 191, and then, from right to left, can be seen the first effects of the changes - the two Youngs Express Rigid Eight vans. Other Fisher Renwick Maudslay, ERF, and Seddon vehicles can be seen. Whilst 'GUILLEMOT' has the first style of BRS green livery, including the Lion and illuminated cab sign, almost all the others retain original liveries. The second Youngs Rigid Eight is also lettered for B.R.S. The second line up shows Atkinson, Scammell, ERF and Seddon vehicles.

Above: The front of White City depot soon after nationalisation. The photograph says it all, now Unit C33 Fisher Renwick Manchester. The same comment applies to the 'Showboat' parked in the front. Note the lack of passing traffic.

Above: Former Fisher Renwick Leyland Octopus 'ROBIN', CVR 503 - was this the other Octopus seen in the pre-war photo of two Leylands at Shadwell, and later transferred to Symington? Replaced by a Scammell Rigid Eight after the war, and sold to McGawn of Ayr, via Allen Grey, it was to be nationalised with their fleet. It is seen at Girvan harbour, the International K8 articulated lorry behind also belonged to McGawn.

Left: A sad end or finale. These two cut down Scammell Rigid Eight 'Low Showboats', having been withdrawn by B.R.S. Parcels, are on their way to TGB Motors, Bury to be dismantled. The picture dates from early 1960.

Right: The three cheques for the acquisition by the British Transport Commission and dated April 1949, June 1952, May 1953.

F/N 053397 London 2 APR 1949

To the Cashiers of the Bank of England

Pay to Gustav Adolph Renwick or Bearer Order

For GLYN, MILLS & CO,

A.W. Thomson

BRITISH TRANSPORT COMMISSION.

55, BROADWAY, LONDON, S.W.1.

151

N.º 1359

Mess.ʳˢ Glyn Mills & Cº
67, LOMBARD STREET, LONDON, E.C.3.

NOT NEGOTIABLE

Date
18th January, 1952 Pay Gustav Adolph Renwick or Order

Two hundred and fifty-three thousand seven hundred pounds and £253,700.0.4d

four-pence————————————— For and on behalf of BRITISH TRANSPORT COMMISSION.

W.E.Morgan
Comptroller.
Director of Funds or Assistant.

J.Hayes
Chief Secretary.
Deputy Secretary.
Principal Staff Officer.

Senior Secretarial Assistant

BRITISH TRANSPORT COMMISSION.

55, BROADWAY, LONDON, S.W.1.

151

N.º 2098

Mess.ʳˢ Glyn Mills & Cº
67, LOMBARD STREET, LONDON, E.C.3.

NOT NEGOTIABLE

Date
15th May, 1953 Pay Gustav Adolph Renwick or Order

Eighteen Thousand Five Hundred and Forty-seven Pounds Seven £18,547.7.6d.

Shillings and Sixpence For and on behalf of BRITISH TRANSPORT COMMISSION.

J.M.Neil
Comptroller.
Director of Funds or Assistant.

J.R.Brazier
Chief Secretary.
Deputy Secretary.
Principal Staff Officer.

Senior Secretarial Assistant

Chapter Eight

1949-1972 – Fisher Renwick Group, The Final Chapter

Fisher Renwick began their contract hire service in 1946, starting as Fisher Renwick Services and Fisher Renwick Contracts, at first operating from Coppetts Road, and then from White City. As the consequences of the nationalisation acquisitions which would result from the proposed Transport Act became known, the potential for Fisher Renwick to provide contract hire vehicles for companies who would wish to carry their own goods on their 'C' licence became apparent.

The Transport Act established this principle in law, and Denis Renwick, with his father as Chairman, recreated Fisher Renwick as a contract hire group, and formed Fisher Renwick Contract Hire Ltd. The Chairman, until his death in 1957, was Major Gustav Renwick. Denis A. Renwick was Director. Building on the base of their existing, small contract fleet, new separate Contract Companies were established, although still based at the two depots. Besides supplying to existing customers, they also began to advise and provide vehicles to small businesses who now preferred to have their own dedicated transport, operated for them by Fisher Renwick, rather than have to use British Road Services contracts.

There were different customer bases at London and at Manchester, with probably more of the smaller, one or two vehicle contracts in London. Although the shortage of new vehicles, and problems operating older vehicles may have been a selling point. The difficulties in obtaining new vehicles for the new Contract operation led to new, unfamiliar makes e.g. Trojan being introduced, or modified ex-army chassis e.g. the Arlington 'forward control' conversions of the Bedford MW chassis being purchased (this was to remind Major Renwick of the situation following the 1918 Armistice). The familiar chassis makes, Albion, Bedford, Ford, and Seddon were also purchased.

Some customers needed only small 'car derived' vans, which were also in limited supply. There were problems in providing the best service possible during the difficult conditions of post war austerity. The dollar shortage meant that petrol, derv and tyres were still rationed or controlled, which added to the problems in developing their new business.

Following nationalisation, and the not unrelated increase in Contract customers, Fisher Renwick Services vehicles were understandably no longer welcome at Coppetts Road or White City, nor were the necessary office facilities available, so other arrangements became necessary. These included a willing, indeed eager transfer of staff to the new Fisher Renwick companies. Their knowledge ensured continuing standard of service for the growth in contracts. Drivers such as Cliff Darlington, who was on the Firestone contract, and Frank Powell, who now drove a Seddon 6ton box van on hire to North British Rayon, both had previously driven Showboats. Key members included Chief Engineer Fred Walpole, who had started as a driver of the first Peerless lorries at Shadwell in 1922 and whose service came close to being equalled by 'Chippy' Muldoon, vehicle electrician at Shadwell, then Muswell Hill, and finally at Hendon. Jane Thorburn, Denis Renwick's secretary 1942-1968, Anne Blair, the Major's secretary - White City 1941, moved to London in 1968 to act as Denis Renwick's secretary to 1972. 'Vi' Coupe, continued as Arthur Marshall's secretary at White City.

As British Road Services increasingly became the only alternative Road transport supplier other than Own Account or 'C' licence operations, old customers were content to let their transport be met by contract hire from either Fisher Renwick Contracts or Services. Some of these e.g. Brooke-Bond, had been customers from the start of the Steamer Liner Service, and Kolynos Pharmaceutical from 1920. Others had used the road transport service and felt able to continue their trust through a vehicle hire contract for their transport needs. These companies included Corn Products, Ingersoll Rand, United Turkey Red (U.T.R.).

This work was taken over from 'ANNAN' and 'NITH', and still running on changeover at Shap, using two Seddon box vans. These were replaced by two Austin FG box vans, to be replaced by two more Seddon vans, the Austins proving to be less reliable. The Firestone Tyre contract had two AEC Mammoth Major 8w. box vans operated on the changeover system, London - Manchester. They took tyres North and returned with tyre cord fabric from mills at Middleton, Hebden Bridge and Todmorden. The first vans were replaced by Mark V versions, in turn to be replaced by AEC badged Maudslay Mustang six wheelers. Each version had a sliding roof for overhead loading at the mills.

Other long time customers changing to contract included Procter & Gamble (previously Thomas Hedley). The

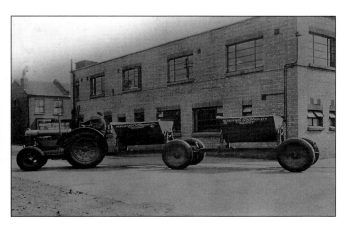

Above: Fordson Standard tractor and 'Dobbin' train of two side tipping dumper trailers. One of the items of plant available for hire from Berresford Atkinson Ltd. Manchester in October 1940.

Above: Difficulties in obtaining new vehicles after the war, were met in part by ex military conversions. This Bedford MW Arlington Motors conversion was one of more than 20 purchased.

Above: This new OL van was delivered at almost the same time for the Brillo contract, note the sequence of the registration numbers. The finish and lining out is a particular feature of the vans for this contract. *(R.P.S. Bevin Family Collection).*

Above: By contrast, at the same period, this new Bedford 30 cwt normal control van was able to be placed on contract hire to International Chemical Company Ltd. delivering amongst other products their 'Kolynos Dental Cream'.

Above: This Bedford JI van was supplied to Osborne Garrett in March 1960. The customer is now Osborne Garrett, Nagele, as a result of the merger between two major firms. Both were using Fisher Renwick Services, who retained the contract to supply the vehicles to the merged business.

Above: Difficulty in obtaining new vehicles could also be met by purchasing less familiar makes, being sometimes more readily obtainable. This Trojan 1-ton van with its unique V two-stroke engine was one of several purchased. They gave satisfactory service but non-standard features meant no more were purchased as Bedford and Fordson vans became more readily available.

Above: This 1951 Oldham registered Seddon six ton van was a familiar make and one of two supplied to a pre-nationalisation customer, United Turkey Red. Built to be operated within the 30 m.p.h. limit, their contract involved a considerable mileage during a year.

Simpson 'Goblin' Foods contract now used an attractive livery featuring their 'Goblin' trade mark on the sides of their vans.

Other early customers included: Metropolitan-Vickers using Austin 3 way vans; A.J.Mills, Bacon merchants, who used two Ford 3 ton 'Cost Cutter' box vans with a red livery (one of these was stolen complete with its load, and was never seen again); Farinol Floor Compound - later Evans Chemicals, Liverpool, who continued the contract - also using a Ford 3 ton 'Cost Cutter' in an orange and blue livery; and Lilia Ltd. Manchester depot, had enjoyed a special relationship with Lilia's Distribution Manager, Robert Vardy, who drove in to his work from Cheadle Hulme, and was happy to state he had come to depend on Fisher Renwick vehicles guiding him to or from home when there were poor motoring conditions.

One contract which started from two car-derived vans was with Porter Lancastrian, who supplied refrigeration and dispensing equipment mostly for the licensed trade, which developed into providing a large fleet of Austin A35 vans for their countrywide customer service. A difficult contract was that for Gervaise Dairy products.

To overcome the need for servicing facilities, and also offices, existing businesses were purchased in 1949. First was 'K' Garage, Watford Way, Hendon, conveniently close to London customers and well placed for the start of journeys northwards. This became the new Fisher Renwick Group Head Office, and base for Denis Renwick, who following Major Renwick's death, became Chairman in 1957. The Management included other Fisher Renwick stalwarts who preferred to remain with the Company. Notable was W. A. (Bill) Rivers, who started as 14 year old Office boy at Shadwell.

During a period of depressed trading for return loads for Manchester, Denis Renwick purchased a quite reasonable car for £5, and sent 'Bill' out to canvass for traffic. He proved to be very successful, among his notable customers were Firestone Tyres. He gained the first order for this traffic standing amid the rubble foundations of the Firestone 'Art Nouveau' building, a much admired structure, which years later would be reduced back to rubble – a victim of property speculation. The Firestone Tyre business was retained as a contract as previously described. 'Bill' Rivers moved to Coppetts Road, and was to become Sales Director, and then senior Director Fisher Renwick, second to Denis Renwick.

Sadly he was to die through cancer.

The Managing Director of both F.R. Contracts and F.R. Services was Len Perkins. The Fleet Engineer for both Companies was Fred Walpole, still with them. Many of the original drivers also transferred back from British Road Services as opportunities arose. Other vital posts were filled by Marion Harding, secretary 'K' Garage - whose service went back to Shadwell, Fred Blackwell and Ken Uzzell who looked after the forecourt, Eddie Hawker, who moved to become Workshop Manager, and Jack Trodd, Managing Director.

To meet the servicing needs at Manchester, the Kingsway Garage Ltd., Didsbury, Manchester, was acquired. The Managing Director with responsibility for the Manchester operations was Major Arthur Marshall. Fisher Renwick had acquired his family's business, during his war service, and upon his demobilisation after Dunkirk, when he was seriously wounded, he joined Fisher Renwick, with responsibility for the Scottish operation, being based at Earlston until nationalisation. He then moved to Manchester. The Managing Director of F. R. Services, Manchester, was John Holding, who started at White City as office boy, (His wife Connie, was the daughter of Dick Thorpe, a F. R. long distance driver). The Engineer was John Millington.

Contracts were not restricted to operating from the two depots, from the start out-placements were normal, the fleet for Crosby Doors was located at their premises, whilst the Kraft contract

Above: A mystery photograph. One of two Albion flats supplied to Hills & Partridge, Millers, Aylesbury. Although used for deliveries of sacks of flour, feeding stuffs and grain they had bolsters rather than headboards to retain the top layer of the load. The possible Durham registration numbers do not match the dates for the contract 1949 to 1955. It may be they were not new vehicles.

Right upper: The 'K' Garage, Watford Way, seen shortly after the acquisition by Fisher Renwick Group to serve as the Head Office, and as a base for London Contract Hire vehicles. The Garage was to be redeveloped during 1970-1972 to be able to meet the demands being made on its car and petrol forecourt sales and services following the extension of the M1 to Hendon, now just behind the Garage premises.

Right: Although Fisher Renwick soon disposed of their first AECs in 1934, they were to choose the Mammoth Major for their contract hire operations where this type of vehicle was required. Firestone Tyres were again a customer who turned to contract hire on nationalisation, this AEC Mammoth Major Mk III being used on an intensive schedule, delivering tyres to the Lancashire area and returning with tyre textiles. The van body had a sliding opening roof to suit the method of loading at the mills, using a hoist to lower the reels from an upper storey doorway.

required multi-depot location. Crosby group's Distribution Manager, Frank Walden was positive about the advantages he gained from the contract hire agreement with Fisher Renwick Ltd., including new Bedford vehicles incorporating the spare servicing allowance, longer 32ft. trailers, and a claimed 10% saving in administration.

There were two other businesses in which Major Renwick was briefly involved. The first was Berresford Atkinson Ltd, Stretford. This was a small contractors plant hire firm with a family connection. Although successful, it was decided to dispose of the interest in it, following the death of 'Berry', the brother-in-law of Denis Renwick. The contract transport business was considered the preferred business.

French Renwick Ltd., Hendon, was started as a partnership with a member of the W. & C. French family business of civil engineers, who had preferred not to return to work in the family concern. Unfortunately the business did not progress in management or performance as Major and Denis Renwick had required, and the building side was closed down. The Company continued as French Renwick, becoming the base for the Kraft Foods contract. This started as a contract to provide some 130 Ford 4D vans, and at its renewal these were replaced with approximately the same number and type of van. Following further renewal of the contract a fleet of some 158 Bedford TK vans was provided, these were to be among the vehicles taken over by Ryder. In the first contracts the whole fleet of vans had to be provided

Above: This mid 1950's Dodge 3 ton van shown at the premises of an unidentified coachbuilder, was one of 13 for a Birmingham based contract. While the Dodge vans gave good service, the contract was not an easy one. Their drivers were roundsmen rather than drivers, and maintenance at a small depot was difficult. The Fisher Renwick fitter in charge, Jack Dennis, had held a variety of jobs with the family, including being Major Renwick's gardener at Holystone. Later he took charge of the Kraft contract at Birmingham.

all at the same time and ready for work at each depot. Because of this, each batch had consecutive registration numbers. To allow for the requirements of plating, and the annual test, the final fleet had a mix of ages.

From the start the vehicles had been based at Kraft's local depots (each chosen to be able to serve each of the commercial television regions), located at Birmingham, Bristol, Croydon, East Kilbride, (this had sub-depots at Dundee and Aberdeen), Leeds, Liverpool, Newcastle-upon-Tyne, and Waltham Cross. All these vehicles had special bodies supplied by Hunter Vehicles Ltd., Enfield, who were to supply the majority of bodies for London based vehicles. The Manchester contract vehicles were usually bodied by Fishwick, Temperence Street, Ardwick, although some, notably for Procter & Gamble, who specified side loading access, were supplied by Salmesbury Engineering, Blackburn. These were not satisfactory in service, and later versions were built by Boalloy and particularly Hunter.

The Managing Director of the French Renwick division was Horace Paine, who joined from B.R.S. His Assistant was George Warner, who had been with the construction from its start. Guy Renwick was an F.R. Executive Director dealing with Kraft depots. The Group had again set up its own Insurance department (created by Horace Paine), as part of French Renwick, managed by Tom Lysaght. The underwriting was undertaken by J.H. Dewey.

H.(Mickey) Wilcock of Dearden, Harper and Miller, auditors to the Dry Dock Company, became their final Company Secretary, later invited to move to Fisher Renwick Group, London as the Company Secretary. Coincidentally, the first secretary appointed by Fisher, Renwick, Manchester London Steamers, also acted as first secretary of the Dry Dock Company, and some 80 years later the final Secretary of the Dry Dock Company became Secretary of Fisher Renwick, albeit operating in a quite different business.

Barbara Castle's Transport Act 1968, made it clear that Fisher Renwick would need to develop their servicing and maintenance facilities. Whilst they had been adequate for the demands of the period prior to the Act, comparing well with those of competitors, increased and better equipped workshops and management of servicing were now necessary. This did of course also mean that new

Right top: Firestone also employed a large contract fleet of Bedford lorries, including articulated vans for delivery of their tyres. They were to become a major user of the workshop capacity at the London depot.

Right: One of twelve AEC Mammoth Major V sided lorries. Wandleside Cables, following their removal to a new factory in Ulster, employed the AECs to take raw material to the factory, via the ferry, and returning with loads of cabling. The company made the move to take advantage of subsidies available to new industry locating in Ulster. Despite this, the business closed twelve years on. At least Fisher Renwick were able to conclude their contract when the AECs had completed their planned life.

The AECs on the Firestone contract proved to be satisfactory, standing up to the considerable mileage travelled. When their replacement was necessary two new Mammoth Major Vs with improved Hunter bodies were provided for this major contract.

Above: This BMC Austin FG van was one of a varied fleet supplied to Peglers. The load would be both heavy and valuable. The 'Threepenny Bit' cab was popular with operators for easy parking in restricted areas, although not essential for Peglers' work.

Below: Cundell Corrugated had several of these Bedford vans for product delivery. They remain in business today.

Below: The Fisher Renwick name and livery was revived, and lived on until the acquisition by Ryder. These vehicles were not used for 'spot' or casual hire, but were spares to cover servicing or satisfy a demand for extra vehicles until these could be built and painted in the appropriate livery. They were mostly located at the London depots. The Manchester-based vehicles were finished in a plain livery, invariably grey.

Left: This smartly turned out LAD-cabbed Albion in the livery of Stevenson & Howell was placed in service during November 1967, the body having shuttered front side loading facilities.

Left below: This Ford 3 Ton ET 'Cost Cutter' 4D van was one of 140 specially bodied vehicles, all placed in service on the same day, for a country-wide Kraft Foods contract. The bodies were provided with racking to accommodate the various types and sizes of packaging of the many types of product carried. These also varied according to the season. The vans were located at the various Kraft depots, and relief vans were provided when major servicing was due. So successful was the management of this contract that it was renewed with the supply of new Ford vans to the same general specification.

Above: Some 15 years after the first Kraft Foods contract, 158 Bedford TK vans were to be placed in service for the third Kraft Foods contract. This 1964 version was one of the first. The livery has stood the test of time although the body, with side access provided, is now bigger - the supermarkets, still in their early stages, requiring larger deliveries. The vans were still operated from 10 depots - to cover each television region - these depots in turn being served by large capacity rigid eight wheeled vans, operated by B.R.S. from Kraft's Kirby factory.

opportunities for hiring vehicles became available, as businesses operating their own vehicles realised that they too needed to operate to the higher, and therefore more costly standards.

The outcome was the acquisition of a site at Abbey Road, Park Royal, which after completion of the purpose built depot by Laing, was opened on 6th April 1970. The purchase of this land, the car park of the former Park Royal Greyhound Track, was the result of negotiations by Guy Renwick with Westminster & Country Properties Ltd., owners of this and other tracks, who were to develop the remainder of the site.

F.R. Contracts, F.R. Services, and F.R. Services, Wimbledon were amalgamated under Reg Cox, who had been Managing Director, Fisher Renwick Services Ltd., Wimbledon. Len Perkins retired from ill health. Fred Walpole also retired. Reg Cox chose to retire on the acquisition by Ryder.

This was followed shortly afterwards by a new depot for Fisher Renwick Services at Globe Lane, Dukinfield, Manchester. This site had been part of Adamson's Boiler and Engineering Works, the new offices being a conversion of the canteen block. (Daniel Adamson, founder of that business had been the driving force behind the building of the Ship canal, so it was appropriate that Fisher Renwick should now occupy some of this site).

Ironically it was the existence of these new purpose designed depots, and the way the Contract Hire services were fulfilling the demands of the 1968 Act, that led Ryder to begin negotiations to acquire the various businesses comprising Fisher Renwick, with the exception of 'K' Garage and Kingsway Garage Ltd., Didsbury. Ryder realised that if they were to succeed in Britain, they needed to acquire a company of Fisher Renwick's calibre. At the take-over some 600 vehicles were being operated on behalf of their customers. Ryder paid £1,580,982-40p for the Fisher Renwick Group and its vehicles, May 1972.

The sale to Ryder arose because Death duties in a wholly owned, two shareholder business would have put their entire enterprise, jobs, everything, at risk.

Prior to the sale, a two year development project at K Garage was started in 1970 at the instigation of Denis Renwick, this following the opening of the Hendon extension of the M1 and to deal with the increasing demand for its services, including a service department and nine petrol pumps to cope with peak demands. K Garage continued as the Head Office for remaining Fisher Renwick businesses. It was now also a major agent for cars under the management of Jack Trodd, holding franchises for Austin, Ford, Jaguar, M.G., Morris, Triumph and Wolseley cars, and a very busy outlet for petrol, with a loyal private customer base for its British car franchises. Guy Renwick had much of the responsibility for the detail of this project, completed without closure during the work.

It was sold later to John Gregory, (then Chairman, Queens Park Rangers), who was to acquire the Blue Star Garage chain at the same time. K Garage remains a well known land mark from the M1, now being known as Alan Day, the Finchley Mercedes distributor.

The sale of Kingsway Garage, Didsbury, marked the end of over a century of family involvement in transport, of goods and then finally personal transport.

The details of the earliest vehicles in the Fisher Renwick Contracts and Services fleets are not available. Details of most vehicles operated from 1965 to March 1972 are provided in the Contract vehicle fleet list.

POSTSCRIPT

Former Fisher Renwick premises Manchester no longer exist.

Cornbrook Road, Pomona. No trace of any of the premises, the site has for many years been used as a scrap merchant's yard.

White City depot, Chester Road. Demolished, (together with the adjacent Greyhound Track) some years ago to become the site of a retail park.

Fisher Renwick Services Group, Diston House, Talbot Road, Stretford (Head Office). Demolished some ten years ago. The site was developed as a purpose built office block, and includes a branch for the Midland Bank.

Kingsway Garage Ltd., Kingsway, Didsbury, Manchester. Half the original frontage on the corner of Fog Lane remains, with an enlarged showroom, now I.L.Kirkham (Car Sales).

The Kingsway frontage comprises a modern 'Total' petrol station, with car wash. The Kingsway Garage workshops no longer exist. The old, former cottages within the main yard remain, these latterly housed Kingsway Auto Electrical Services (no connection with the Garage or Group, although their services were used). The Fisher Renwick Services workshops at the bottom of the yard also remain, and are used for a commercial vehicle and bodywork repair business. The original wooden office block used by Fisher Renwick Services has been replaced with a brick built office/garage/workshop unit.

Simpsons Motors, Whalley Range, Manchester. The complete building remains in use as a Kwik-Fit centre. The front of the building is now only recognisable with their standard facing and livery.

Right: A Scammell Routeman 2, this special tanker was the result of joint development by Fisher Renwick Services and their contract customer, Procter & Gamble. It was used to deliver shortening (a special type of catering fat). The tank was heavily insulated to ensure the hot liquid did not fall below the critical point at which it would solidify. In addition to the insulation, heating coils were fitted in the tank so that the temperature could be maintained in the event of any delay. The coils were designed to operate with every type of electric supply likely to be encountered. This specification made for a heavy unladen weight and, to help overcome this, the Routeman was also very special in being fitted with a Rolls Royce petrol engine. It was also the last Scammell to be purchased by a Fisher Renwick company, or a member of the Renwick family.

Above top: Johnsons Wax Products was also a long established customer, and were to increase their van hire following their acquisition of the manufacturers of Brillo and Lifeguard products. This Bedford TK entered service in 1964, replacing a Bedford J van. The livery is particularly effective. Note the large Royal Warrant.

Above: A less common vehicle supplied. This Bedford CA based 'Dormobile' personnel carrier is a further example of the Fisher Renwick willingness to satisfy their customers requirements. The small body has an attractive variation of Johnson's livery, the Royal Warrant is seen, as is their advertising slogan.

Above: Fisher Renwick Contracts always supplied smaller vans if required. This one is a 1965 registered Commer 'Walk-Thru' van for Lintafoam, another long established customer.

Above: In contrast, this Bedford with a much greater capacity was one of several KG based vans supplied to deliver this bulky load. The livery is equally attractive on either small or large body areas. Lintafoam also had nine Bedford KFA articulated vans on contract hire from Fisher Renwick at this time.

Above top: The Scammell Routeman 2 tanker operation was generally successful, which led to this Leyland Beaver articulated outfit being placed in service in 1964. The shortening is now carried in three vertical tanks, allowing more flexibility at delivery. The insulation was designed to hold the critical temperature and the tanks each had heating coils. The ability to operate these from any likely electric power source was again provided for.

Above: One of the earliest side loading bodies, a Bedford TK with Salmesbury Engineering body, was developed by Fisher Renwick jointly with Procter & Gamble. It was designed for loading with forklift trucks fitted with side loading clamps. The plastic roof flexed in service causing problems with the runners for the aluminium sliding side doors. They were to be replaced with Bedford TK vans having 'linkliner' bodies, with sliding side doors.

Above: This maximum capacity Bedford TK Luton van operated on another long-standing contract. McIntosh were based in Kirkcaldy, their vans travelled tens of thousands of miles yearly, delivering new furniture. At first, the height of the vans used was limited by the relatively low height of various services pipes located at their works. However, these were later moved. They were not easy vehicles to drive in high winds when empty.

Right top: One of several Bedford KGA articulated vans provided for Charles Phillips, an early food stores chain, having branches in the Greater London area. This successful business was later to be acquired by Tesco.

Right: Among the major contracts was that for Turner & Newall. This Bedford KGA articulated van was one of a number placed in service in 1967. Turner's factory area was so vast that the Fisher Renwick mechanic used a van to get around the site when carrying out the routine vehicle services and checks.

Left: This Park Royal based Bedford - Scammell KF articulated unit YGK 778G was a Contract Hire spare unit. Although in Fisher Renwick livery, the picture was taken after their acquisition by Ryder. An appropriate photograph with which to conclude.

Above: The new Park Royal Depot premises; the workshops comprised 25,000 square feet of space, or a quarter of the site, and were opened April 1970. It provided the maintenance facilities for some 500 vehicles then operated by Fisher Renwick Services for their South of England contract customers. Ford D and various Bedford vans can be seen in Fisher Renwick livery, including the Manchester & London legend - a harbinger of the past. However, they were only spare contract vans. Note too, the many new Bedford chassis by the pylon, waiting for their bodies.

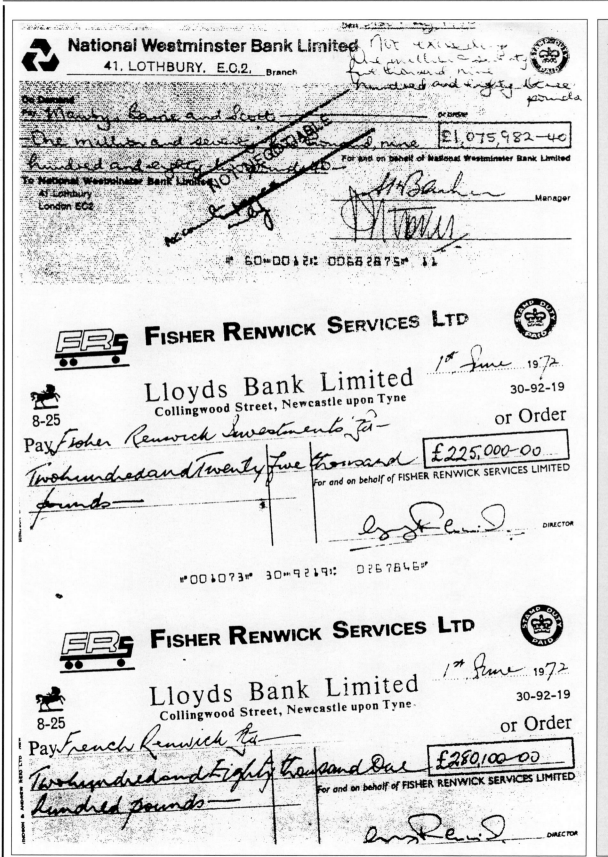

Left: The three cheques for the acquisition by Ryder; one dated May 1972, and two for June 1972.

Chapter Nine

Chapter Nine

1891-1971
Manchester Dry Docks Co. Ltd

This brief account of the Dry Dock Company is correctly included in the Saga because of the continuing association with the Steamer Company, and for the period lasting 80 years when first Sir George Renwick, then Major Renwick and finally Denis Renwick were to be consecutively Chairmen of the Dock Company.

Following the visit to Manchester to take part in the 'Official' tour arranged for Shipowners to be shown the scope for business that would result once the Canal and its Docks were completed, George Renwick was sufficiently impressed to deliberately ensure his partner, Joseph Fisher returned to Newcastle without him, while he stayed over in Manchester to meet again with the Directors of the Canal Company, to negotiate rights for the Dry Docks, and for the Steamer Service. George Renwick's enthusiasm for the Steamer Service operating out of the Canal being enhanced by his recognising the potential of the business the Dry Docks would also attract.

He was much better at negotiation than the Directors of the Canal Company, for he actually acquired an area of land at Mode Wheel considerably larger than was required for the Dry Dock facilities. Following the continuing financial problems of the Canal Company and the involvement of Manchester Corporation, there was a renegotiation of the agreement and the land not actually to be used by the Dry Dock Company reverted to the Canal Company.

As already related George Renwick formed the Manchester Pontoons and Dry Docks Co. Ltd., the first meeting of the Company, on the 12th October 1891, confirmed the appointment of George Renwick as Chairman, and Thomas Bell, Horace Eltringham, (also a Director of Joseph T. Etlringham & Co. Ltd., Shipbuilders, Wallsend), and Alexander Taylor, who was to be Engineer to the Company and Designer of the Pontoons and Dry Docks. The meeting

Above: The Pontoon dry dock at Ellesmere Port, 29th January 1900. This rare view of an improved pontoon shows the method used by Alexander Taylor to lighten the deadweight by making the well reduction in the depth of the sides. The four-masted sailing ship PURITAN would have brought timber from a Baltic port.

finalised the agreement to purchase the 17 acre Mode Wheel site, together with the site at Ellesmere Port.

Following the successful raising of capital from Newcastle's businessmen for the new Company, a contract was placed with James Nuttall for the construction of No. 1 Dry Dock, Mode Wheel. The cost of £29,400 did not include the dry dock gates nor the pumps. The pumps were to be obtained from Tangyes Ltd. Smethwick, for £1,925, the gates being ordered a little later from Joseph T. Eltringham, for £2,740.

The first Pontoon was ordered from Edwards and Company, for £20,983. To prepare for its delivery and the operation of the facility Mr. Norman was appointed Manager at Ellesmere Port. The first ship to use the Pontoon was the Sailing ship 'BEESWING', (previously there had been work carried out on a dredger and on barges).

The Directors meeting of 1st December 1893 appointed J. A. Grice to be the Dry Docks Company Secretary, taking over from R. Teasdale, secretary for the Steamer Company, who had also been acting as the temporary secretary for the Dry Dock Company.

The No.1 Dry dock was officially opened 14th February 1894, the second Pontoon was opened 8th September 1894. No. 2 Dry dock was opened 21st February 1907, and No. 3 Dry dock on 5th April 1917. An extension in length of No. 2 Dry dock was opened 13th June 1951.

During the company's first 10 years the Manchester Pontoon averaged 40 ships per year, with No.1 Dry dock averaging 60 ships per year. No records of dockings for Ellesmere Pontoon survive.

Ellesmere Port also built coastal steamers. It is a reasonable assumption that up to 69 barges or similar constructions had already been built at Ellesmere to 1920, and then the Pontoon was also to be used for the construction of these steamers. Following the general shortage of repair work with the end of the Great War, Sir George Renwick decided that a coastal steamer of a relatively simple design should be constructed, as a means of keeping the Pontoon occupied. It also fulfilled Sir George Renwick's commitment to shipbuilding. He was also involved with his project to create a new shipyard on the Tyne.

The design settled upon was for a Short Raised Quarter Deck Coaster, with a single hatch and derrick. Four coasters were to be built, each approximately 120 feet long, 22 feet breadth, and 9 feet depth. They had a single Scotch boiler, working at 130 lbs pressure, and a compound engine with two cylinders 15" and 32" bore and 24" stroke. The boilers and engines were also manufactured by the Dry Dock Company using the foundry and other facilities at Mode Wheel, it is possible that help with the design of these came from Joseph T. Eltringham & Co. Ltd. All four had a remarkably similar gross tonnage.

The first coaster to be built was yard no.71, 265 gross tons, commissioned April 1920 for the Ramsay Steamship Co. Ltd., Isle of Man, and named BEN SEYR. She remained in their service until being lost without trace during a gale on 2nd October 1938, while carrying a load of oats to Cardiff.

The second coaster, yard no.72, 266 gross tons, was commissioned May 1923 for A.M. Ralli and Son, Liverpool, and named MIA. Ralli were well established traders in cotton, jute and other textile fibres. She was sold to William F. Cook, Aberdeen in 1932, and then in 1937 to T.W. Dixon, Whitehaven, and renamed BEACONIA. In 1954 she was purchased by the Ramsay Steamship Co. Ltd. being renamed BEN VERREY. She was finally sold by them for breaking March 1957.

The third coaster, yard no.73, 266 gross tons, was commissioned April 1924 for Thomas Brothers Shipping Co. Ltd., Liverpool, being named DORIS THOMAS. Following a break-up of the partnership in 1936, she was owned by Thomas Coasters Ltd., (Owen Thomas). Sold to A.F. Henry and MacGregor Ltd. Leith, renamed DENNIS HEAD. In 1938 she was bought by the Ramsay Shipping Co. Ltd. replacing the BEN SEYR. She was renamed BEN AIN, continuing in their service until sold for breaking June 1963.

The last coaster built was yard no. 74, 267 gross tons, commissioned December 1926 for William A. Savage, Liverpool, Managing Owners for the Zillah Shipping and Carrying Co. Ltd., Liverpool. Named PENSTONE, she sank following collision 31st July 1948, with the Norwegian Motor ship VILLANGER, with loss of three of the ship's five crew.

The coasters were obviously a successful design, and well constructed, with three of the four becoming operated by one company, the Ramsay Shipping Company.

During this period the Ellesmere site employed some 50 men, and would have also carried out repair work, using the Pontoon, whilst the coasters were being fitted out. When the Ellesmere Port business was closed down 3rd October 1969 some 150 employees were made redundant. The Pontoon was broken up.

In 1971 Manchester Dry Docks Company was the subject of a take-over by an investment company, who changed the name to Manchester Marine Ltd. In May 1974 this company was taken over by Manchester Liners, who restored the name Manchester Dry Docks. The continuing decline in use of the Ship Canal resulted in the Pontoon at Manchester also being scrapped. Late 1979 it was necessary to place the Dry Docks in liquidation. Nos. 1 and 2 Dry docks were taken over by former redundant staff of the Company, trading as United Ship Repairers and Engineers (Manchester) Ltd. Amongst their customers is the Isle of Man Steam Packet Co. Ltd. The Dry Docks are still working, but are now trading as Lengthline Ltd.

No. 3 Dry dock was used for a period by Stretford Shipbreakers Ltd who appear to be no longer operating.

Below: An aerial view of the Manchester Dry Docks, mid 1930's. The Manchester pontoon can be seen centre left, with the Ship Canal Company's 60 ton floating crane seen beside it. The photograph serves its purpose in showing the size of the Docks, and the extensive workshops. The identities of the ships pictured are not known, but the first was one of Manchester Liners fleet.

Appendices

1.   Shipping List (1) Manchester and London Shipping Co., Ltd   130
     & Fisher Renwick Co., Manchester-London Steamers (1908) Ltd

2.   Shipping List (2) Fisher Renwick Manchester-London Steamers Ltd   131

3.   Fleet List of Steamers owned by Fisher Renwick, Newcastle upon Tyne   132

4.   Years in Service of Steamers on line with Manchester- London Steamers   133
     & Fisher Renwick Manchester-London Steamers Ltd
    Years in Service of Steamers with Fisher Renwick, Newcastle upon Tyne

5.   Fisher Renwick Road Fleet - Scammell Fleet List to 1932   134
     & Fleet Additions 1933-1935

6.   Fisher Renwick Road Fleet - Fleet Additions 1936-1949   135
    Named Vehicles - Not Muswell Hill-based vehicles

7.   Fisher Renwick Road Fleet - Other Manchester, Birmingham   137
     & other depot-based vehicles
    Muswell Hill Fleet Nationalised to B.R.S.

8.   Fisher Renwick Road Fleet - Muswell Hill numbered vehicles   138
     & Other Fisher Renwick numbered vehicles
    Fisher Renwick Contract Hire vehicles

9.   Fisher Renwick Contract Services, London - Select List   139

10.   Fisher Renwick Contract Services, Manchester - Select List   142

11.   Fisher Renwick Directory of Places   144

Shipping List (1)

MANCHESTER and LONDON SHIPPING Co., Ltd.
SALTPORT DOCK 1892-1903, LONDON WHARF, 4 DOCK, POMONA 1904-1908

LLOYDS REG'TR NUMBERS and SAIL LETTERS	NAME of STEAMER (and type)	Gross Tonnage	SHIP BUILDER ENGINE BUILDER	L. B. D.	N.H.P.	MACHINERY	REMARKS
1875 80555 STGM	LODORE	650 (Reg.)	Wigham Richardson Wigham Richardson	200.2' 28.3' 14.0'	99	Cpd. 2 cyls. 26",46"x 30" Blr Pr. 75lb	Owned F.R.N.o-T. Chartered to M.-L. Shipping
1891 98287	VOLUNTEER(i)	112	Hepple & Co. Ltd. Hepple & Co. Ltd.	96.6' 19.6' 10.6'		Cpd. 2 cyls. 16^1/$_2$",32^1/$_2$" Blr Pr. 80lbs.	Chartered to F.R. Only Steamer of J.Murphy S.Sh'lds.
1890 95954 MBGR	RENWICK	664	Tyne Iron S'bldg. N.E.Marine & Eng.	180.0' 28.1' 13.7'		T.E. 3 cyls. 13^1/$_2$",22^1/$_2$"36" -27". B.Pr.160 lbs.	Owned F.R. N.-o-T Chartered to M.-L. Shipping
1881 83911 WBVL	BLENCOWE (Well Deck)		J.T.Eltringham. J.P.Reynolds.	165.0' 26.1' 13.0'	70	Cpd. 2 cyls. 25",40"-30" Blr.Pr. 80"	Owned F.R. N.-o-T. Chartered to WBVL M.-L. Shipping.
1896 97549 MKBL	FISHREN (formly ROBERT THORBURN)	983	Sunderland S'bldg N.E.Marine & Eng.	210.0' 30.0'	149	T.E. 3 cyls. 19",31",51" -33''. Blr. Pr. 160"	Owned F.R. N.-o-T. Chartered to M.-L. Shipping.
1900 110367 SCQD	FUSILIER (Well Deck)	963	J.P.Reynolds. J.P.Reynolds.	206.7' 32.2' 14.3'	138	T.E. 3 cyls. 17^1/$_2$",28",47" -33" Blr.Pr. 170"	Owned F.R. N.-o-T. Chartered to M.-L. Shipping.

FISHER, RENWICK Co's MANCHESTER-LONDON STEAMERS (1908) Ltd.

1899 95670 LCMH	WHITBY (Part Awning)	2081	J.L.Thompson. J.L.Thompson.	283.9' 38.1' 19.8'	203	T.E. 3 cyls 21",31",57^1/$_2$" -39" Blr.Pr. 160"	Operated by M.-L. Shipping 1906-08 Transferred to N.-o-T. 1908.
1901 112434 SFTQ	BLAIRMORE (formerly MOUNTFIELD)	3038	Wm.Gray. W.H'pool. Marine Eng. Works, W.H'pool.	325.0' 47.2' 22.4'	257	T.E. 3 cyls. 24",38",64" -42" Blr.Pr.160"	Added to Fleet 1919. Fitted with Electric Lighting. N.-o-T 1908
1901 114401 SGHT	VOLUNTEER(ii) (Well Deck)	837	J.P.Reynolds & Son. J.P.Reynolds & Son.	200.2' 30.2' 13.1'	99	T.E. 3 cyls. 16^1/$_2$",25^1/$_2$",44" -30" Blr. Pr.160"	Transferred from F.R. N.o.T. 1908
1901 114431 SHNM	YEOMAN (Well Deck)	1009	Wood, Skinner. N.E.Marine & Eng.	220.0' 31.7' 14.8'	135	T.E. 3 cyls. 17^1/$_2$",28",46" -33" Blr.Pr.180"	Transferred from F.R. N.o.T. 1908

Shipping List (2)

FISHER, RENWICK, MANCHESTER – LONDON STEAMERS Ltd

DATE, LLOYDS REG'TR. No. Signal Letter	NAME of STEAMER (and type)	Gross Tonnage	SHIP BUILDER ENGINE BUILDER	L. B. D.	N.H.P.	MACHINERY	REMARKS
1902 113116 SUND	TROOPER (Well Deck)	950	J.P.Reynolds & Son. J.P.Reynolds & Son.	206.5' 22.2'	137	T.E. 3 cyls. 17",28",47" - 33" Blr.Pr. 170"	Used at Saltport,1902. Transferred from F.R. N.-o-T. 1908
1903 113122 VENF	HUSSAR (Awning Deck with Freeboard)	1255	Tyne Iron S'building. N.E. Marine & Eng'g.	220.4' 32.9' 14.4'	149	T.E. 3 cyls. 17",28",46" - 33" Blr.Pr.180lbs.	Transferred from F.R. N.-o-T. 1908
1907 124283 HKPJ	CARBINEER (Awning Deck with Freeboard)	1266	Tyne Iron S'building. N.E. Marine & Eng'g,	230.1' 33.6' 14.9'	144	T.E. 3 cyls. 17",28",46" - 33" Blr.Pr.180lbs.	First New Steamer for F.R. M.-L. Steamers.
1908 124286 HMDF	MUSKETEER (Awning Deck with Freeboard)	1285	Tyne Iron S'building N.E. Marine & Eng'g,	220.1' 33.1' 14.8'	143	T.E. 3 cyls. 17",28",47" - 33" Blr.Pr.180lbs.	One Scotch Boiler, with 4 Corrugated Furnaces. 72 sq.ft. Grate Area.
1909 124207 HPRT	LANCER (Awning Deck with Freeboard)	1363	Tyne Iron S'Building N.E. Marine & Eng'g.	230.1' 34.0' 21.8'	163	T.E. 3 cyls. 18",30".49" - 30" Blr.Pr.180lbs.	
1914 135360 JNGP	CUIRASSIER (Shelter Deck with Freeboard)	1045	Wm. Dobson & Co. N.E. Marine & Eng'g	230.6' 35.0' 14.9'	170	T.E. 3 cyls. 18",30",49" - 33" Blr.Pr.180lbs.	
1915 135364 JKHQ	HALBADIER (Shelter Deck with Freeboard)	1049	Ropner & Son. N.E.Marine & Eng'g.	230.0' 35.0' 14.9'	170	T.E. 3 cyls. 18",30",49" - 33" Blr.Pr.180lbs.	Torpedoed by U-boat 6th Jan 1918.
1923 147391	SAPPER (Shelter Deck with Freeboard)		Wm. Dobson & Co. N.E.Marine & Eng'g.	230.6' 35.0' 14.9'	170	T.E. 3 cyls. 18",30",49" - 33' Blr.Pr.180lbs.	With Electric Lighting and Power.
1924 147403 KRGH	SENTRY (Shelter Deck with Freeboard)		Tyne Iron S'building. N.E.Marine & Eng'g.	230.1' 34.0' 21.8'	193	T.E. 3 cyls. 18",30".49" - 33" Blr.Pr.180lbs.	With Electric Lighting and Power. Last Steamer built for Fisher Renwick.

Fleet List of Steamers owned by Fisher Renwick, Newcastle-upon-Tyne, 1877-1927

Does not include Steamers which were chartered in by Fisher Renwick
in the 1890's. Newcastle-upon-Tyne had some 50 shipowners with some 270 steamers,
Fisher Renwick, Newcastle, owning some 20 vessels around this time.

Steamer	Gross Tonnage	In Service
is. TRIO	310	1877 - 1898
is. GUSTAV BITTERN	351	1879 - 1889 *
is. HENRY FISHER	335	1879 - 1903
is. BRANKSTON	450	1880 - 1881
is. CLAREMONT	1032	1880 - 1894
is. KATE FORSTER	373	1880 - 1896 *
is. LODORE	480	1880 - 1897 Ch.
is. WETHERALL	372	1880 - 1896
is. MAIRE FLEURE	391	1881 - 1903
is. TYNE	435	1881 - 1903
is. BAINES HAWKINS	480	1882 - 1903
is. BLENCOWE	350	1882 - 1901 Ch.
is. ALBERTINA	470	1883 - 1904
is. FANNY BERTHA	479	1883 - 1900
is. MILLICENT	491	1883 - 1904
is. TROUTBECK	526	1883 - 1900
is. WILTSHIRE	325	1883 - 1899
is. ELLA SAYER	1126	1884 - 1918 (torpedoed).
is. LADY BERTHA	460	1884 - 1889 *
is. PANDORA	445	1884 - 1895
is. LOUGHBROW	488	1885 - 1903
ss. NEWMARK	683	1888 - 1904
ss. SPRINGHILL	1507	1888 - 1917 (mined). *
ss. DENIA	469	1889 - 1893 (wrecked).
ss. WHITBY	2081	1889 - 1902 Ch.
ss. CRAGG	404	1892 - 1901 *
ss. CARADOC	861	1893 - 1899
ss. EASTHAM	631	1893 - 1897
ss. RENWICK	650	1893 - 1897 *
ss. W.D.CRUDDAS	1661	1897 - 1901
ss. FUSLIER	963	1900 - 1902 Ch.
ss. ROBERT THORMAN re-registered as ss. FISHREN	983	1902 - 1904 Ch.
ss. VOLUNTEER	837	1901 - 1908 Tr.
ss. YEOMAN	1009	1901 - 1923 Tr.
ss. TROOPER	950	1902 - 1911 Tr.
ss. HUSSAR	1255	1903 - 1915 Tr.
ss. AMSTELDAM	1233	1914 - 1917 (torpedoed).
ss. WOODLEIGH	2664	1916 - 1917 (wrecked)
ss. NEWMINSTER ABBEY	3114	1917 - 1917 (torpedoed). *
ss. BLAIRMORE	3038	1918 - 1919 Tr.
ss. EVERELDA	2662	1919 - 1927

Key:

* - Family name derivation.
Ch. - Chartered into Manchester-London Shipping Ltd.
Tr. - Transferred to Fisher Renwick, Manchester-London Steamers Ltd.

Note:
Some steamers, possibly sequestered 1914 - 1918, were managed for
the Admiralty by Fisher Renwick, Newcastle-upon-Tyne.

Years in Service of Steamers on line with Manchester-London Steamers and Fisher Renwick, Manchester – London Steamers Ltd

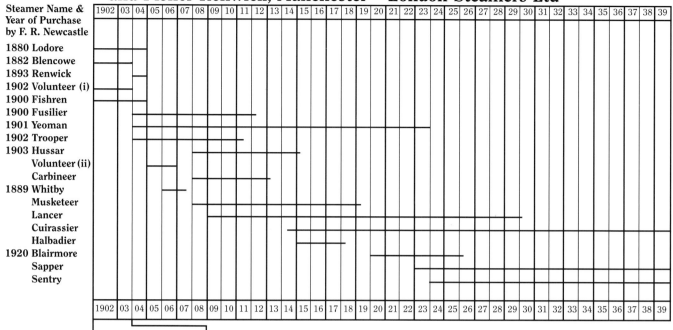

Steamer Name & Year of Purchase by F. R. Newcastle

	1902	03	04	05	06	07	08	09	10	11	12	13	14	15	16	17	18	19	20	21	22	23	24	25	26	27	28	29	30	31	32	33	34	35	36	37	38	39

1880 Lodore
1882 Blencowe
1893 Renwick
1902 Volunteer (i)
1900 Fishren
1900 Fusilier
1901 Yeoman
1902 Trooper
1903 Hussar
Volunteer (ii)
Carbineer
1889 Whitby
Musketeer
Lancer
Cuirassier
Halbadier
1920 Blairmore
Sapper
Sentry

Saltport Dock
1892-1903
Steamers on charter
from Fisher Renwick
Newcastle upon Tyne

No.4 Wharf
1892 - 1939
London Wharf
Pomona
Manchester

Manchester Wharf
1892 - 1939
Shadwell Basin
Glamis Road
Wapping

Years in Service of Steamers with Fisher Renwick, Newcastle upon Tyne

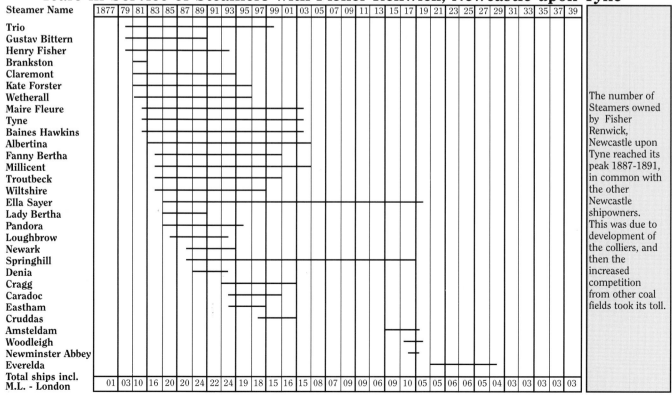

Steamer Name

	1877	79	81	83	85	87	89	91	93	95	97	99	01	03	05	07	09	11	13	15	17	19	21	23	25	27	29	31	33	35	37	39

Trio
Gustav Bittern
Henry Fisher
Brankston
Claremont
Kate Forster
Wetherall
Maire Fleure
Tyne
Baines Hawkins
Albertina
Fanny Bertha
Millicent
Troutbeck
Wiltshire
Ella Sayer
Lady Bertha
Pandora
Loughbrow
Newark
Springhill
Denia
Cragg
Caradoc
Eastham
Cruddas
Amsteldam
Woodleigh
Newminster Abbey
Everelda
**Total ships incl.
M.L. - London**

| 01 | 03 | 10 | 16 | 20 | 20 | 24 | 22 | 24 | 19 | 18 | 15 | 16 | 15 | 08 | 07 | 09 | 09 | 06 | 09 | 10 | 05 | 05 | 06 | 06 | 05 | 04 | 03 | 03 | 03 | 03 | 03 |

The number of Steamers owned by Fisher Renwick, Newcastle upon Tyne reached its peak 1887-1891, in common with the other Newcastle shipowners. This was due to development of the colliers, and then the increased competition from other coal fields took its toll.

FISHER RENWICK ROAD FLEET

SCAMMELL FLEET LIST TO 1932

VEHICLE NAME	REGIST. NO.	MAKE	MODEL	TYPE	BODY	DATE	NOTES
	NC 3718	Scammell	7T.	H	Flat	08/21	
	NC 3744	Scammell	7T.	H	Flat	08/21	
FUSILIER	NC 5037	Scammell	7T.	H	Flat	09/21	
	NC 5895	Scammell	7T.	H	Flat	09/21	
	NC ?	Scammell	7/10T.	S10	SP. Tilt	??/22	
ENGINEER	XM 8895	Scammell	12T.	S12	Cable Float	03/2?	
GUARDSMAN	XM 9590	Scammell	12T.	S12	Cable Float	03/23	
HUSSAR	NE 6097	Scammell	12T.	S12	Flat	03/26	
YEOMAN	NE 6871	Scammell	10T.	S10	Flat	03/26	
	NE ?	Scammell	10T.	S10	Flat	04/26	
HALBADIER	UL 1852	Scammell	15T.	SE15	Flat	10/28	
VOLUNTEER	XV 5213	Scammell	15T.	SE15	Flat	10/28	
MUSKETEER	? ?	Scammell	15T.	SE15	Flat	10/28	
FUSILIER	XV 5547	Scammell	15T.	SE15	Flat	12/28	
CAVALIER	XV 9921	Scammell	15T.	SE15	Flat	12/28	
PIONEER	YV 5155	Scammell	15T.	SE15	Box	04/28	
BRIGADIER	YV 5156	Scammell	15T.	SE15	Box	06/28	
MERLIN	YW 5024	Scammell	15T.	SE15	Cable Float	09/28	S/h 4/32.
LANCER	YW 5207	Scammell	15T.	SE15	Box	06/28	
PARTRIDGE	YW 5208	Scammell	15T.	SE15	Cable Float	06/28	
DRUMMER	YX 5267	Scammell	15T.	SE15	Box	09/28	
PHEASANT	GK 642	Scammell	15T.	SE15	Cable Float	10/28	
DRAGOON	GU 9561	Scammell	15T.	SE15	GP/H.S.Tilt	04/29	
GROUSE (1)	GJ 8257	Scammell	10T.	S10	Box	06/30	Pneu.tyres
BLACKCOCK (1)	GJ 8258	Scammell	10T.	S10	Box	06/30	
SNIPE	GJ 8259	Scammell	10T.	S10	Box	06/30	
WOODCOCK (1)	GJ 8260	Scammell	10T.	S10	Box	06/30	
LAPWING (1)	GK ?	Scammell	10T.	S10	Sided	06/30	
MALLARD	GK 643	Scammell	10T.	S10	Box	08/30	
WIDGEON	GN 892	Scammell	10T.	S10	Box	01/31	
GREYHEN	GN 893	Scammell	10T.	S10	Box	01/31	
PTARMIGAN (1)	GN 894	Scammell	10T.	S10	GP/S.Tilt	01/31	
MOORHEN (1)	? ?	Scammell	10T.	S10	GP/S.Tilt	08/31	
CURLEW (1)	GT 202	Scammell	10T.	S10	GP/S.Tilt	08/31	
PLOVER (1)	GT ?	Scammell	10T.	S10	GP/S.Tilt	08/31	

FLEET ADDITIONS 1933-1935

Only chassis no's	GY 2093	Scammell	13T.	R6RC13	H.Sided	To FR.1/36	
known for these	1816	Scammell	13T.	R6RC13	Box	10/33	(Petrol)
RC13 chassis.	1830	Scammell	13T.	R6RC13	Box	10/30	
	1831	Scammell	13T.	R6RC13	Box	10/30	
	1841	Scammell	13T.	R6RC13	Box	03/34	
	1842	Scammell	13T.	RC13	Box	03/34	
	2017	Scammell	13T.	RC13	Flat	11/34 5LW	

(The above vehicle was transferred to R. Wynn 09/1939)

	2018	Scammell	13T.	RC13	Flat	11/34 6LW	
	2019	Scammell	13T.	RC13	Flat	01/35	
	2024	Scammell	13T.	RC13	Box	02/35	
	2025	Scammell	13T.	RC13	Box	02/35	
	2026	Scammell	13T.	RC13	Box	03/35	
	2027	Scammell	13T.	RC13	Box	03/35	

FLEET ADDITIONS 1933-1935 (continued)

VEHICLE NAME	REGIST. NO.	MAKE	MODEL	TYPE	BODY	DATE	NOTES
only chassis	2028	Scammell	13T.	RC13	Box	03/35	
Nos. known	2065	Scammell	13T.	RC13	Box	06/35	
for these	2066	Scammell	13T.	RC13	Flat	06/35	
RC13 chassis	2067	Scammell	13T.	RC13	Box	06/35	
	2068	Scammell	13T.	RC13	Box	10/35	
	2069	Scammell	13T.	RC13	Box	10/35	

(The last eleven RC13 chassis were supplied with Gardner 6LW Diesel engines)

The following Registration Nos and names, SHELDRAKE ? ?, REEVE AXT 676, AXT 853, and ALW 665 were some of those allocated to these vehicles, also TF 8235 A.E.C. with Box Body.

FLEET ADDITIONS: 1936 - 1949

VEHICLE NAME	REGIST. NO.	MAKE			
REDSTART (1)	BLL ?	Scammell	Lightweight SKA Rigid Six Van
KITE (1)	BLL 248	Scammell	Lightweight SKA Rigid Six Flat
	BLT 949	Scammell	Lightweight SKA Rigid Six
	BLY 525	Scammell	Lightweight SKA Rigid Six
	BUC 793	Scammell	Lightweight SKA Rigid Six
	BUC 794	Scammell	Lightweight SKA Rigid Six
	BYU 933	Scammell	Lightweight SKA Rigid Six
	CGD 341	Scammell	Lightweight SKA Rigid Six
	CGD 342	Scammell	Lightweight SKA Rigid Six

Other known named Boxvans were: HAWK, EAGLE, PETREL, REDSHANK

NAMED VEHICLES: Not Muswell Hill Based Vehicles

VEHICLE NAME	REGIST. NO.	MAKE	MODEL	TYPE	BODY	NOTES
MERLIN	GK 642	Scammell	S5.	8w.	Artic Cable Float	
YARROW	SY 5384	ERF	CI.54	4w.	Flat	(ex Brown)
MEDWAY (1)	BLG 800	ERF	CI.68	8w.	Flat	(ex Brown)
CAM (1)	CMB 111	ERF	CI.68	8w.	Flat	(ex Brown)
ESK	CMB 883	ERF	CI.56	6w.	Flat	(ex Brown)
BITTERN	? ?	Leyland	Hippo	6w.	Van	
SANDPIPER	? ?	Leyland	Hippo	6w.	Van	
PUFFIN	CNF 991	Leyland	Octopus	8w.	Flat	
CALDER	CUD 650	Seddon		4w.	Flat	
ROBIN (1)	CVR 503	Leyland	Octopus	8w.	Flat	(ex Brown)
KITTIWAKE (1)	CVR 802	Leyland	Octopus	8w.	Flat.	
MERGANSER (1)	? ?	Leyland	Octopus	8w.	Flat.	
ISIS (1)	DLG 307	?		?	?	
CARRON	DMA 225	ERF	C.I.54	4w.	Flat.	(ex Brown)
DEVRON	DMA 757	ERF	C.I.54	4w.	Flat.	(ex Brown)
LIDDLE	DMB 771	ERF	C.I.54	4w.	Flat.	(ex Brown)
YARROW	DMB 969	ERF	C.I.54	4w	Flat.	(ex Brown)
JED	DMP 370	ERF	C.I.68	8w.	Flat.	(ex Brown)
DUNLIN (1)	DNC 715	Leyland	Octopus	8w.	Flat.	
COOT (1)	DNE 57	Leyland	Octopus	8w.	Flat.	
SANDPIPER	? ?	Leyland	Octopus	8w.	Flat.	
CRANE (1)	DNE 699	Leyland	Octopus	8w.	Flat.	
SCAUP	DNK 162	Scammell	Rigid Eight	8w	High Sided.	
WHIMBREL	DMV 911	Leyland	Octopus	8w.	Box.	
TEVIOT	DTU 52	ERF	C.I.54	4w.	Flat	(ex Brown)
TWEED	DTU 287	ERF	C.I.68	8w.	Flat.	(ex Brown)
TAY (1)	DTU 288	ERF	C.I.56	6w.	Flat.	(ex Brown)
DOCHARD	DTU 523	ERF	C.I.54	4w.	Flat.	(ex Brown)
TUMMEL (1)	ELG 55	ERF	C.I.56	6w.	Flat.	(ex Brown)
DEE	ELG 56	ERF	C.I.68	8w.	Flat.	(ex Brown)

NAMED VEHICLES: Not Muswell Hill Based Vehicles (continued)

VEHICLE NAME	REGIST. NO.	MAKE	MODEL	TYPE	BODY	NOTES
ROBIN (2)	ELG 357	ERF	CI.4.	4w.	Flat.	(ex Brown)
IRWELL (1)	ELG 763	ERF	CI.68	8w.	Flat.	(ex Brown)
MALLARD (2)	FGC 171	Scammell	Rigid Eight	8w.	Flat.	
SNIPE	FGO 168	Scammell	Rigid Eight	8w.	Flat.	
TEAL	FGO 169	Scammell	Rigid Eight	8w.	Flat.	
WOODCOCK (2)	FGO 172	Scammell	Rigid Eight	8w.	Flat.	
GREYHEN (2)	FGU 792	Scammell	Rigid Eight	8w.	Flat.	
SWALLOW	FLG 140	ERF	CI.4.	4w.	Flat.	(ex Brown)
REDWING	FLG 337	ERF	CI.4.	4w.	Flat	(ex Brown)
LAPWING (2)	FLG 362	ERF	CI.4.	4w.	Flat	(ex Brown)
MARTIN	FLG 363	ERF	CI.68	8w.	Flat.	
MERSEY	FLG 747	ERF	CI.68	8w.	Flat.	
NITH	FTB 332	ERF	CI.4.	4w.	Box.	
ANNAN	FTB 333	ERF	CI.4.	4w.	Box.	
FORTH	FTB 383	Scammell	Rigid Eight	8w.	Flat.	
QUAIL	FTB 540	Scammell	Rigid Eight	8w.	Flat.	
CLYDE (1)	FTB 884	Scammell	Rigid Eight	8w.	Low Showboat.	
EAGLE	FTE 529	Scammell	Rigid Eight	8w.	Low Showboat.	
DON	FTE 634	Scammell	Rigid Eight	8w.	Low Showboat.	
HAWK	FTE 82X	Scammell	Rigid Eight	8w.	High Showboat.	
CLYDE (2)	FTE 829	Scammell	Rigid Eight	8w.	High Showboat.	
ROOK	FXJ 129	Scammell	Rigid Eight	8w.	High Showboat.	
RAVEN	FXJ 360	Scammell	Rigid Eight	8w.	High Showboat.	
PTARMIGAN (2)	FXJ 68X	Scammell	Rigid Eight	8w.	Flat.	
GROUSE (2)	FXJ 951	Scammell	Rigid Eight	8w.	Flat.	
DUNLIN (2)	GJF 792	Scammell	Rigid Eight	8w.	Low Showboat.	
WIDGEON (2)	GNA 773	Scammell	Rigid Eight	8w.	Flat.	
EGRET	GNB 385	Scammell	Rigid Eight	8w.	Flat.	
EIDER	GNB 925	Scammell	Rigid Eight	8w.	High Showboat.	
SPEY	GNX ?	Scammell	Rigid Eight	8w.	Box.	
MOORHEN (2)	GNC 227	Scammell	Rigid Eight	8w.	Flat.	
SHELDRAKE (2)	GNC 119	Scammell	Rigid Eight	8w.	High Sided.	
GREBE	GNC 451	Scammell	Rigid Eight	8w.	Flat.	
CORMORANT	GNC 434	Scammell	Rigid Eight	8w.	Box.	
KITE (2)	GNC 709	Scammell	Rigid Eight	8w.	Box.	
KESTREL	GNC 763	Scammell	Rigid Eight	8w.	Box.	
BUZZARD	GTB 34	Scammell	Rigid Eight	8w.	Flat	
GUILLEMOT	GTD 191	Scammell	Rigid Eight	8w.	High Showboat.	
GANNET	GTE 190	Scammell	Rigid Eight	8w.	High Showboat.	
PUFFIN (2)	GTF 782	Scammell	Rigid Eight	8w.	Flat.	
	GTF 791	Scammell	Rigid Eight	8w.	Box.	
LINNET	HTB 763	Seddon		4w.	Flat.	
TYNE	HTE 708	Scammell	Rigid Eight	8w.	Low Showboat.	
	JTJ 690	Scammell	Rigid Eight	8w.	Flat. (Claimed to be last R8 to F.R.)	
WAGTAIL	LMY292	Maudslay	Mogul	4w.	Flat.	
DIVER	LUW 908	Maudslay	Meritor	8w.	Flat.	
LEADER	MMH 10	Scammell	Rigid Eight	8w.	Flat.	
LYNN	MMH 11	Scammell	Rigid Eight	8w.	Flat.	
	MMH 209	Scammell	Rigid Eight	8w.	Flat.	
FULMAR	OMY 392	Scammell	Rigid Eight	8w.	Flat.	
TERN	SME 311	Scammell	Rigid Eight	8w.	Flat.	
TRENT	SME 262	Seddon	Artic.	6w.	Flat.	
CALDER	? ?	Seddon		4w.	Flat or Artic. Flat?	Alloc. to Leeds.
SWALE	? ?	Seddon		4w.	Box or Artic. Flat?	Alloc. to Leeds.
WHARFE	SME 339	Seddon		4w.	Box or Artic. Flat?	Alloc. to Leeds.

NAMED VEHICLES: Not Muswell Hill Based Vehicles (continued)

VEHICLE NAME	REGIST. NO.	MAKE	MODEL	TYPE	BODY	NOTES
MERGANSER (2)	SMF 709	Scammell	Rigid Eight	8w.	Flat.	
BLACKADDER	SH 7119	Scammell	Artic Eight	8w.	Flat	
WHITEADDER	SH 7061	ERF	Artic	6w.	Flat	
COQUET	SH 7275	Scammell	Rigid Eight	8w.	Flat.	

Other MANCHESTER, BIRMINGHAM and other depot - based vehicles

VEHICLE NAME	REGIST. NO.	MAKE	MODEL	TYPE	BODY	NOTES
ARIES		Albion			Box,	also AJAX, PERSEUS.
CERES		Commer	Q4 Superpoise	4w.	Box.	
CETUS	ETJ 432	Commer	Q4 Superpoise	4w.	Box.	
HERMES		Commer	Q4 Superpoise	4w.	Box.	
HERCULES		Commer	Q4 Superpoise	4w.	Box.	
CANOPUS	CTJ 428	Commer	Q4 Superpoise	4w.	Box.	
CAPELLA	ETJ 469	Commer	Q4 Superpoise	4w.	Box.	

Also Studebaker F.C. Box LYRE, MARS. Also others

MUSWELL HILL Fleet Nationalised to B.R.S.

VEHICLE NAME	REGIST. NO.	MAKE	MODEL	TYPE	BODY	NOTES
EARN	WS 5384	ERF	CI.4	4w.	Flat.	(ex Brown)
PARTRIDGE	YW 5208	Scammell	S15	8w.	Artic. Cable Float.	
GADWALL	DJH 768	Scammell	Rigid Eight	8w.	Box.	(First Rigid 8 to F.R.)
GAGANEY	DJH 769	Scammell	Rigid Eight	8w.	Box.	
SCAUP	DNK 162	Scammell	Rigid Eight	8w.	Sided.	
SCOTER	DNK 165	Scammell	Rigid Eight	8w.	Flat.	
PINTAIL	ETJ 721	Scammell	Rigid Eight	8w.	High Showboat.	
POCHARD	ETJ 950	Scammell	Rigid Eight	8w.	High Showboat.	
BLACKCOCK	FGU 979	Scammell	Rigid Eight	8w.	Flat.	
PLOVER (2)	FYR 489	Scammell	Rigid Eight	8w.	High Showboat.	
CURLEW (2)	FYR 591	Scammell	Rigid Eight	8w.	High Showboat.	
RUFF	GNA 422	Scammell	Rigid Eight	8w.	High Showboat.	
REEVE	GNA 576	Scammell	Rigid Eight	8w.	High Showboat.	
HERON	GNB 266	Scammell	Rigid Eight	8w.	Flat.	
EGRET (1)	GNB 385	Scammell	Rigid Eight	8w.	Flat.	
SHANNON	LMH 767	ERF	CI.56	6w.	Flat.	
WAGTAIL	LMY 292	Maudslay	Mogul III	4w.	Flat.	
THRUSH (2)	LUC 281	Maudslay	Meritor	8w.	Flat.	
?	MME 99	Scammell	Rigid Eight	8w.	Flat.	
BRENT	MMH 166	Seddon		4w.	Flat.	
?	MMH 205	Scammell	Rigid Eight	8w.	Flat.	
CAM (2)	OML 206	Seddon		4w.	Flat.	
WEAVER	OMY 880	Seddon		4w.	Flat.	
LEA	SMF 150	Seddon		4w.	Box.	
LUNE	SMF 696	Seddon		6w.	Box.	
MEDWAY (2)	SMY 446	Seddon		6w.	Flat.	
THAMES (2)	SMY 728	Seddon		6w.	Flat.	
ROM	TMG 511	Seddon	Artic.	6w.	Flat.	
EGRET (2)	TMG 519	Scammell	Rigid Eight	8w.	Flat.	
LOWTHER	TMG 526	Seddon	Artic.	6w.	Flat.	
LANDRAIL	TMG 530	Scammell	Rigid Eight	8w.	Flat.	
LAPWING (3)	TMG 531	Scammell	Rigid Eight	8w.	Flat.	
ISIS (2)	TMG 683	Seddon	Artic.	6w.	Flat.	
COOT (2)	TMG 694	Maudslay	Meritor	8w.	Flat.	
MERSEY (2)	TMG 840	Seddon	Artic.	6w.	Flat.	
RIBBLE (2)	TMG 841	Seddon	Artic.	6w.	Flat.	
HUMBER	TMK 406	Seddon	Artic.	6w.	Flat.	
TEES	TMK 586	Seddon	Artic.	6w.	Flat.	

MUSWELL HILL Fleet Nationalised to B.R.S. (continued)

VEHICLE NAME	REGIST. NO.	MAKE	MODEL	TYPE	BODY	NOTES
GREYHEN (2)	TMV 567	Scammell	Rigid Eight	8w.	Flat.	
TEAL (2)	TMV 896	Maudslay	Meritor	8w.	Flat.	
DERWENT	TMV 907	Seddon		4w.	Luton.	(Showboat Pup.)
EAMONT	TMV 909	Seddon		4w.	Box.	

MUSWELL HILL Numbered Vehicles - most were Collection and Delivery

1(i)	DXV 576	Bedford O	Box.	25	FYR 362	Bedford O	Box.
3	DYF 301	Bedford O	Box.	26	CLO 736	Bedford O	Box.
4	DYF 302	Bedford O	Box.	27	CGC 856	Bedford O	Box.
5	EUC 268	Fordson 7V	Box.	29	DTU 987	ERF	?
6(i)	EUC 267	Fordson 7V	Box.	30	FYU 436	Bedford O	Box.
8	EUC 270	Fordson 7V	Box.	33	LMT 427	Bedford O	Box.
11	ELT 941	Fordson 7V	Box.	34	LMT 428	Bedford O	Box.
1(ii)	FGO 169	Fordson 7V	Box.	35	LMT 540	Bedford O	Box.
12	FGO 170	Fordson 7V	Box.	36	LMT 539	Bedford O	Van.
13(i)	FYE 201	Fordson 7V	Box.	37	LMV 116	Bedford O	Box.
14	FYE ?	Fordson 7V	Box.	38	LMV 373	Bedford O	Box.
16(i)	FYE 826	Fordson 7V	Box.	40	LMV 374	Bedford O	Box.
17	GMK 322	Fordson 7V	Box.	41	LMV 375	Bedford O	Box.
19	SML 488	Austin K4	Box.	46	LMV 376	Bedford O	Box.
20	CXO 239	Bedford O	Van.	13(ii)	MMY 103	Bedford O	Box.
21	DGJ 549	Bedford O	Van.	47	OML 99	Austin K4	Artic. 6w. Sided.
22	BYL 118	Bedford O	Van.	16(ii)	OML 589	Austin K4	Flat.
23	EXX 86	Bedford O	Van.	50	?	?	Bedford O	Box.

MUSWELL HILL Austin K4 Chassis. No Fleet Numbers Available

SME 261	Box.	SML 490	Box.	TMG 532	?
SMF 93	Box.	SML 500	Box.	TMG 685	?
SMF 710	D/Side.	SML 771	Box.	TMG 832	?
SML 479	Box.	SML 782	D/Side.	TMG 834	?
SML 481	Box.	SMY 441	Flat.	TMG 837	?
SML 485	Box.	SMY 450	Box.	TMV 57	Box.
SML 487	Box.	SMY 730	D/Side.	TMV 738	?
SML 488	Box.	TMV 906	Flat.		

Other FISHER RENWICK numbered Vehicles

65	BLN 454	?		73	CXD 919	Bedford O	Box.
66	AXT 939	Leyland Octopus		74	BYL 547	Bedford O	Box.
67	AXT 940	Leyland Octopus		75	BYT 540	Bedford O	Box.
68	BLC 921	Bedford O	Box.	76	CKD 918	Bedford O	Box.
69	BLC 920	Bedford O	Box.	78	DGP 288		?
70	BLN 811	?		79	DGP 289		?

CONTRACT HIRE Vehicles

Rockman Bros.

R 1	BAN 102	Bedford O Box.
R 2	BAN 103	Bedford O Box.
R 3	BAN 104	Bedford O Box.
R 4	BAN 105	Bedford O Box.
R 5	BAN 106	Bedford O Box.
R 6	BAN 205	Bedford O Box.
R 7	BAN 207	Bedford O Box.
R 8	BAN 208	Bedford O Box.
R 9	BAN 510	Bedford O Box.
R10	BAN 104	Bedford O Box.

Wright Hire (Kingsbury).

W 1	?	Bedford O Box.
W 2	?	Bedford O Box.

Arthur Pannell Ltd.

AP 1 - AP 8		Bedford O	Box Vans
AP 9	MMH 4	Bedford O	Box.
AP10	MMH 3	Bedford O	Box.
AP11	MMH 2	Bedford O	Box.
AP12	?		?
AP13	?		?
AP14	MMH 360	Seddon 4w.	6t. Flat.

Wolfendale Bros. Salford. *(In Fisher Renwick livery)*

1.		? ?	Atkinson 6w
2. KINGFISHER		HGJ 646	Atkinson 8w.
or BEA ? and CBA ?			

FISHER RENWICK CONTRACT SERVICES

FISHER RENWICK SERVICES, LONDON
Select List

ASSOCIATED BRITISH MALTSTERS

1.	PUL 767F	Albion Clydesdale Box Van.
2.	GLO 443J	Bedford CF Luton.
3.	GMH 852J	Bedford CF Luton.
4.	HMM 884K	Bedford CF Luton.
5.	GLY 17J	Bedford KG Box Van.
6.	GLY 18J	Bedford KG Box Van.
7.	LBY 635K	Bedford KG Box Van.
8.	LBY 636K	Bedford KG Box Van.
9.	LGH 249K	Bedford KG Box Van.

BRILLO

1.	LMG 477C	Bedford CA Van
2.	VMC 413G	Austin A40 Van
3.	LYT 867D	Bedford KD Luton.
4.	DJJ 911H	Bedford KG Box Van.

BROOKE BOND OXO

1.	OLT 996E	Bedford KE Box Van.
2.	OYP 246F	Bedford KE Box Van.
3.	OYP 247F	Bedford KE Box Van.
4.	VMV 348G	Bedford KE Box Van.
5.	VMV 349G	Bedford KE Box Van.
6.	VMV 350G	Bedford KE Box Van.
7.	VMV 351G	Bedford KE Box Van.
8.	VYV 196G	Bedford KE Box Van.
9.	CGX 502H	Bedford KE Box Van.
10.	CHV 226H	Bedford KE Box Van.
11.	CHV 227H	Bedford KE Box Van.
12.	CHV 228H	Bedford KE Box Van.
13.	DRK 572J	Bedford KE Box Van.
14.	DYM 766J	Bedford KE Box Van.
15.	DYM 767J	Bedford KE Box Van.
16.	DYP 146J	Bedford KE Box Van.
17.	DLD 716J	Bedford KG Container/Box.
18.	DLD 717J	Bedford KG Container/Box.
19.	HYE 681K	Bedford KHL Flat.
20.	HYE 682K	Bedford KHL Flat.
21.	HYE 683K	Bedford KHL Flat.
22.	HYE 684K	Bedford KHL Flat.
23.	HMM 890K	Bedford KHA Artic Unit.
	Trailer.	Crane Fruehauf 32 ft.

CATERERS BUYING ASSOCIATION

1.	LGC 329D	Bedford KC Box Van.
2.	HBY 664D	Bedford KC Box Van.
3.	HBY 665D	Bedford KC Box Van.
4.	OGJ 800E	Bedford KB Box Van-spare.

CATERERS BUYING ASSOCIATION (Continued)

5.	OHV 880E	Bedford KF Box Van
6.	OHV 882E	Bedford KF Box Van.
7.	LYT 870D	Bedford KG Box Van
8.	HYR 327K	Bedford KG Box Van
9.	HYR 328K	Bedford KG Box Van
10.	HYR 329K	Bedford KG Box Van

CPC (United Kingdom) Ltd
CORN PRODUCTS (formerly Brown & Polson)

1.	CGX 503H	Bedford KD Box Van.
2.	DGF 481H	Bedford KD Box Van.
3.	DGF 482H	Bedford KD Box Van.
4.	DRK 575J	Bedford KD Box Van.
5.	FGF 112J	Bedford KD Box Van.
6.	FGP 675J	Bedford KD Box Van.
7.	GLK 634J	Bedford KD Flat.
8.	GLO 445J	Bedford KD Box Van.
9.	GLO 446J	Bedford KD Box Van.
10	VYW 17G	Bedford KG Box Van.
11.	YLD 693G	Bedford KG Box Van.
12.	YLD 694G	Bedford KG Box Van.
13.	YLD 695G	Bedford KG Box Van.
14.	CHV 225H	Bedford KG Box Van.
15.	DGF 479H	Bedford KG Box Van.
16.	DYV 292J	Bedford KG Box Van.
17.	HYR 324K	Bedford KG Box Van.
18.	DGF 480H	Bedford KG Flat.
19.	FGP 676J	Bedford KG Flat.
20.	EYP 495J	Bedford KG Flat.
21.	DYV 293J	Bedford KM Flat.

CHARDEN

1.	TGT 184F	Bedford KD Dropside.

CHESEBOROUGH-PONDS

1.	CLL 601H	Bedford KC Box Van.
2.	YMF 343G	Bedford KD Box Van.
3.	VMV 343G	Bedford KD Box Van.
4.	VYK 200G	Bedford KD Box Van.
5.	VYW 16G	Bedford KD Box Van.
6.	YHX 482G	Bedford KD Box Van.
7.	VYW 18G	Ford D 750 Flat.

CROSBY & CO.

1.	GFJ 878D	Commer CCTV Artic. Unit
2.	PPL 667E	Commer CCTV Artic. Unit
3.	HDP 742E	Commer CCTV Artic. Unit

CROSBY & CO. (continued)

4.	JDP 318E	Commer CCTV Artic. Unit
5.	HRD 908E	Commer CCTV Artic. Unit
6.	LPD 621F	Commer CEGW Artic. Unit
7.	VPB 727F	Commer CEGW Artic. Unit
8.	ORD 621G	Commer CEGW Artic. Unit
9.	CPF 381H	Dodge KP 950 Artic. Unit
10.	CPF 395H	Dodge KP 950 Artic. Unit
11.	CPF 394H	Dodge KP 950 Artic. Unit
12.	DPB 571J	Dodge KP 950 Artic. Unit
13.	FGP 671J	Bedford KHA Artic. Unit
14.	FGP 672J	Bedford KHA Artic. Unit
15.	FGP 673J	Bedford KHA Artic. Unit
16.	FGT 807J	Bedford KHA Artic. Unit
17.	FJD 416J	Bedford KHA Artic. Unit
18.	FJD 417J	Bedford KHA Artic. Unit
19.	FJD 422J	Bedford KHA Artic. Unit
20.	EYY 792J	Bedford KHA Artic. Unit
21.	EYY 793J	Bedford KHA Artic. Unit
22.	EYY 794J	Bedford KHA Artic. Unit
23.	HLR 984K	Bedford KHA Artic. Unit
24.	FGP 674J	Bedford KD Flat.
25.	TUU 354F	Bedford KD Flat.
1-3.		Tasker 26ft. Flat.
4-9.		York 26ft. Flat.
10-17,23-24,29.		York 32ft. Flat.
18-20.		York 26ft. Flat.
21-22,28.		York 28ft. Flat.
25-27.		Pitt 28ft. Flat.
30-39.		Crane 32ft. Flat.
40-42.		Crane 39ft. Flat.

DART EXPRESS
1.   LLX 479D   Albion Reiver Flat.

DECCA
1.   VYY 78G   Ford D 750 Box Van.
2.   YHX 483G   Ford D 750 Box Van.

DUCKHAM OIL
1.   OLN 910E   Bedford CA Van.
2.   EYY 795J   Bedford KD Box Van.
3.   EYY 796J   Bedford KD Box Van.

ELECTRO ACOUSTIC
1.   VYO 923G   Ford D 300 Box Van.
2.   YLH 236G   Ford D 300 Box Van.
3.   CLC 8H   Ford D 300 Box Van.

FANFOLD
1.   LUW 705D   Bedford CA Van.
2.   LYW 767D   Commer 35 cwt. Van.
3.   LYU 154D   Bedford KC Box Van.

FIRESTONE TYRES
1.	LYE 106D	Bedford CA Van.
2.	LLh 437D	Bedford J Van.
3.	OMH 10E	Bedford J Van.
4.	LGC 327D	Bedford KFA Artic. Unit.
5.	LYU 158D	Bedford KFA Artic. Unit.
6.	LYU 160D	Bedford KFA Artic. Unit.
7.	OGJ 798E	Bedford KFA Artic. Unit.
8.	TMF 483F	Bedford KFA Artic. Unit.
9.	TMT 142F	Bedford KFA Artic. Unit.
10.	VUU 132G	Bedford KFA Artic. Unit.
11.	VUU 133G	Bedford KFA Artic. Unit.
12.	VUU 134G	Bedford KFA Artic. Unit.
13.	LLX 477D	Bedford KGA Artic. Unit Spare
14.	LLX 478D	Bedford KGA Artic. Unit Spare

GEIGY
1.   HMX 487K   Bedford CF Van.
2.   DYV 291J   Bedford KF Box Van.
3.   FGF 114J   Bedford KF Box Van.
4.   LGH 250K   Bedford KF Box Van.

GRACE
1.   PUL 764F   Ford D 300 Box Van.
2.   TRK 486F   Ford D 300 Box Van.

GROSSMITH
1.   LBY 633K   Ford D 300 Box Van.

GUTHRIE PULLAN
1.   OHV 878E   Bedford CA Van
2.   OHV 879E   Bedford KD Dropside.

HATCHAM RUBBER
1.   VYK 198G   Bedford KD Flat.
2.   YLU 315H   Bedford KM Artic Unit.
    Crane-Fruehauf 35ft. Flat.

J. JEFFERIES
1.   TUU 355F   Bedford KF Dropside.
2.   VYV 197G   Bedford KF Dropside.
3.   TJD 266F Ford   D 300 Dropside.

S.C. JOHNSON
1.	OLT 992E	Bedford J1 Box Van.
2.	OLT 993E	Bedford J1 Box Van.
3.	LGC 321D	Bedford KC Box Van. (Spare)
4.	VYO 917G	Bedford KC Box Van.
5.	VYW 15G	Bedford J1 Box Van.
6.	YHX 484G	
7.	FGF 115J	Bedford KD Box Van.
8.	FJD 421J	Bedford KD Box Van.
9.	FGY 21J	Bedford KD Box Van.

J - WAY
1. GLO 442J   Bedford CF Box Van.
2. DYK 967J   Bedford Hawson 35 cwt Van.
3. FGJ 102J   Bedford KC Box Van.

LINTAFOAM
1. PUL 763F   Bedford KF Luton Van.
2. VUC 128G   Bedford KF Luton Van.
3. DJJ 912H   Bedford KG Luton Van.
4. YLU 311H   Bedford KG Luton Van.

L.H.P.
1. LYE 101D   Bedford CA Pick Up.
2. LUV 710D   Bedford KC Truck.

McKAY
1. TGT 183F   Bedford KD Luton Van.
2. VYY 80G   Ford D 550 Box Van.

JAMES MARTIN
1. TRK 488F   Bedford CA Van.
2. VYO 924G   Ford Transit Van.
3. TJD 267F   Ford D 300 Dropside.
4. TJD 268F   Bedford KD Dropside.

OSBORNE GARRETT
1. TGH 374F   Bedford CA Van.
2. TUU 356F   Bedford CA Van.
3. VMV 346G   Bedford CA Van.
4. VYO 446G   Bedford CA Van.
5. VYO 921G   Bedford CA Van.
6. VYO 922G   Bedford CA Van.
7. VYW 19G   Bedford CA Van.
8. LYE 100D   Bedford J1 Van.
9. LYE 103D   Bedford J1 Van.
10. FGT 806J   Bedford KD Box Van.

OSBORNE, GARRETT & NAGLE (Strood).
1. TJD 269F   Bedford Van.
2. OGU 505E   Bedford KF Box Van.
3. CLL 602H   Bedford KF Box Van.

PLASTIC COATINGS
1. HYR 330K   Ford D 300 Box Van.
2. LYW 762D   Bedford KE Luton Van (Spare)
3. OYP 248F   Bedford KE Luton Van
4. PUL 760F   Bedford KE Luton Van
5. PUL 761F   Bedford KE Luton Van
6. TRK 489F   Bedford KE Luton Van
7. VYO 918G   Bedford KE Luton Van
8. CLR 970H   Bedford KE Luton Van
9. GLO 444J   Bedford KE Luton Van
10. HMX 486K   Bedford KE Luton Van
11. YLM 897G   Bedford KF Luton Van

PLASTIC COATINGS (continued)
12. YLM 898G   Bedford KF Luton Van
13. YLM 896G   Bedford KM Dropside.
14. YLU 312H   Bedford KM Dropside.

S.M. METAL
1. DLD 725J   Bedford CF Van.
2. GME 973J   Bedford CF Van.

SNOWDEX
1. HMX 490K   Ford D 800 Dropside.

SPUR ENGINEERING
1. TMF 487F   Bedford KE Dropside.

STEVENSON & HOWELL
1. OYV 413F   Bedford J1 Van.
2. YHX 485G   Bedford KC Box Van.
3. MYX 882D   Bedford KC Box Van.
4. LRK 518D   Bedford KC Box Van.
5. LRK 517D   Bedford KC Box Van.

H. H. TALLENT
1. OYL 691F   Bedford KD Luton Van.

TRIUMPH B. SYSTEMS
1. DJJ 914H   Bedford KD Box Van.
2. DJJ 915H   Bedford KD Box Van.
3. FGJ 103J   Bedford KD Box Van.

U. P. O.
1. OYV 414F   Bedford KD Dropside.
2. TMT 148F   Bedford KD Dropside.
3 YLU 308H   Bedford KD Dropside.

UNIVERSAL CATERERS
1. VYY 81G   Ford D 300 Box Van.
2. TGH 379F   Bedford KD Box Van.

WILLIAMES
1. FGY 216J   Ford D 550 Luton Van.
2. FGY 217G   Ford D 550 Luton Van.

W. WOODS
1. LLX 475D   Bedford KD Luton Van.
2. TUU 357F   Bedford KD Luton Van.
3. GMH 851J   Ford Transit Luton Van.

ZOPPAS
YGP 883G   Bedford KG Flat.

CONTRACT POOL VEHICLES
1. PUU 97F   Ford Transit Van.
2. FGY 220J   Bedford CF Van.

CONTRACT POOL VEHICLES (continued)

3.	TGT 176F	Austin Van.
4.	OHV 883E	Bedford KB Box Van.
5.	YLH 232G	Bedford KC Box Van.
6.	OYV 411F	Ford D 300 Box Van.
7.	VVB 437G	Ford D 300 Dropside.
8.	LYU 153D	Bedford KD Box Van.
9.	MYN 49D	Bedford KD Box Van.
10.	YLC 782G	Bedford KD Box Van.
11	OGJ 799E	Bedford KD Box Van.
12.	OHV 885E	Bedford KD Box Van.
13.	YGP 885G	Ford D 550 Box Van.
14.	VYY 79G	Ford D 550 Box Van.
15.	NGH 139D	Bedford KD Luton Van.

POOL VEHICLES ('Plastic Coatings' Livery)

16.	VLC 217C	Bedford KF Luton Van
17.	LRK 515D	Bedford KF Artic. Unit.
18.	YGK 778G	Bedford KF Artic. Unit.
19.	YGK 780G	Bedford KG Flat.
20.	FGF 113J	Bedford KM Artic. Unit.
21.	NPD 61D	Commer CCTW Artic Unit.

WORKSHOP SERVICE VEHICLES

1.	TUL 368F	Bedford HA 6 cwt Van.
2.	VYF 869G	Bedford HA 6 cwt Van. (Based at Crosby Factory)
3.	VYF 888G	Bedford HA 6 cwt Van.
4.	VYN 552G	Ford Transit 22 cwt Van.

FISHER RENWICK SERVICES (M/CR.) Ltd. Select List

JAMES CARR

KXJ 129G	Austin 30 cwt. Van.

DUSMO FARINOL

VYO 919G	Austin EA 360 Van.
LVU 489G	Ford D 400 Box Van.

J.D.ENTWISTLE

MND 371G	Bedford KEL Insul. Box Van.
OXJ 307H	Bedford KEL Dropside.

W.C.EVANS

ATU 467K	Bedford KC Box Van.

FERGUSON SHIERS

HNE 498E	Bedford KDL Box Van.
JND 76F	Bedford KDL Box Van.
CNF 343C	Bedford KGL Box Van.
KNC 341F	Bedford KGL Box Van.
KNC 342F	Bedford KGL Box Van.
KVR 488F	Austin A60 Van.
LVR 340G	Austin A60 Van.

CIBA GEIGY

MNF 440G	Bedford KEL Box Van.
FNE 867D	Bedford KGL Box Van.
LVR 341G	Ford Transit 22 cwt Van.
BMB 838K	Bedford KGL Box Van.
BMB 839K	Bedford KGL Box Van.

LINTOFOAM

NGH 131D	Bedford KGL Luton Van.
HVM 891F	Bedford KFL Luton Van.
HVM 892F	Bedford KFL Luton Van.
HVM 893F	Bedford KFL Luton Van.
KND 649F	Bedford KFA Artic. Unit.
KVM 211F	Bedford KFA Artic. Unit.
KVM 212F	Bedford KFA Artic. Unit.
LNE 313G	Bedford KFA Artic. Unit.
LNE 316G	Bedford KFA Artic. Unit.
NVM 753H	Bedford KFA Artic. Unit.
PXJ 733J	Bedford KFA Artic. Unit.
DLG 98K	Bedford KFA Artic. Unit.
DLG 99K	Bedford KFA Artic. Unit.
1 - 3	B.T.C. Van. 28ft.
4 - 14	B.T.C. Van /Cradle. 25ft & 26ft. (5)
15 - 17.	York. Freightmaster. 33ft.

MINTO & TURNER

MNF 803G	Bedford KEL Luton Van.

A.H. McINTOSH, Kirkcaldy

FNB 197D	Bedford KDL Luton Van. Spare.
FVR 976D	Bedford KDL Luton Van.
FVU 832D	Bedford KDL Luton Van.
FXJ 83D	Bedford KDL Luton Van.
GVM 93E	Bedford KDL Luton Van.
FNE 301D	Bedford KEL Luton Van.
GNC 466E	Bedford KEL Luton Van.
JND 77F	Bedford KEL Luton Van.
KNC 34F	Bedford KEL Luton Van.
KVM 736F	Bedford KEL Luton Van.
KXJ 130 G	Bedford KEL Luton Van.
MNA 438G	Bedford KEL Luton Van.
MNF 802G	Bedford KEL Luton Van.
ONA 661H	Bedford KEL Luton Van.
ATU 468K	Bedford KEL Luton Van.
ATU 469K	Bedford KEL Luton Van.
EMA 349K	Bedford KEL Luton Van.

TURNER & NEWALL

HXJ 458F	Ford D 800 Artic. Unit.
JND 125F	Bedford KGA Artic Unit.
JND 126F	Bedford KGA Artic Unit.
JND 127F	Bedford KGA Artic Unit.
JND 128F	Bedford KGA Artic Unit.
JND 129F	Bedford KGA Artic Unit.

TURNER & NEWALL (continued)

	JND 130F	Bedford KGA Artic Unit.
	JND 131F	Bedford KGA Artic Unit.
	JND 132F	Bedford KGA Artic Unit. Spare
	KVR 289F	Bedford KGA Artic Unit.
	MNB 467G	Bedford KGA Artic Unit.
	MNB 468G	Bedford KGA Artic Unit.
	MNF 801G	Bedford KGA Artic Unit.
	MNF 805G	Bedford KGA Artic Unit.
	OVR 869H	Bedford KGA Artic Unit.
100.		York Flat. 25ft.
102.		York Flat. 32ft.
103		York Flat. 33Ft.
104 - 118.		York. Freightmaster. 33ft.

ORBEX

	PNB 661J	Bedford KDL Box Van.

PEGLER (Manchester)

	ONE 940H	Bedford KB Box Van.
	CMB 622K	Bedford KB Box Van.

PEGLER (Washington)

	KNC 343F	Bedford KEL Box Van.
	ATU 464K	Bedford KDL Box Van.

PLASTIC COATINGS Ltd. (Winsford)

	PUL 762F	Bedford KEL Luton Van.
	TRK 493F	Bedford KF Dropside.
	VMV 345G	Bedford KEL Luton Van.
	NVM 752H	Bedford KMA Artic. Unit/Hiab
	NXJ 81H	Bedford KMH Dropside
	WMA 918J	Bedford KMH Dropside
1 - 2.		York. Dropside. 35ft.

PLASTIC COATINGS Ltd. (Kingswinford)

	OLE 574E	Bedford KEL Luton Van.
	VVB 439G	Bedford KEL Luton Van.
	NND 538H	Bedford KEL Dropside.

PROCTER & GAMBLE

	EMG 603B	Leyland Beaver Artic. Tanker.
	FVR 825D	Scammell Routeman Tanker.
	WTU 756J	ERF Artic.Tractor
	HVM 84F	Bedford KEL Box Van.
	HXJ 971F	Bedford KEL Box Van.
	HXJ 972F	Bedford KEL Box Van.
	HXJ 973F	Bedford KEL Box Van.
	HXJ 974F	Bedford KEL Box Van.
	HXJ 975F	Bedford KEL Box Van.
	HXJ 976F	Bedford KEL Box Van.
	JND 74F	Bedford KEL Box Van.
	JND 75F	Bedford KEL Box Van.
	JND 78F	Bedford KEL Box Van.

PROCTER & GAMBLE (continued)

	JNE 955F	Bedford KEL Box Van. Spare
	TMT 143F	Bedford KEL Box Van.
	TUV 765F	Bedford KEL Box Van.
	MNA 439G	Bedford KEL Box Van.
	MNF 804G	Bedford KEL Box Van.
	NNB 128H	Bedford KEL Box Van.
	MVU 488G	Ford D.400 Box Van.
	KND 521F	Bedford KMH Skeletal.
	KND 522F	Bedford KGA Artic. Unit.
	LNE 314G	Bedford KGA Artic. Unit.
	CLG 693K	Bedford KFL Tautliner Van.
	CLG 694K	Bedford KFL Tautliner Van.
	CLG 695K	Bedford KFL Tautliner Van.
	CLG 696K	Bedford KGL Tautliner Van.
	DLG 113K	Bedford KGL Linkliner Van.
	DLG 114K	Bedford KGL Linkliner Van.
	DLG 115K	Bedford KGL Linkliner Van.
	DLG 116K	Bedford KFL Linkliner Van.
		Crane. Bulk Transporter.
		Hands Skeletal. 20ft. x 2

RATCLIFFE BROTHERS

	WMA 916J	Bedford KEL Luton Van.
	WMA 917J	Bedford KEL Luton Van.

U.P.O. (U.K.) Ltd.

	DJJ 913H	Bedford KDL Flat (Tail-lift).

FISHER RENWICK-M/TER. - Spare Vehicles.

	LNE 311G	Bedford CAL Van
	KVR 217F	Bedford Hawson 35 cwt.
	JXJ 485F	Bedford KDL Box Van.
	GNF 543E	Bedford KDL Luton Van.
	JNF 796F	Bedford KEL Box Van.
	KVM 735F	Bedford KEL Box Van.
	LNC 987G	Bedford KEL Box Van.
	LNE 312G	Bedford KEL Box Van.
	LNR 342G	Bedford KEL Box Van.
	XMA 680J	Bedford KEL Box Van.
	LXJ 793G	Bedford KEL Box Van.
	FGX 71C	Bedford KGL Luton Van
	ATU 465K	Bedford KGE Luton Van
	HHV 403D	Bedford KGL Dropside.
	ATU 466K	Bedford KHE Dropside.
	HVM 894F	Bedford KFA Artic Unit.
	LVM 689G	Bedford KFA Artic Unit.

WORKSHOP SERVICE VEHICLES

	JXE 841D	Bedford KGS Recovery Wagon
	HND 100E	Bedford HA Van.
	LNB 423G	Bedford HA Van.
	NNF 739H	Bedford HA Van. (Washington)
	OVU 133H	Bedford HA Van.
	Reserve Trailer	York W2 Flat 33ft.

This is a Transcript of the FISHER RENWICK Directory of 'Places', or Towns served by their own vehicles. It was issued to each Driver,whether Trunk, Long-distance, or Local collection and delivery. It was kept with them at all times. The original was published in 1945.

FISHER   RENWICK   LTD
85, MAIN STREET, BELLSHILL, LANARKSHIRE
Telephone: Bellshill 2292

The Company operates nightly trunk services for the carriage of goods by road, with depots and warehousing facilities at :—

MANCHESTER
LONDON
BIRMINGHAM
LIVERPOOL
LEEDS
GLASGOW
EDINBURGH
DUNDEE
KIRKCALDY

FISHER   RENWICK   LTD.
depot addresses and telephone numbers:—

MANCHESTER	White City, Old Trafford. Trafford Park 1864
LONDON	Coppetts Road, Muswell Hill. Tudor 6480
BIRMINGHAM	Castle Bromwich Hall. Castle Bromwich 2655
LIVERPOOL	52, Vauxhall Road. Central 8751
LEEDS	Balm Road Mills, Hunslet. Leeds 75539
GLASGOW	85, Main Street, Bellshill. Bellshill 2292
EDINBURGH	Westfield Road, Earlston. Earlston 293
KIRKCALDY	Wellesley Road, Methil. Buckhaven 2169
DUNDEE	Claypots, Broughty Ferry. Broughty Ferry 7489

This Directory shews towns continuously served by the Company's own vehicles. The Company will be pleased to quote for towns beyond its normal delivery area. Such services are usually performed in conjunction with local carriers.

The Company segregates its local cartage boundaries into radii of 10, 15, 20, 25, 30 and 35 miles from the centre of each depot town.

Thus the routing code "L1" denotes a district within the London free delivery area, and "L3" denotes a district between 15 and 20 miles from London centre.

TOWN	ZONE
A	
Abbey Wood	L.2
Abbots Langley	L.3
Aberford	LE.1
Accrington	M.3
Acocks Green	B.1
Ackworth	LE.2
Acton	L.1
Addingham	LE.3
Addlestone	L.3
Adlington	M.3
Aigburth	LP.1
Ainsdale	LP.2
Aintree	LP.1
Albrighton	B.3
Alcester	B.3
Alderley Edge	M.2
Aldridge	B.1
Allerton	LP.1
Allesley	B.2
Almondbury	LE.3
Alperton	L.1
Altrincham	M.1
Alum Rock	B.1
Alvechurch	B.1
Amblecote	B.2
Amersham	L.4
Anerley	L.1
Anfield	LP.1
Appley Bridge	M.4
Apsley End (Herts)	L.4
Ardsley	LE.2
Ardsley (Barnsley)	LE.3
Ardsley, East	LE.1
Ardsley, West	LE.1
Ardwick	M.1
Ardwick-le-Street	LE.4
Armley	LE.1
Ashby-dela-Zouche	B.5
Ashford (Middx)	L.2
Ashtead (Surrey)	L.3
Ashton/Makerfield	M.3
Ashton/Lyne	M.1
Ashton/Mersey	M.1
Ashton/Ribble	M.5
Astley (Lancs)	M.1
Astley Bridge	M.2
Astley Green	M.1
Aston (Warwk)	B.1
Atherton	M.2
Atherstone	B.3
Attercliffe	LE.5
Audenshaw	M.1
Aughton	LP.1
Aylesbury	L.6
Aylestone	B6
B	
Bacup	M.3
Baginton	B.3
Baguley	M.1
Baildon	LE.1
Baldock	L.6
Balham	L.1
Balsall	B.2
Balsall Common	B.2
Balsall Heath	B.1
Bamber Bridge	M.4
Banstead	L.2
Bardsey	LE.1
Bardsley	M.1
Barking	L.1
Barkingside	L.2
Barnes	L.1
Barnet	L.2
Barnoldswick	LE.5
Barnsley	LE.3
Barnt Green	B.1
Barton Grange	M.1
Barton/Irwell	M.1
Barwell	B.4
Barwick-in-Elmet	LE.1
Batley	LE.1
Battersea	L.1
Baxenden	M.3
Bayswater	L.1
Beaconsfield	L.4
Bearwood	B.1
Bebbington	LP.1
Beckenham	L.1
Beckton	L.1
Becontree	L.1
Bedworth	B.3
Beeston (Yorks)	LE.1
Belmont (Lancs)	M.3
Bell Green	B.3
Belle Vue	M.1
Belvedere	L.2
Bengeworth	B.5
Berkhamstead	L.4
Bermondsey	L.1
Bethnal Green	L.1
Bewdley	B.3
Bexley	L.2
Bexley Heath	L.2
Bickenhill	B.1
Bickerstaffe	LP.2
Bidford	B.4
Biggin Hill	L.2
Billinge	LP.3
Bilston	B.1
Bilton	B.5
Bingley	LE.2
Binley	B.4
Birkdale	LP.3
Birkenhead	LP
Birmingham	B.1
Birstall	LE.1
Blackburn	M.4
Blackheath (Birmingham)	B.1
Blackheath (London)	L.1
Blackley	M.1
Blackpool	M.6
Blackrod	M.3
Blakedown	B.2
Blakenhall	B.1
Bloxwich	B.2
Blundell Sands	LP.1
Bolehall	B.2
Bollington	M.2
Bolton	M.1
Boothtown	M.1
Bootle	LP.1
Bordsley	B.1
Boreham Wood	L.2
Boroughbridge	LE.4
Boughton	LP.3
Bounds Green	L.1
Bournbrook	B.1
Bournville	B.1
Bow	L.1
Bowden	M.1
Boxmoor	L.4
Bradford (Lancs)	M.1
Bradford (Yorks)	LE.1
Bramhall	M.1
Bramley	LE.1
Bredbury	M.1
Brentford	L.1
Brentwood	L.3
Brereton	B.3
Bretherton	LP.3
Bridgnorth	B.4
Brierfiel	M.4
Brierley	LE.3
Brierley Hill	B.1
Brighouse	LE.2
Brighton-le-Sands	LP.2
Brimsdown	L.2
Brixton	L.1
Broadheath	M.1
Brockmoor	B.1
Bromborough	LP.1
Bromford	B.1
Bromley (Kent)	L.1
Bromley-by-bow	L.1
Bromsgrove	B.2
Broseley (Salop)	B.5
Broughton (Salford)	M.1
Broughton (Preston)	M.6
Brownhills	B.2
Buckhurst Hill	L.2
Burley (Leeds)	LE.2
Burley-in-Wharfdale	LE.2
Burnage	M.1
Burnley	M.4
Burnt Oak	L.1
Burntwood	B.2
Burscough Bridge	LP.2
Burton-upon-Trent	B.5
Burtonwood	M.3
Bury	M.1
Bushey	L.2
Byfleet	L.3
C	
Calverley	LE.1
Camberwell	L.1
Camden Town	L.1
Canley	B.3
Canning Town	L.1

TOWN	ZONE
Cannock	B.3
Cantley	LE.5
Carshalton	L.1
Castle Bromwich	B.1
Castleford	LE.2
Castleton	M.1
Caterham	L.3
Catford	L.1
Catshill (Bromsgrove)	B.2
Cawthorne	LE.3
Chadderton	M.1
Chadwell Heath	L.2
Chalfont St. Giles	L.4
Chalfont St.Peters	L.4
Chalk Farm	L.1
Chapel Allerton	LE.1
Chapel End	B.3
Chapel-en-le-Frith	M.3
Chapelfield (Lancs)	M.1
Chapelfields	B.3
Charing Cross	L.1
Charlestown (Lancs)	M.1
Charlesworth	M.2
Charlton	L.1
Chaseside	L.2
Chasetown	B.2
Chatham	L.5
Cheadle (Cheshire)	M.1
Cheadle Heath	M.1
Cheadle Hulme	M.1
Cheam	L.2
Cheetham	M.1
Cheetham Hill	M.1
Chelmsford	L.6
Chelsea	L.1
Chertsey	L.3
Chesham	L.4
Cheshunt	L.2
Cheslyn Hay	B.2
Chester	LP.3
Chigwell	L.2
Chingford	L.2
Chinley	M.3
Chislehurst	L.2
Chiswick	L.1
Chobham	L.4
Chorley	M.3
Chorley Wood	L.3
Chorlton-cum-Hardy	M.1
Chorlton-on-Medlock	M.1
Church	M.4
Churchtown	LP.3
Clapham	L.1
Clapham Common	L.1
Clapton	L.1
Clayton (Lancs)	M.1
Clayton (Yorks)	LE.2
Clayton-le-Moors	M.4
Cleckheaton	LE.2
Clent	B.1
Cleveleys	M.6
Clifton	M.1
Clifton Junction	M.1

Clitheroe	M.6
Cloughfold	M.3
Coalbrookdale	B.5
Coalport	B.5
Coalville	B.5
Cobham (Kent)	L.4
Cobham (Surrey)	L.3
Codsall	B.3
Coleshill	B.1
Colindale	L.1
Collyhurst	M.1
Colnbrook	L.3
Colne	M.6
Colwich	B.4
Compshall	M.1
Congleton	M.4
Conisborough	LE.4
Connah's Quay	LP.2
Cookham	L.4
Cookley	B.2
Coombe	L.1
Copsewood	B.3
Coseley	B.1
Cotteridge (Warwk)	B.1
Coulsdon	L.2
Coventry	B.3
Cowley (Middx)	L.3
Cradley	B.1
Cradley Heath	B.1
Crawshawbooth	M.3
Crayford	L.2
Cricklewood	L.1
Cronton	LP.1
Crosby	LP.1
Crossens	LP.3
Cross Gates (Yorks)	LE.1
Croston	LP.3
Crouch End	L.1
Croxley Green	L.3
Croydon	L.1
Crumpsall	M.1
Curdworth	LE.3

D

Dagenham	L.2
Dalston	L.1
Darenth	L.3
Darfield	LE.3
Darlaston	B.1
Dartford	L.3
Darton	LE.3
Darwen	M.3
Davyhulme	M.1
Dawley	B.5
Delph	M.3
Denham	L.3
Denton	M.1
Deptford	L.1
Dewsbury	LE.1
Didsbury	M.1
Diggle	M.2
Disley	M.2
Ditton	LP.1
Dobb Cross	M.2

Dodworth	LE.3
Doncaster	LE.5
Donisthorpe	B.4
Donnington	B.5
Dorking	L.4
Drightlington	LE.1
Droitwich	B.3
Droylesden	M.1
Duddeston	B.1
Dudley	B.1
Dukinfield	M.1
Dulwich	L.1
Dunstable	L.6

E

Ealing	L.1
Earlsdon	B.3
Earlsfield	L.1
Earl Shilton	B.5
Earlstown	B.5
East Barnet	L.1
East Finchley	L.1
East Ham	L.1
East Moseley	L.2
East Tilbury	L.4
Eatington	B.5
Eccles	M.1
Eccleshill	LE.3
Eccleston (Chester)	LP.3
Edenbridge	L.4
Edenfield	M.2
Edgbaston	B.1
Edge Hill	LP.1
Edgware	L.1
Edgeworth	M.2
Edmonton	L.1
Egerton	M.2
Egham	L.3
Ellesmere Port	LP.1
Elland	LE.2
Elstree	L.2
Eltham	L.1
Elton	M.1
Emscote	B.3
Enderby	B.6
Enfield	L.2
Epping (Essex)	L.3
Epsom	L.2
Erdington	B.1
Erith	L.2
Esher	L.2
Essington	B.2
Everton	LP.1
Evesham	B.5
Ewell	L.2

F

Failsworth	M.1
Fairfield	LP.1
Fallings Heath	B.1
Fallowfield	M.1
Farnborough (Kent)	L.2
Farningham (Kent)	L.3
Farnworth	M.1

TOWN	ZONE
Farsley	LE.1
Fazackerley	LP.1
Fazeley	B.2
Featherstone	LE.2
Feckenham	B.3
Feltham	L.2
Fillongley	B.2
Finchley	L.1
Finsbury	L.1
Finsbury Park	L.1
Fletchamstead	B.3
Flixton	M.1
Foleshill	B.3
Foots Cray	L.2
Forest Gate	L.1
Forest Hill	L.1
Formby	LP.1
Four Oaks	B.1
Freckleton	M.6
Freshfield	LP.1
Friern Barnet	L.1
Frodsham	LP.1
Fulham	L.1
Fulwood	M.5

G

Garforth	LE.1
Gargrave	LE.5
Garstang	M.6
Garston	LP.1
Gateacre	LP.1
Gathurst	M.3
Gerrards Cross	L.3
Gildersome	LE.1
Gillingham	L.5
Glazebury	M.2
Glossop	M.2
Godley	M.1
Golbourne	M.3
Golders Green	L.1
Golcar	LE.3
Gomersal	LE.3
Goodmayes	L.2
Goole	LE.5
Gorton	M.1
Grappenhall	M.2
Grassendale	LP.1
Gravelly Hill	B.1
Gravesend	L.4
Grays	L.3
Great Barr	B.1
Great Bridge	B.1
Great Crosby	LP.1
Great Harwood	M.4
Great Heath	B.3
Greenford	L.1
Greengates (Bradford)	LE.1
Greenhithe	L.3
Greenwich	L.1
Greet	L.1
Greetland	LE.3
Guide Bridge	M.1
Guildford	L.5
Guiseley	LE.5
Gunnersbury	L.1

H

Hackbridge	L.1
Hackney	L.1
Hadfield	M.2
Hadley (Salop)	B.5
Hagley	B.2
Hale	M.1
Halesowen	B.1
Halewood	LP.1
Halifax	LE.1
Hall Green	B.1
Hallsall	LP.1
Hammersmith	L.1
Hampstead	L.1
Hampton	L.1
Hampton-in-Arden (Warwk)	B.1
Hamstead	B.1
Handforth	M.1
Handsworth (B'ham)	B.1
Handsworth (Yorks)	LE.5
Hanwell	L.1
Hanworth	L.2
Harborne	B.1
Harefield	L.3
Harlesden	L.1
Harlington	L.2
Harlow	L.2
Harmondsworth	L.2
Harpenden	L.4
Harpurhey	M.1
Harringay	L.1
Harrogate	LE.2
Harrow	L.2
Harrow Weald	L.2
Hartlebury	B.3
Hartshill (N.Warwk)	B.3
Haskayne	LP.2
Haslingden	M.3
Hatfield	L.3
Hatton (Warwk)	B.3
Hawksworth	LE.2
Haworth	LE.3
Haydock	LP.3
Hayes (Kent)	L.2
Hayes (Middx)	L.2
Hazelgrove	M.1
Headingley	LE.1
Headless Cross	B.2
Heald Green	M.1
Heath Town	B.2
Heaton Chapel	M.1
Heaton Mersey	M.1
Heaton Norris	M.1
Hebden Bridge	LE.1
Heckmondwike	LE.1
Hednesford	B.3
Helmshore	M.2
Helsby	LP.2
Hemel Hempstead	L.4
Hemsworth	LE.2
Hendon	L.1
Henley-on-Thames	L.6
Herne Hill	L.1
Hertford	L.3
Heston	L.2
Heyside	M.1
Heywood	M.1
Highbury	L.1
Highams Park	L.1
Highgate	L.1
Hightown (Formby)	LP.1
High Wycombe	L.5
Hillingdon	L.2
Hillmorton	B.6
Hill Top	B.1
Hinckley	B.4
Hindley	M.2
Hindley Green	M.2
Hipperholm	LE.2
Hitchen	L.6
Hither Green	L.1
Hoddesdon	L.3
Hockley Heath	B.2
Holborn	L.1
Holloway	L.2
Hollinwood	M.1
Holmes Chapel	M.4
Holmfirth	LE.3
Homerton	L.1
Honley	LE.3
Hooton	LP.1
Horbury	LE.1
Hornchurch	L.3
Hornsey	L.1
Horsforth	LE.1
Horton	LE.1
Horton Kirby	L.3
Horwich	M.3
Hounslow	L.2
Hoxton	L.1
Hoylake	LP.1
Huddersfield	LE.2
Hulme	M.1
Hunslet	LE.1
Hunston	LP.1
Huyton Quarry	LP.1
Hyde	M.1

I

Ibstock	B.5
Idle	LE.1
Ilford	L.2
Ilkley	LE.2
Ince (Wigan)	M.3
Irlam	M.1
Irlam o' th' Heights	M.1
Ironbridge	B.5
Isleworth	L.1
Islington	L.1
Iver	L.3

K

Kearsley	M.1
Keighley	LE.3
Kenilworth	B.3

TOWN	ZONE
Kennington	L.1
Kensal Green	L.1
Kensington	L.1
Kenton	L.1
Kentish Town	L.1
Kew	L.1
Kidbrook	L.1
Kidderminster	B.3
Kilburn	L.1
Kingsbury (Middx)	L.1
Kingsbury (Warwk)	B.2
Kings Cross	L.1
Kings Heath	B.1
Kings Langley	L.3
Kings Norton	B.1
Kingston	L.1
Kingswinford	B.2
Kinver	B.2
Kippax	LE.1
Kirkby	LP.1
Kirkburton	LE.2
Kirkdale	LP.1
Kirkham	M.6
Kirkheaton	LE.2
Kirkstall	LE.2
Knaresborough	LE.3
Knottingley	LE.2
Knotty Ash	LP.1
Knowle	B.1
Knowlesley	LP.1
Knutsford	M.2

L

Ladywood	B.1
Lambeth	L.1
Langley (B'ham)	B.1
Langley (Bucks)	L.3
Langley (Warwk)	B.3
Lea Marston	B.1
Leamington	B.4
Leamore	B.1
Leatherhead	L.3
Lee	L.1
Leeds	LE.1
Lees	M.1
Leicester	B.6
Leigh (Lancs)	M.2
Leigh-on-Sea	L.6
Letchworth	L.6
Levenshulme	M.1
Lewisham	L.1
Leyland	M.4
Leyton	L.1
Leytonstone	L.1
Lichfield	B.2
Lickey End	B.2
Linthwaite	LE.2
Liscard	LP.1
Litherland	LP.1
Littleborough	M.2
Little Crosby	LP.1
Little Heath	B.3
Little Hulton	M.1

Little Lever	M.1
Liverpool	LP.1
Liversedge	LE.1
Lofthouse	LE.1
London	L.1
London Colney	L.3
Longbridge (B'ham)	B.1
Longbridge (Warwk)	B.4
Longford	B.3
Longridge	M.5
Longsite	M.1
Lostock Junction	M.3
Loughton	L.2
Lower Edmonton	L.1
Lowton	M.2
Lozells	B.1
Luton	L.5
Lye	B.1
Lydiate	LP.1
Lymm	M.2
Lytham	M.6

M

Macclesfield	M.3
Maghull	LP.1
Maida Vale	L.1
Maidenhead	L.4
Maidstone	L.6
Malden	L.2
Malvern	B.6
Manchester	M.1
Manor Park	L.1
Marple	M.1
Marsden (Yorks)	LE.4
Marston Green	M.1
Marylebone	L.1
Measham	B.4
Meltham	LE.3
Menston	LE.2
Mere	M.2
Mere Green	B.1
Merstham	L.3
Merton	L.1
Methley	LE.1
Mexborough	LE.4
Micklefield	LE.1
Mickleton	LE.1
Middleton	M.1
Middleton Junction	M.1
Middlewich	M.4
Miles Platting	M.1
Mill Hill	L.1
Millwall	L.1
Milnrow	M.2
Milnesbridge	LE.3
Minworth	B.1
Mirfield	LE.2
Mitcham	L.1
Mobberley	M.2
Molesey	L.2
Monton	M.1
Morden	L.1
Morley	LE.1
Mortlake	L.1

Moseley	B.1
Mossley	M.2
Mossley Hill	LP.1
Moston	M.1
Moxley	B.1
Much Wenlock	B.5
Muswell Hill	L.1
Mytholmroyd	LE.3

N

Narborough	B.6
Neasden	L.1
Nechells	B.1
Nelson	M.4
Netherton	B.1
New Barnet	L.2
New Brighton	LP.1
New Cross	L.1
New Eltham	L.1
Newhall	B.5
New Hey	M.5
New Malden	L.1
New Mills (Lancs)	L.1
Newport (Salop)	B.5
New Southgate	L.1
Newton (Hyde)	M.1
Newton Heath	M.1
Newton-le-Willows	M.3
Newtown (Wigan)	M.3
Norbiton	L.1
Norbury	L.1
Normanton	LE.1
Northendon	M.1
Northfield (Warwk)	B.1
North Finchley	L.1
Northfleet	L.4
Northolt	L.2
Northwich	M.3
Northwood	L.2
North Woolwich	L.1
Norton Canes	B.2
Norwood	L.1
Notting Hill	L.1

O

Oakengates	B.5
Oldbury (Worcs)	B.1
Old Ford	L.1
Oldham	M.1
Old Hill	B.1
Old Swinford	B.2
Old Trafford	M.1
Olton	B.1
Ombersley	B.4
Ongar	L.4
Ormskirk	LP.2
Orpington	L.2
Orrell (Bootle)	LP.1
Ossett	LE.1
Oswaldthwistle	M.3
Otley	LE.2
Oulton	LE.1
Oughtibridge	LE.5
Oxenhope	LE.3

TOWN	ZONE
P	
Paddington	L.1
Padiham	M.4
Palmers Green	L.1
Parbold	LP.3
Park Royal	L.1
Partington	M.1
Pateley Bridge	LE.4
Paticroft	M.1
Peckham	L.1
Pelsall	B.1
Pemberton	M.3
Pendleton	M.1
Penge	L.1
Penistone	LE.3
Penketh	LP.2
Penkridge	B.3
Perivale	L.1
Perry Barr	B.1
Pershore	B.5
Pimlico	L.1
Pinner	L.2
Plaistow	L.1
Plumstead	L.1
Ponders End	L.1
Pontefract	LE.2
Poplar	L.1
Port Sunlight	LP.1
Potters Bar	L.2
Powick	B.5
Poynton	M.2
Prescot	LP.1
Preston	M.5
Prestwich	M.1
Pudsey	LE.1
Purfleet	L.3
Purley	L.2
Putney	L.1
Q	
Quarry Bank	B.1
Queensbury (Yorks)	LE.2
Quinton (B'ham)	B.1
R	
Radcliffe	M.1
Radford (Coventry)	B.3
Rainford	LP.2
Rainham (Essex)	L.2
Rainhill	LP.1
Ramsbottom	M.2
Rastrick	LE.2
Ratby	B.6
Ravensthorpe	LE.2
Ravenstone	B.5
Rawcliffe	LE.5
Rawdon	LE.1
Rawmars	LE.4
Rawtenstall	M.3
Raynes Park	L.1
Reading	L.6
Redbourn	L.4
Reddish	M.1
Redditch	B.2
Redhill	L.3
Rednal	B.1
Reigate	L.3
Rhodes	M.1
Richmond	L.1
Rickmansworth	L.3
Ringway	M.1
Ripon	LE.1
Ripponden	LE.3
Rishton	M.4
Roby	LP.1
Rochdale	M.2
Rochester	L.5
Rodley	LE.1
Roehampton	L.1
Romford	L.2
Rossendale	M.3
Rotherham	LE.5
Rotherhithe	L.1
Rothwell	LE.1
Roundhey	LE.1
Rowley Regis	B.1
Royston (Yorks)	LE.2
Royton	M.1
Rubery	B.1
Rubery Hill	B.1
Rufford (Lancs)	LP.3
Rugby	B.5
Rugeley	B.3
Ruislip	L.2
Runcorn	LP.2
Rushall	B.1
Rusholme	M.1
Ryhill	LE.1
Ryton-on-Dunsmore	B.4
S	
Saddleworth	M.2
St. Albans	L.3
St. Annes-on-Sea	M.6
St. Helens	LP.2
St. Johns Wood	L.1
St. Mary Cray	L.2
St. Pancras	L.1
Sale	M.1
Salford	M.1
Salford Priors	B.4
Saltaire	LE.2
Saltley	B.1
Saltney	LP.3
Sandal Magna	LE.1
Sandbach	M.4
Sanderstead	L.2
Scarisbrick	LP.2
Scholes (Yorks)	LE.1
Seacroft	LE.1
Seaforth	LP.1
Sedgley	L.1
Sedgley (Prestwich)	M.1
Sefton Park	LP.1
Selby	LE.3
Selley Oak	B.1
Seven Kings	L.2
Sevenoaks	L.4
Shadwell (Leeds)	LE.1
Shadwell (London)	L.1
Shaw	M.1
Shawforth	M.2
Sheffield	LE.5
Shelf	LE.2
Shenstone	B.2
Shepherds Bus	L.1
Shepley	LE.3
Shepperton	L.3
Shepshed	B.6
Shevington	LP.3
Shifnal	B.4
Shipley	LE.1
Shire Oak	B.2
Shirley (Warwk)	B.1
Shirley Heath	B.1
Shoreditch	L.1
Short Heath (Staffs)	B.1
Shortheath (Warwk)	B.1
Shotton	LP.2
Sidcup	L.2
Silkstone	LE.3
Silsden	LE.3
Silvertown	L.1
Skelmanthorpe	LE.3
Skelmersdale	LP.2
Skipton	LE.4
Slaithwaite	LE.3
Slough	L.3
Small Heath	B.1
Smethwick	B.1
Snaith	LE.4
Solihull	B.1
Southall	L.1
South Croydon	L.2
Southend	L.6
Southgate	L.1
South Norwood	L.1
Southport	LP.3
Southwark	L.1
Sowerby Bridge	LE.3
Sparkbrook	B.1
Sparkhill	B.1
Speke	LP.1
Springfield (B'ham)	B.1
Stafford	B.4
Stainburn (Yorks)	LE.1
Staines	L.3
Stalybridge	M.1
Stamford Hill	L.1
Stanford-le-Hope	L.4
Standish	M.3
Stanley (Yorks)	LE.1
Stanmore	L.2
Stanningley	LE.1
Stanwell	L.3
Stapenhill	B.5
Stechford	B.1
Stepney	L.1
Stepney Green	L.1
Stevenage	L.5
Stirchley (B'ham)	B.1

TOWN	ZONE
Stockport	M.1
Stocksbridge	LE.4
Stockton Heath	M.3
Stockwell	L.1
Stoke Newington	L.1
Stonebridge Park	L.1
Stoneclough	M.1
Stoneleigh	B.3
Stourbridge	B.2
Stourport	B.3
Stourton (Yorks)	LE.1
Stratford	L.1
Stratford-on-Avon	B.4
Streatham	L.4
Streetley	B.1
Stretford	M.1
Strood	M.1
Studley	B.2
Sudbury	L.1
Sunbury-on-Thames	L.2
Surbiton	L.2
Sutton	L.2
Sutton Coldfield	B.1
Swadlincote	B.5
Swanley	L.3
Swanscombe	L.3
Swinton	M.1
Sydenham	L.1
Sydenham,Lower	L.1

T

Tadcaster	LE.2
Tamworth	B.2
Tardebigge	B.2
Teddington	L.2
Tettenhall	B.2
Thames Ditton	L.2
Thorne	LE.5
Thorner	LE.1
Thornton (Bradford)	LE.1
Thornton Heath	L.1
Tilbury	L.4
Tile Hill	B.2
Timperley	M.1
Tipton	B.1
Todmorden	M.3
Tolworth	L.2
Tooting	L.1
Tottenham	L.1
Tottenham Hale	L.1
Tottington	M.1
Trafford Park	M.1
Tring	L.6
Tulse Hill	L.1
Twickenham	L.1
Tyburn	B.1
Tyldesley	M.2
Tyseley	B.1

U

Upholland	LP.2
Upminster	L.3
Upper Edmonton	L.1
Upper Esholt	LE.1
Upper Mill	M.2
Upper Norwood	L.1
Uper Tooting	L.1
Urmston	M.1
Uttoxeter	B.5
Uxbridge	L.3

V

Vauxhall (London)	L.1
Vauxhall (B'ham)	B.1
Victoria	L.1

W

Wakefield	LE.1
Walham Green	L.1
Walkden	M.1
Wallesley	LP.1
Wallington	L.1
Walmersley	M.1
Walsall	B.1
Walsall Wood	B.2
Walthamstow	L.1
Waltham Abbey	L.2
Waltham Cross	L.2
Walton	LP.2
Walton-on-Thames	L.3
Walton-le-Dale	M.5
Walworth	L.1
Wanstead	L.1
Wandsworth	L.1
Ward End	B.1
Wardle	M.2
Wardleworth	M.2
Ware	L.4
Wargrave	M.3
Warrington	M.3
Warstock	B.1
Warwick	B.3
Washwood Heath	B.1
Waterfoot	M.2
Waterloo (L'pool)	LP.1
Waterloo (London)	L.1
Watford	L.3
Wath-upon-Dearne	LE.4
Wavertree	LP.1
Wealdstone	L.2
Wednesbury	B.1
Wednesfield	B.2
Welling	L.2
Wellington	B.5
Welwyn Garden City	L.4
Wembley	L.1
West Bromwich	B.1
Westcliff	L.6
West Croydon	L.1
West Derby	LP.1
West Drayton	L.2
West Ham	L.1
Westerham	L.3
Westhoughton	M.2
West Kirby	LP.1
Westminster	L.1
West Smethwick	B.1

West Thurrock	L.3
West Wycombe	L.5
Wetherby	LE.2
Weybridge	L.3
Whaley Bridge	M.3
Whalley Range	M.1
Whiston (Lancs)	LP.1
Whetstone	L.1
Whitefield	M.1
Whitwick	B.6
Whitworth	M.2
Wibsey	LE.1
Widnes	LP.2
Wigan	M.3
Willesden	L.1
Willenhall (Staffs)	B.1
Willenhall (Warwk)	B.4
Wilmcote	B.3
Wilmslow	M.2
Wilnecote	B.2
Wimbledon	L.1
Winchmore Hill	L.1
Windsor	L.4
Winsford	M.4
Winson Green	B.1
Winton	M.1
Withington	M.2
Witton	B.1
Woking	L.4
Wollaston (Worcs)	B.2
Wolston	B.4
Wolverhampton	B.2
Wombourn	B.2
Wombwell	LE.4
Wood Green	L.1
Woodford	L.1
Woodhouse	LE.1
Woodlesford	LE.1
Woodley	M.1
Woodville	B.5
Woolfold	M.1
Woolton	LP.1
Woolwich	L.1
Worcester	B.4
Wordsley	B.2
Worsley	M.1
Wortley	LE.1
Wraysbury	L.3
Wrotham	L.4
Wyken	B.3
Wylde Green	B.1
Wythall	B.1
Wythenshawe	M.1

Y

Yardley	B.1
Yeadon	LE.1
Yiewsley	L.2
York	LE.4

Index

AEC: 51
    Mammoth Major 51, 108
    Mammoth Major Mk III Van - Firestone *111*
    Mk V Sided - Wandleside Cables *113*
    Mk V Van - Firestone *114-115*
Adamson, Daniel 117
Albion:
    Flat- Hills & Partridge *111*
    LAD-cabbed Van - Stephenson & Howell 117
Allison, (Dundee) 84
Armstrong-Saurer 'Samson' 53
ARO (Associated Road Operators) 62
Austin:
    Fleet line up, Muswell Hill *103*
    FG Vans 108
    FG Van - Peglers *116*
    K4 Flat *102*
    K4 Sided *96*

Bacon's End 59, 77
Barlow, A.H. 104
Barnes, Alfred, Minister of Transport 91
Barrington, Claude 67
Battle of Messines Ridge 23, 26
Bedford:
    Fleet line-up, Muswell Hill *103*
    30cwt MW F.C. conversion - Brillo *109*
    30 cwt N.C. van - Kolynos *109*
    CA Dormobile Personnel Carrier - Johnsons Wax *118*
    JI Van - Osborne Garrett *109*
    KF Luton Van - Fisher Renwick Contract Hire *116*
    KG Luton Van - Lintafoam *119*
    KGA Artic Van - Charles Phillips *121*
    KGA Artic Van - Turner & Newall *121*
    ML Van - Cosmos Lamps *101*
    OL Box Van - Brillo *109*
    OL Box Van(s) *93, 103*
    OLB Box Van *97*
    OWL Flat *81*
    TK Van - Cundell Corrugated *116*
    TK Van - Johnsons Wax *118*
    TK Van - Kraft *117*
    TK Luton Van - McIntosh *120*
    TK Van - Procter & Gamble *120*
    WHL Van *81*
    WTL *55, 90*
    WTL 'Orion' *61*
Bedford-Scammell:
    Artic - Firestone *113*
    KF Artic - Fisher Renwick Contract Hire *117*
Beecham's 55
Bell, Thomas 125
Berrisford Atkinson 109, 112
Bethell, I 12
Bingham, Alf 74, 77, 90
Blackford Brothers (Leeds) 80
Blackwell, Fred *111*
Blair, Anne 108
Blue Star Garages 118
Boalloy 112
Bouts 38
Bouts-Tillotson 51, 98
Box, Norman E. 18
B.O.C.M. (British Oil and Cake Mills) 12
British & Irish Steam Packet Co. Ltd 23
British Road Services (BRS) 104, 108
British Transport Commission 104
Brooke-Bond Tea 38, 108
Brown, Alexander (Symington) 80, 84
    Fleet list *85*
Bruce, 'Willy' 86, 88
Burton's Wagon Wheels 98
Butler & Crisp 41

Caledonian Omnibus Co. (Parcels) 84
Carter Paterson 57, 98
CMUA (Commercial & Motor Users Association) 62
Coast Lines 24, 37, 58, 77
Cole E.K. 56
Commer:
    Superpoise Vans 56
    'Walk-Thru' Van - Lintafoam *117*
Cook, Siddle C. 96
Cornbrook Wheelwrights 51, 54, 57, 72, 85, 87
Corn Products 108
Coulson, Henry *22*
Coulson & Co. 7
Coupe, 'Vi' 108
Coventry 74, 77
Cowan & Co. 15, 21, 23, 33, 64
Cox, Reg. 117
Crosby Doors 111
Cunningham, J 23
C.W.S. Flour Mill 12

Daimler 27, *43*
Dalgliesh, Stanley 33
Darlington, Cliff 108
Darlington Royal Show 27
Dennis, Jack 112

Deuchar, Mabel 15
Dewey, J.H. 112
Dobson, W & Co. 33
Dodge:
    3 ton Van - Procea *112*
Dominion Cash Registers 38
Dyson drawbar trailer 38

Eastern Roadways 100
Edwards & Company 125
Elliot Fisher Typewriters 60
Eltringham, Horace 125
Emergency Road Transport Organisation 62, 69
English Electric 86
ERF:
    Ex A Brown Fleet List 85
    Artic Flat 'Whiteadder', Ex Rogers (Earlston) *92*
    C1.5 Flat 'Devron' *86*
    C1.5 Flat 'Liddle' *87*
    C1.5 Van 'Annan' *91, 108*
    C1.5 Van 'Nith' *108*
Evans, Henry & Sons 16, 22, 33

Farinol Floor Compound 110
Firestone Tyres 108, 110
Fisher, Harbron and Renwick 7, *11*
Fisher Renwick:
    Depots:
        Bellshill 84
        Castle Bromwich Hall, Birmingham 74, 77
        Coppetts Road, Muswell Hill 13, 53, 58, 62, 63, 77, *78, 79*, 88, *90*, 94, 95, *103*, 104, 108, 110
        Balm Road Mills, Hunslet, Leeds 80
        Vauxhall Road, Liverpool 74, 77, *80*, 90
        Barr Bank, Lymm 80, 88
        Rutherglen site 100
        Town End Garage, Symington, Biggar 80
        White City, Old Trafford 58, 63, 74, *75, 76*, 88, 95, 100, 103, 104, *105*, 108, 118
    Directory of Places 144-150
    Mechanics at Symington *85*
    Offices, Symington *84*
    Road Fleet Lists 134-138
    Vehicle Pairings 95
Fisher Renwick, Newcastle-upon-Tyne 7, 13, 40
    Shipping In Service:
        1882, 8
        1888, 8
        1905, 14
    Steamers On Line Record 133
    Steamers Owned 1877-1927 132
    Steamers:
        'Amsteldam' 22
        'Ella Sayer' 8, 17, 22
        'Everelda' 22
        'Newminster Abbey' 22
        'Springhill' 22
        'Trio' 7, 8, *11*
        'Whitby' 17
        'Wiltshire' 8
        'Woodleigh' 22
Fisher Renwick Co's Manchester-London Steamers (1908) Ltd 16, 18, 22, 26, 30, 37
    Shipping List 130
    Steamers On Line Record 133
Fisher Renwick, Manchester-London Steamers Ltd. 18
    Collection & Delivery Schedule 67
    Garages & Offices:
        Cornbrook Road 14, 15, 17, 20, 29, 30
        Medland Street 29, 40, 62
        London Wharf, Pomona Dock, Manchester 12, 14, 22, 27, 29, 33, 36, 38, 39, 40, *43*, 57, 58, 118
        Manchester Wharf, Shadwell Basin, London 13, 14, 15, 16, 18, 19, 22, 24, 26, 27, 29, 30, 33, 38, 39, 40, *51, 55*, 64
    Roll of Honour 22, *23*
    Shipping In Service:
        1905, 14
        1908, 17
        1914, 22
        1920, 27
        1936, 51
        1877 to 1927 129
    Shipping List 131
    Shipping On Line Record 133
    Steamers:
        'Blairmore' 24, 30, 37
        'Blencowe' 14
        'Carbineer' 16, *16*, 21
        'Cuirassier' 22, 27, 33, *33*
        'Fusilier' 19, *19*
        'Halbadier' 22, 24
        'Hussar' 19, 22

        'Lancer' 17, 18, *18*, 29, 36, 51
        'Lodore' 13, *15*
        'Musketeer' 22
        'Sapper' 33
        'Sentry' *20*, 33, 34, 43
        'Trooper' *19*
        'Volunteer' (i) 13
        'Volunteer' (ii) 16
        'Yeoman' *16, 20*, 21, 22, *32*
    Trade Card *21* and rear cover
Fisher Renwick (BTC) Ltd. 104
    Acquisition Cheques (BTC) *107*
Fisher Renwick Contracts 108, 117
Fisher Renwick Contract Hire Ltd. 108
Fisher Renwick Contract Services:
    Select Fleet List: London 139-142
    Select Fleet List: Manchester 142-143
    K Garage, Watford Way, Hendon 110, *111*, 117, 118
    Kingsway Garage, Didsbury 111, 117, 118
    Park Royal Depot *122*
    Acquisition Cheques (Ryder) *124*
Fisher Renwick Services 108, 117
Fisher, George Forster 13, 16
Fisher, Harbron & Renwick 7
Fisher Joseph 7, 13, 125
Fisher, Percy 23
Ford:
    3 ton GT 'Cost-Cutter' Van - Kraft *117*
    Model T *42*
    Model T Flat 27, 39, *39*, *42*
    Model AA 39
    Model B *54*
    Model B Flats *57*
    Model B Luton FC Conversion *54*
    Model B Van, *79, 80, 81*
Fordson 7V Fleet 56
    7V 3 ton 50
    7V Vans *56, 79*, 90
    Standard Tractor *109*
Foster and Seddon 97
W & C French 112
French Renwick 112
FTA (Freight Transport Association) 63
Charles Fryer & Co. 26

Gardner Engines 53, 97
Garner 58
Garke Report 69
General Steam Navigation 39
Gervais Dairy 110
Glamis Road 13
Glovers Cables 12
Goblin Foods 110
Goddard, Teddy 74
Goodfellow, William (Methill) 84
Gregory, John 118

Halls of Finchley 97
Harding, Marion 111
Hawker 'Eddie' 111
Hawthorn, R.W. 7
Hays Wharf Cartage Co. 16, 39, 42, 57
    Horse Drawn Van *63*
Thomas Hedley 56
Heinz Foods 56
Hinchliffe J & H 56, 95
Hinchliffe, Herbert 64, 72, 74, 84, 89, 90, 91, 94, 95
Hinchliffe, John H. 64, 72, 74, 84, 89, 90, 91, 94, 95
HMV 56
Holding, John 111
Holdsworth & Hanson 77, 98, 100
Holystone 112
Home Guard, Coppetts Road, Muswell Hill *90*
Hoover 56
Hudson of Milnthorpe 86
Hugh, Percy C. 26, 30
Hulton Press 98
Hunter Vehicles 112
Imperial Lighterage 46
International K8 Artic Flat *93*
Ingersoll-Rand 108
John, Sir Gatcombe 25
R Johnson & Nephew 27
Jungle Café, Shap 88, 91, *101*

Kellogg's Corn Flakes 38, 56
Knox tractors & articulated unit 26, 27, 30
Kolynos Pharmaceuticals 41, 108
Kraft Foods 111, 112, 117

Lancashire & Yorkshire Railway 20
Leathers, Lord Minister of Transport 72
Lengthline Ltd 127
Lewis, Bert & Norman 74
Leyland Lorries 51, 53
Leyland:
    Beaver 'LAD' Artic - Procter & Gamble *120*
    Bull *52*, 53
    Hippo 51,
    Hippo Flat *89*

Hippo Van 'Tern' *68*
Hippo Ex A. Brown *89*
Octopus 51, *55*, *65*, 68
Octopus Flat 'Kittiwake' *65*
Octopus Flat 'Robin' *106*
Octopus Van 'Diver' 74
Octopus Van 'Dunlin' 74, *81*
Lilia Ltd. 110
Lloyds Bank, Newcastle-upon-Tyne 46
London & India Dock Co. 13
London & North Eastern Railway 32
London, Midland & Scottish Railway 40
Lots Road Power Station 17
Love, William (Bellshill) 84
Lysaght, Tom 112

Macdonald's Penguin Wafers 98
Manchester Corporation 125
Manchester Lines 127
Manchester London Cargo Liner Service 7, 12
Manchester - London Steamers 7, 21, 24
Manchester and London Shipping Co. Ltd 12
   Shipping List (1902-1908) *131*
   Steamer Fleet list 1905 14
   Steamers:
      'Blencowe' 14
      'Fishren' 14, 17, 19
      'Lodore' 13, 15
      'Volunteer' (i) 13
   Trade Bill *13*
Manchester Marine 127
Manchester Oil Refineries 56
Manchester Pontoons and Dry Docks Co. Ltd 12, 125
   Manchester Pontoon 126
   Ellesmere Pontoon *125*, 126
   Contracts (vessels):
      Beeswing 12, 126
      Bittern 12
      Martin 12
      Puritan *125*
Manchester Dry Docks Co. Ltd. 23, 112, 125, *126-127*
   Contracts (vessels)
      'Woodleigh' 23
   Steamers Built:
      'Ben Seyr' 126
      'Doris Thomas' 126
      'Mia' 126
      'Penstone' 126
Manchester Ship Canal 12, 14, 19, 36, 127
Maritime Lighterage Company 16
Margarine Union 40
Marks & Spencer 55, 89
Marshall, Arthur (Major) 108, 111
Maudslay:
   Fleet List 86
   Meritor Flats 104
   Meritor, 'Teal' *102*
   Mogul III 'Perseus' *96*
   Mustang 108
McGovern, Grove Parcels 74
McNamara & Co Ltd 36, 100
Meat Transport Organisation 72
Meat Transport Pool 69
Meriden, The Café *49*, 58, 59, *71*, *89*
Metropolitan-Vickers 18, 110
Miller, Henry 98
Millington, John 111
Mills A.J. 110
Ministry of War Transport (M.o.W.T.) 72, 89, 91, 95
Mode Wheel Locks 12, 125
M.R.S. (Marston Road Services) 23
Muldoon, 'Chippy' 108
Murdoch, William. Methill 84

NCEC (National Conference of Express Carriers) 62
N.G. & S.F. 98
N.M.U. /Northern Motor Utilities 29
North O.D. 53
North Eastern Marine Engineering Co Ltd 7
North West Licensing Authority 49
NRTEF (Nat. Road Transport Employers Federation) 62
James Nuttall & Co. 125

Omnibus & General Insurance Co. 60

Paine, Horace 112
Peerless Lorries *25*, *39*, *41*, *42*, *43*, 44
Perkins, Len. 110, 117
Pickfords 39, *51*, 57, 98
Port of London Authority(PLA) 13, 16, 20, 24, 40, 59, 62
Porter Lancastrian 110
Powell, Bacon & Hough Lines 23
Powell, Frank 108
Procter & Gamble 108, 112
PX Ltd. 100
Pyman, George & Co. 7

Raeburn, Driver 86
Railways' Square Deal Campaign 62
Ramsay Steamship Co. Ltd 126

Read A.H. 23, 24, 26
Red Arrow (Parcels) 84
Renwick, Denis 7, *10*, 37, 63, 95, 97, 100, 104, 108, 110, 112, 117, 125
Renwick, Guy 7, *10*, 103, 112, 117, 118
Renwick, George (later Sir George) 7, *8*, 12, 13, 14, 20, 23, *24*, 27, 30, 32, 3, 35, 36, 40, *43*, 125, 126
Renwick, George (ii) *24*
Renwick, Gustav Adolphus (Major) 7, *10*, 14, 21, 22, 23, *24*, 26, 27, 29, 30, 32, 33, 34, 35, 37, 38, 40, *43*, 47, *48*, 50, 51, 53, 58, 60, 62, 64, 69, 72, 74, 89, 95, 97, 100, 104, 108, 112, 125
Renwick, John *24*
Renwick, Mary Jane (later Lady) 12, 13, 23, 34, *43*
Renwick, Septimus (Capt.) 23, *24*
Renwick, William Henry 13
Renwick War Memorial 24, *25*, 25
Renwick, Dagliesh Ltd. 8, 33
Rivers W.A. (Bill). 110
Road & Rail Central Conference 62
Road & Rail Traffic Act, 1933 48
Road Haulage Association 63,
Road Haulage (Operations) Advisory Committee 72
Road Haulage Organisation 69, 77, 89, 95
Road Haulage Organisation:
   Fisher Renwick 'Units' 90
Rodgers, William R. Earlston 84
Roe A.V. (Woodford) 80, 83
Rolls Royce 80
Rudd, Edward Whitten 26, 27, 28, 30
Rutherglen 86
Ryder 117

Salmesbury Engineering 112
Salt Union 12, 14
Saltport 12, 13, 14
G Scammell & Nephew 26, 30
Scammell Col. A.G. 9, 26, 30, 35, 36
Scammell Lorries 27, 28, 30, 36, 53
   Agents & Depots:
      Pollen & Crisp, Manchester 30
      Birmingham (Wharfedale Road) 30
      Manchester (Stretford) 30
      Glasgow 30
   Models & Types:
      'lurry' 27
      Demonstration Motive Unit & Carrier 26, 27, *28*
      7 ton H:
         NC 3718 28, *35*, 36
         NC 3744 28, *30-31*, *32*, *33*, *35*
         NC 5037 'Fusilier' *28*, *35*, *36*
         NC 5895 28, 33, *35*
         NC ?? *35*
      10 ton S10:
         NE ?? *35*
         NE 6871 'Yeoman' 35, *43*
         S10 Lorries at Shadwell *55*
         S10 40, *55*
         S10 'Curlew' 46
         S10 'Greyhen' *46*, 47
         S10 'Lapwing' *47*
         S10 'Mallard' *46*
         S10 'Ptarmigan' *47*
      12 ton S12:
         NE 6097 'Hussar' 35, 44
         XM 8895 'Engineer' 32, *37*
         XM 9590 'Guardsman' 32
      SE15 Articulated Lorries:
         List 37
         At Meriden Café 49
         'Drummer' *46*
         'Lancer' *45*
         'Merlin' 51, 53, 98
         'Partridge' *48*, 51, 52, 53, 98, *104*
         'Pioneer' *45*
      45 ton Low Loader
         'Electrician' *92*
         'Engineer' *92*
      RC13 Rigid Six:
         44, 45, 46, 49, *65*
        Vans: 46
         'Reeve' 46, *58*
         'Sheldrake' *60*
      Lighweight Rigid Six:
         44, *53*, *64*, 68
        Van & Flats - names 53
         'Redstart' *61*
      Rigid Eight:
         53-58, *64*, 86
        Vehicle Pairings 95
        Line up, Muswell Hill *103*
        Line up White City *105*
        Flats:
           MMH 167 *98-100*
           'Blackcock' *92*
           'Lapwing' 68
           'Lyne' 86
           'Ptarmigan' *70-71*
           'Teal' 74, *81*
           'Tern' 74

Sided:
   'Grouse' *79*
   'Scaup' *66*
Vans:
   At Shadwell 68
   Showboat in trouble *88*
   'Low' Showboats *106*
   'High' 'Clyde' *104*
   'Low' 'Clyde' *87*
   'Don' *97*, 101
   'Eider' *72*
   'Curlew' *82-83*
   'Forth' *89*
   'Gadwall' *66*
   'Guillemot' *105*
   'Hawk' *97*
   'Pintail' 74
   'Pochard' 74
   'Plover' *77*
LA 20 Articulated
   'Blackadder' (Ex Rogers, Earlston) *92*
Routeman 2 Tanker - Procter & Gamble *119*
Schneider artillery tractors 26
Seddon:
   Post-War Purchases 97
   'Showboat pup' 'Derwent' 97
   Mk VL Van - United Turkey Red *110*
   Mk VL Flat - A Pannell *102*
Seddon-Carrimore Artic-Flat 'Tees' *106*
Shadow Factory, Castle Bromwich 74
Shand-Kydd Wallpapers 38
Shap 86, 88, 91, 93, 96, 108
Shelvoke & Drewry Ltd 58
Slough Trading Co. 41
Smith, 'Dougie' 88
Southampton Docks 17, 32
Southern, Alderman J. W. 12
Standerwick & Scout 62
Standing Joint Committee 62
Steamers, Other Owners:
   'British Hero' *19*
   'Drake' 19, 20
   'Herald' 21
   'Lochside' 15
   'Neptunia' *64*
   'Titanic' 25
   'Villanger' 126
Stretford Shipbreakers 127
Studebaker 51
   Normal Control Dropside *59*
   Flat *61*, *75*
   Luton Van *60*
   Forward Control 'Camelbacks' List 56
   'Lyre' 74, *81*
   Van 68
Sultan & Co. 36
Sutton & Co. 100
Swan's Shipbuilders 7
Swan Hunter & Wigham Richardson Ltd 7

Tapp, P.J.R. 69
Taylor, Alexander 7, 12, 125
Teasdale, R. 12, 126
T.G.B. Dealers 86
Thames River 19, 20
Thomas Bros. Shipping Co. 127
Thorburn, Jan 108
Thorpe, Dick 111
Timpson Shoes 91
Trafford Park Industrial Estate 14, 27, 38, 56
Transport Act, 1968 112
Transport Advisory Council 62
Transport Bill, 1947 98, 108
Transport, Minister of , 72
Trodd, Jack 111, 118
Trojan 1 ton Van - Osborne & Garrett *109*
TRTA (Traders' Road Transport Association) 63, 72
Tyne Iron & Shipping Co., Ltd 16, 33

United Turkey Red (UTR) 91, 108
Uzzell, Ken. 111

Vardy, Robert 110
Vickers Armstrong, Castle Bromwich 74

Walden, Frank 112
Walpole, Fred *25*, *41*, *42*, 47, *58*, 108, 111, 117
Warner, George 112
Watkins Transport 74
Westinghouse 17, 18
Wigham, Richardson 7
Wilcox, H. (Mickey) 112
Wilson, George. (Pittenweem) 84
Withrington, Harold 73

Youngs Express Deliveries 56, 91, 98, *105*

Zillah Shipping & Carrying Co. Ltd 127